Reinhard Gotzhein

Open Distributed Systems

Informatics

J. M. Schneider
Protocol Engineering
A Rule-based Approach

R. Gotzhein
Open Distributed Systems
On Concepts, Methods, and Design
from a Logical Point of View

W. Bibel
Automated Theorem Proving

E. Eder
Relative Complexities of First Order Calculi

F. Kurfeß
Parallelism in Logic

Vieweg

Reinhard Gotzhein

Open Distributed Systems

On Concepts, Methods, and Design from a Logical Point of View

Die Deutsche Bibliothek - CIP-Einheitsaufnahme

Gotzhein, Reinhard:
Open distributed systems : on concepts, methods, and design from a logical point of view / Reinhard Gotzhein.- Braunschweig ; Wiesbaden : Vieweg, 1993
(Vieweg advanced studies in computer science)

Verlag Vieweg, P.O. Box 5829, D-65048 Wiesbaden

Vieweg is a subsidiary company of the Bertelsmann Publishing Group International.

Originally published by Friedr. Vieweg & Sohn Verlagsgesellschaft mbH, Braunschweig/Wiesbaden, 1993

Printed on acid-free paper

ISBN 978-3-528-05358-1 ISBN 978-3-322-86009-5 (eBook)
DOI 10.1007/978-3-322-86009-5

Foreword

A variety of technological advances have taken place since the early days of computer networking in the sixties and the present distributed systems of the nineties. The major concern of the past was the distribution of functions aimed at providing reliable and high perfomance data transmission facilities for different geographical spans, from local to global areas. Currently, the area of greatest interest appears to focus on that of distributed applications. M. Stonebraker's *"Your company is distributed so should your data be"* augurs this shift of focus towards a more complete coverage of distributed systems technology.

One of the reasons that this process of technological advance required approximately thirty years was the relatively slow acceptance of the concept *"Openness"*. Openness means, intuitively, that different components from different manufacturers produced by different groups are able to interact and cooperate with each other. It is clear that the need for Openness arose step by step with the consequence that the technological implications and concepts were developed in parallel with the need for using them. The work on *"Open Systems Interconnection (OSI)"* began in the late seventies (1977) under the sponsorship of the International Standardization Organization. Five years later the *"Open Systems Interconnection Reference Model (OSI-RM)"* was born. This framework for the development of standards covers data transport issues (up to Layer 4) as well as some application issues (File Transfer, etc.; up to Layer 7).

The work on the Open Systems Interconnection Architecture (another name for the OSI-RM) and the use of this model for the development of new standards in the application area made apparent the importance of a communication model as an abstraction of a distributed system. In particular, it promoted (and still does) an understanding of distributed systems before their construction and allows this knowledge to be communicated to other developers and users. The differentiation between *"Service"* and *"Protocol"*, for example, provides a very clear understanding between the "What" and the "How" when extended to distributed systems (layering concept). A further result of this OSI-RM work was that the model could be comprehended without dealing with the functional details. Time showed, however, that the modeling concepts developed in the OSI-RM context were not sufficient and needed to be extended in various ways. To obtain a thorough understanding the service concept offered was rather limited because the dynamic aspects were not covered adequately. Rigorous service definitions, for example, were not part of the basic architectural concepts.

This book addresses open distributed systems design questions and offers solutions based on appropriate logical frameworks for specifying and reasoning about dynamic properties of distributed systems. The concepts and methods investigated and developed are suitable for expressing system architectures, system behaviour and complete system specifications. A wide spectrum of applications, in particular for the key architectural concept of the interaction point as well as for communication services in general, illustrate the broad applicability of the proposed approach.

A lucid introduction assists the reader's learning of the main concepts of distribution such as interaction, concurrency and the rule of systems environments. A well-accepted definition of *"Openness"* is offered, that is, the criteria of conformity for which distributed systems development is aiming. The consequences in fulfilling the aim are drawn by first developing the basic concepts and models for the description of system architectures, system behaviours and their surrounding environments. Secondly, different formal description techniques are used to place the necessary rigour for the different properties to be stated. Finally, it is not just one single method but a set of different methods (including epistemic logic) which are proposed, appropriate and suited for the application context to be formally specified.

Flexibility and rigour of the architectural concepts proposed herein give rise to the hope that they will be used in a wide context of distributed applications and as such stimulate further advances in the existing area of distributed systems in general.

Hamburg, April 1993 Friedrich Vogt

Preface

One may safely assume that almost all substantial future computer systems will be distributed systems, and that distributed systems will include our most important and most critical computer systems. Also, with more international standards becoming available, more systems will be open by conforming to these standards. Open distributed systems are, however, very difficult to design and implement, particularly because of the risk of timing-related design errors. The rate of failure of distributed systems is many times higher than for single sequential programs. Thus, the topic of design techniques for open distributed systems is currently one of the most important research areas in Computer Science.

Current activities in the area of formal methods are focussing mainly on the development and the application of *operational* description techniques. These techniques support the widely spread, execution-oriented way of thinking, therefore, a good acceptance can be expected. Also, operational techniques are well suited for the automatic generation of prototype implementations. On the other hand, some essential aspects of open distributed systems cannot or not sufficiently be characterized with existing operational techniques. In particular, the capabilities to describe system architecture and the semantics of architectural concepts are unsatisfactory. Moreover, formal reasoning, an important prerequisite for a deepened system understanding, is usually not sufficiently supported.

This book presents a new, abstract, and comprehensive view of open distributed systems. Starting point is a small number of core concepts and basic principles, which are informally introduced and precisely defined using mathematical logic. It is shown how the basic concepts of *Open Systems Interconnection (OSI)* and *Open Distributed Processing (ODP)*, which are currently the most important standardization activities in the context of open distributed systems, can be obtained by specialization and extension of these basic concepts. Application examples include the formal treatment of the interaction point concept and the hierarchical development of communication systems.

The organization of the text is as follows. After an introduction to the development of open distributed systems, formal methods in the system design process are discussed. The book then focusses on the requirement specification of open distributed systems, consisting of system architecture and system behaviour. A small number of elementary concepts is identified, and it is shown how these concepts can be composed into system architectures and system behaviours. To formally express system requirements, a temporal epistemic logic to refer to past, present, and future as well as to the knowledge of active system components is designed. Also, a notion of conformance that incorporates both system architecture and system behaviour is defined. Several simple examples illustrate the application of the logic in the hierarchical development of open distributed systems. Moreover, the interaction point and the service, which both are key concepts of open distributed systems design, are studied in detail. A number of interaction point properties are specified, and their interdependencies are investigated. Further results concern the representation of interaction points in other description techniques, and their role in the definition and verification of conformance. Then, a communication service and a service provider are specified, and it is proved that the service provider indeed provides the given service. As it turns out, the notion of service is closely related to the notion of interaction point.

This book is a contribution to the field of software engineering in general and to the design of open distributed systems in particular. It is oriented towards the design and implementation of real systems and brings together both formal logical reasoning and current software engineering practice.

Acknowledgements

This book is a revised version of my habilitation thesis, which I completed in 1992. The work reported here has been inspired and written during my position as researcher and lecturer at the Computer Science Department of the University of Hamburg. Preliminary results on some of the topics presented in this book have appeared in [Got90], [Got90b], [Got92a], [Got92d], and [GoVo92]. I am particularly indebted to Prof. Dr. F. H. Vogt for his continuous support and constructive criticism. Also, I wish to express my gratitude to Prof. Dr. G. v. Bochmann, Prof. Dr. F. Kröger, Prof. Dr. L. Moser, and Prof. Dr. K. Turner for many valuable comments and suggestions. The financial support by the *Stifterverband für die Deutsche Wissenschaft* and the *Deutsche Forschungsgemeinschaft (DFG)* is gratefully acknowledged. Also, my thanks go to all my colleagues in Hamburg and in the world, in particular to Dr. R. Groz, Dr. P. Ladkin, Dr. J. Schneider, and Dr. E. Werner, with whom I had many long discussions on the subject of the book. Finally, I thank my wife Karin and our daughter Anja for their remarkable patience and care, especially towards the completion of this book.

Hamburg, April 1993 Reinhard Gotzhein

Contents

Figures

Tables

About the author

Reinhard Gotzhein received the Diplom (M.S.) and Dr. Ing. (Ph.D.) degrees in computer science from the University of Erlangen, Germany, in 1982 and 1985, respectively. In 1992, he habilitated at the University of Hamburg, Germany. From 1985 until 1986, he has been post-doctoral fellow at the University of Montreal, Canada. From 1987 until 1991, he worked as assistant professor at the University of Hamburg. From 1991 until 1992, he has been visiting professor of the computer science department of the University of Montreal. Currently, he is assistant professor at the University of Hamburg. His research interests include open distributed systems, architectural modeling, communication protocols, formal specification, and verification.

0 Introduction

0.1 Key topics of open distributed systems design

The design of open distributed systems has received much attention from practitioners and from theoreticians during the past 15 years. Several computational theories have been developed, and many techniques for the specification of these systems have been proposed by the computer science community, with some of them being internationally standardized. Moreover, much effort has been devoted to the problem of verifying and testing open distributed systems, and to the development of international standards. So, is there anything else that ought to be said about open distributed systems design?

We believe there is. Although much progress has been made in the foundations of open distributed systems design, many problems are far from being adequately solved. Their adequate treatment is and will perhaps always be extremely difficult. Partially, this difficulty is due to the *behavioural complexity*, which is inherent in distributed systems. How should a global behaviour be decomposed such that the joint behaviour of its parts is *conforming*? And if local behaviour is defined, how can the joint behaviour be safely predicted and described?

Another difficulty arises from the *openness of these systems*. "The term 'open' was chosen to emphasize the fact that by conforming to ... international standards, a system will be open to all other systems obeying the same standards throughout the world" ([Zim80]). It is the nature of standards that they should be minimal, that is, capture essential aspects only. However, in the development of international standards there is often need for compromises, leading to options or even to omission of essential aspects, which both can result in loss of interoperability and thus of openness. How can the relationship between design decisions and openness be made more transparent? What is the right balance between the generality of the design and assumptions that are provably sufficient to guarantee interoperability?

An important factor of open systems that is sometimes underestimated is the *role of the environment.* A characteristic of an open system is that it is embedded in an environment, and that the system and its environment mutually influence each other. Typically, the behaviour of the environment is not known in advance. However, there is a mutual dependency between the behaviour of the open system under consideration and a given environment. We can say that the possible system behaviour is partially determined by the possible environment behaviour. It follows that the behaviour of an open system can not be completely characterized independently of the environment. How can such an interrelationship be made explicit? Is it really possible to reason about open systems independently of the environment? Given the description of an open system and some information about the environment, under which circumstances and to which degree is it possible to predict their joint behaviour?

These and other questions arise when we are dealing with open distributed systems. In this thesis, we will study each of these questions in some depth, arriving at perhaps some surprising answers. To do that, we will motivate and introduce a formal framework that, although not simple, we have found particularly intuitive and useful.

0.2 The role of standards

"*Openness* is the quality that a distributed system possesses when it is not required that all its components must be of the same manufacturer/vendor, follow the same technology, use one operating system, etc." ([Gri89]). As pointed out earlier, a system becomes open by conforming to international standards. Two key areas for the development of such standards are *Open Systems Interconnection (OSI)* and *Open Distributed Processing (ODP).*

OSI is mainly concerned with the exchange of information between systems, where "a system is a set of one or more computers, the associated software, peripherals, terminals, human operators, ... etc., that forms an autonomous whole capable of performing information processing" ([ISO81]). The objective of OSI is the definition of a set of standards that allow "different sorts of systems and from different manufacturers [to communicate] without requiring changes in the philosophy of those systems" ([Her89]). As a general framework and a common basis for the coordination and integration of standardization activities with the purpose of systems interconnection, the *International Standardization Organization (ISO)* has developed the *Basic Reference Model (BRM)* of OSI. The BRM introduces a number of elementary architectural concepts, such as service, protocol, entity, connection, service access point, etc., which are composed to form a layered architecture. To each layer, the BRM assigns particular tasks that contribute to the objective of communication between systems.

The objective of ODP is to generalize the concepts of OSI and to address issues of cooperation between systems, which includes communication aspects. "Any task which requires more than one application process to accomplish is within the scope of [ODP]", so "the field of application of distributed processing is virtually unlimited" ([Gri89]). To make distributed processing 'open' in the above sense, specific standards for all kinds of applications will have to be developed. To achieve a coherent set of standards, a Basic Reference Model of ODP which will include the definition of common concepts and a generalized model of distributed processing is under development.

It should be pointed out that the mere existence of international standards is not sufficient to make conforming systems open in the above sense. The standards have to be defined such that conformance guarantees *interoperability*. This means that if two manufacturers independently develop products conforming to the same international standard, these products can safely work together. There are several obstacles that can prevent openness to be achieved in this way, some of which will be briefly addressed in the following.

Firstly, under which circumstances does a system conform to a standard? An answer to this question can only be given if it is clear what conformance actually means. In the context of OSI, static and dynamic conformance requirements are distinguished. Static requirements concern the combination of implemented functions. Dynamic requirements are related to the dynamic behaviour of the system. Moreover, there can be a Protocol Implementation Conformance Statement (PICS) specifying the functions and options which have been chosen in the implementation. In the sense of OSI, a system is *conforming*, if it satisfies the static and dynamic conformance requirements, and if it is consistent with the PICS. In our opinion, this definition of conformance is too weak, it is rather an identification and a separation of concerns. It does, for instance, not tell us how the implemented behaviour should be related to the standard. In other words, it is left to the intuition what conformance really is. There should be a more systematic and complete definition which is independent of a particular standard.

Secondly, how can conformance be validated? To check conformance requirements, usually a number of test cases is defined. An implementation is called "*conforming*" if it passes these test cases. It is obvious that this approach cannot *guarantee* conformance in a more general sense, which is required to achieve interoperability. Protocol software is far too complex to be tested exhaustively, therefore testing can only increase the degree of confidence. In general, the question of defining conformance should be dealt with independently of the specific approach to validate conformance. On the other hand, the validation approach will to some extent depend on the (formal) framework in which conformance has been defined.

Thirdly, is conformance to a standard sufficient to guarantee interoperability between implemented systems? Again, this will largely depend on the definition of conformance, which has to be "strong enough". Moreover, it will depend on the standard itself. The existence of options in a standard, for instance, can prevent interoperability: although systems conform to the same standard, they can fail to interoperate, because they realize different options. As a tribute to this problem and "with some prompting from the Technical Level Feeders Forum, ... ISO has launched the concept of the Internationally Standardized Profiles (ISP)" ([Dav89]). An ISP is a subset of the functionality of a base protocol standard reflecting the choice of options for a particular purpose. Several pilot ISPs are currently under development.

To (partially) remove or circumvent these obstacles, it will be necessary to make the notion of conformance precise, which in turn requires the use of formal methods for specifying standards.

0.3 The need for formal descriptions

It is widely recognized that in order to solve the problems outlined before, the *use of formal methods* during the design process of open distributed systems is indispensable. This concerns the description of the open system on different levels of abstraction as well as every validation activity along the design trajectory, i.e., from problem analysis to implementation.

Of fundamental relevance is the *formal description* of the problem itself, which forms the starting point for all other rigorous design activities. The problem description shall capture the essential aspects of the open system in a precise, concise, complete, and unambiguous way without restricting the multitude of correct solutions, i.e., the description shall be minimal. Under "*essential aspects*", we summarize the essential system properties (which characterize the system's external behaviour) and the visible system architecture. It is evident that the formal description can fulfil these expectations only if it can be written on the right level of abstractness.

The formal description of an open system can serve as an exact definition of an international standard or as a contract between user and implementer. In both cases it is vital that - besides being precise - the description is *intelligible*. "To avoid a mismatch between a reader's intuition and the formal interpretation of the text, a specification must support the intuitive understanding of its contents" ([Bri88a]). This is not just a question of the "right" formalism, but also a matter of specification style and the degree of abstraction. The specification of too much detail, structure, and mechanism can render understandability more difficult and will most likely offend against the principle of minimality.

Intelligibility of the specification of an open distributed system also means that a relationship between the formal description and the modeled reality can be established in a natural and straightforward way. This leads us to architectural considerations and to the question of which basic constituents shall be used to describe a system. In the context of open distributed systems, *basic architectural concepts* such as event, interaction, interaction point, entity, service, and protocol are often used on the requirement level. What is the meaning of these concepts? How are they represented in a formal description? Which of them need to be represented in an implementation? It should be evident that the existence of corresponding architectural concepts is a precondition for the (formal) definition of conformance relating an implemented system to a specification. Therefore, intelligibility is an indispensable element for the effective realization as well as for the analysis of open systems.

Other important features of specifications are *modularity and modifiability*. The specification of a system is called "*modular*", if it consists of a number of segregatable parts which can be easily replaced. In this sense, the specification of an open distributed system should be modular with respect to its architecture and to the behaviour of its components. We speak of architectural modularity if the specification has clearly identified pieces which are related to basic architectural concepts, and which can be segregated from the rest of the specification. Behavioural modularity refers to the identification and segregation of functional units or properties in the specification. Modifiability is required because specifications of open distributed systems can be subject to changes, either during the design itself or in the period of maintenance. Clearly, modularity furthers modifiability, because in a modular system changes will most likely be locally limited.

The formal specification of an open system forms the basis for the development of an implementation and for validation activities. In general, *validation* comprises all measures to check properties of specifications and implementations, such as consistency[1], absence of deadlock or unspecified receptions[2], absence of livelock or divergence[3], or conformance. Validation can be exhaustive - in which case we speak of *verification* - or non-exhaustive. Approaches to exhaustive validation include program verification, reachability analysis, and algebraic transformations; testing and reduced reachability analysis, for instance, are non-exhaustive. Generally, it will depend on the applied formalism and the relationship between formal descriptions what kind of validation can be performed.

0.4 Distributed systems from the point of view of DAI

So far, we have considered open distributed systems mainly from a global point of view. This is certainly justified by abstractness and the principle of minimality. But in many cases, for instance in OSI, it is required to give some internal structure to a system which leads to distribution and concurrency. "Designing a concurrent program is a difficult task; no formalism can make it easy" ([Lam83]). However, some formalisms appear to be more appropriate than others, and the degree of abstractness and intelligibility of a specification can vary considerably with the design methodology. So the consciousness that distributed systems design will always be difficult is important, since it prevents us from entertaining unrealistic expectations; but it does not release us from the obligation to search for better formalisms and methodologies.

Problems related to the aspects of internal structure and concurrency are also studied in the area of *distributed artificial intelligence* (DAI). In DAI, "the central problem is the *cooperation* among multiple intelligent agents to achieve a common goal", also referred to as *social goal.* A social goal is "a goal that is not achievable by any single agent alone but is achievable by a group of agents" ([Wer88]). Examples of social goals are the construction of a car, the operation of a factory, the running of a university, or the provision of a communication service.

Achieving social goals requires cooperation; a social goal is "not, in general, decomposable into separate subgoals that are achievable independently of the other

1 A description is consistent if it is not possible to derive contradictions.

2 An unspecified reception ([Zaf80]) is a typical design error in the specification of a communication protocol.

3 A livelock is a non-terminating loop of internal events. The mere possibility of a livelock is called "divergence" in [Hoa85]. This means that livelock implies divergence, but not vice versa.

agents' activities" ([Wer88]). Cooperation, in turn, requires communication to resolve uncertainty about intentions of other agents, or to find out which alternatives have been chosen. Between humans, there are many forms of communication, for instance, verbal and non-verbal communication, direct and indirect communication, etc. The purpose of communication can be understood as the increase of the agents' knowledge, for instance, knowledge about the world, about other agents, about intentions and plans.

There is a close relationship between *knowledge and action* ([HaFa88]). Actions can be triggered by an agent's knowledge; for instance, if Bob knows that he has an appointment with Alice, he will go to meet her. Actions can also be inhibited by an agent's knowledge; for instance, if Bob knows that Alice has already done the shopping, he can stay at home.

Can the view of DAI help us in the design of open distributed systems? How can notions such as cooperation, agent, goal, or knowledge be adapted to OSI and ODP? Can they lead to a more natural and better understanding and specification of open distributed systems? In particular, is it a good idea to describe an agent's behaviour by referring to his knowledge, leaving it open how that knowledge will be acquired? These and other questions immediately emerge from the previous discussion.

1 Formal methods in the system design process

1.1 A model for the system design process

The design process of open distributed systems starts with the problem and finally leads to a physical implementation solving the problem. In between, depending on the refinement of the design process, there is a varying number of design stages. Figure 1.1 shows a coarse model for the design process with two intermediate documents, the requirement specification and the operational specification.

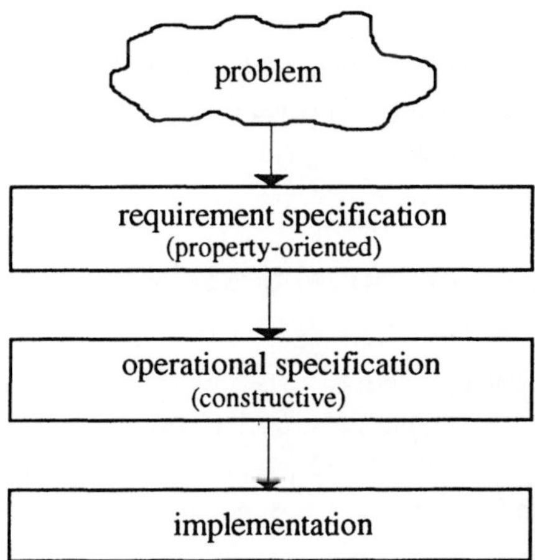

Figure 1.1: A model for the system design process

The cloudy shape in Figure 1.1 shall indicate that initially the problem exists, but is not described in any way. The task of the first design phase leading to the requirement specification, therefore, is a precise and authoritative description of what the problem actually is. Ideally, all the details as to how a possible solution might look like are omitted as long as they are not part of the problem. More comprehensively, the requirement specification may also contain information about reliability, efficiency, feasibility, machine environment, etc. However, we restrict attention to the description of the problem from a conceptual point of view.

To bridge the gap between the requirement specification and the physical implementation, one or more intermediate specifications can be inserted, each of them carrying a number of additional design decisions that finally lead to a problem solution. The design decisions can concern the selection of interface mechanisms, the refinement of the internal structure, the representation of states, the choice of strategies and algorithms, etc. We collectively refer to these intermediate descriptions by "*operational specification*" in order to emphasize that they substantially differ from the requirement specification. Typically, specifications resulting from this design stage are constructive in the sense that it is in principle possible to make them executable.

There is a broad consensus that the design process should be supported by formal methods. This means that first of all, every description is written in a formal language with a mathematically defined semantics called "*Formal Description Technique (FDT)*". Moreover, the transition between two formal descriptions of different levels of abstraction has to be substantiated. This requires a notion of correctness and suitable synthesis and analysis techniques.

1.2 Requirements for formal description techniques

From the general requirements on specifications mentioned earlier, a number of properties for FDTs can be derived. The following list, which is certainly not exhaustive, can serve as a starting point for the design or selection as well as for the comparison of FDTs. It should be emphasized that there is no universal method. This can already be inferred from the fact that some of the following properties depend on the area of application.

1.2.1 Expressiveness

"In order to produce precise and complete formal specifications an FDT must be sufficiently expressive with respect to its area of application" ([Bri88a]). The right degree of expressiveness is a criterion for the design of any mathematical formalism that is applied to specification. As this degree strongly depends on the area of application, it is necessary to investigate the kinds of requirements that are typical for a particular area. Also, it should be taken into account that only essential requirements need to be described, so a formalism that can cover these essential aspects suffices. However, dispute may arise which requirements are considered essential, which then could lead to the design of different formalisms. In other words, each choice of expressiveness made for a particular area of application should be seen as one of a variety of possible selections.

How is the degree of expressiveness affected by the area of application? When describing an open system, it is, for instance, necessary to express interfaces with the environment. Also, it has to be defined what may or may not happen at these interfaces (safety), and often it shall be stated what *will* occur there (liveness). If the system is distributed, we have to express its internal structure and the behaviour and composition of its parts. Is the system reliable or unreliable? In the first case it can be sufficient to express inevitable behaviour, whereas in the latter case potential or even probabilistic behaviour can be relevant, too. Is it a real-time system? If so, the specification of timing constraints and priorities can become a crucial aspect. For some areas of application, it can be natural to give a state-based description, and so on.

Generally, expressiveness can exist with respect to qualitative and quantitative aspects. *Qualitative aspects* are related to the system architecture and the logical appearance of system parts. For instance, the active parts of the system and their internal and external points of contact can be defined, restrictions can be imposed on the relative order of events, or the relation between input and output values can be specified. *Quantitative aspects* are related to measures such as absolute time and probabilities. This allows expressing restrictions on delays, durations, indeterminism, or unreliability.

In general, it would be desirable to combine qualitative and quantitative means of expressiveness into one FDT. However, this would cause considerable difficulties in modeling, and would cut down the reasoning capabilities. "In particular, probabilistic models usually involve concepts from mathematics dealing with continuous phenomena, which are difficult to combine with the discrete nature of the models used for the qualitative descriptions" ([Bri88a]). Therefore, FDTs for open distributed systems usually focus on qualitative aspects, which has "the advantage ... that designs and reasoning about them are simplified, and furthermore can be applied to physical and computing systems of any speed and performance. In cases where timing of responses is critical, these concerns can be treated independently of the logical correctness of the design" ([Hoa85]).

1.2.2 Abstraction

Abstraction - sometimes called "*information hiding*" - means reduction of detail, which is of particular importance during the early stages of systems design. Abstraction can help us to concentrate on essential aspects and thus to improve the quality of the design. However, it can also lead to the reduction of relevant detail, and subsequently to design errors or wrong conclusions, so care should be taken in applying this design principle.

Depending on what details are omitted, several kinds of abstraction can be distinguished. A well-known example is the functional abstraction, which stands for the reduction of algorithmic details. Another example is the data abstraction, which is used to hide the concrete representation of data objects. Both kinds of abstraction can be applied in the context of abstract data types. Furthermore, if data objects are shared between several processes, the incorporation of coordination into these objects allows the processes to abstract from synchronization.

With respect to open systems, several other forms of abstraction can be identified. They can be roughly classified into:

- abstraction from qualitative aspects
    - internal structure
    - behaviour
- abstraction from quantitative aspects
    - time
    - probabilities

A global description, for instance, hides the distribution aspects of an open system, which can be understood as abstraction from internal structure. A well-known example is the service concept of OSI. Here, the idea is to consider a system from the user's point of view and to omit detail about its internal structure and operation ([ViLo85], [Got90b]). The concealment of certain events or the restriction on events occurring at certain locations are possible ways to abstract from behavioural aspects.

With respect to a given FDT, we can distinguish between forced and deliberate abstraction. Using a particular FDT forces us to abstract from all aspects which are not expressable in that formalism. If this concerns relevant aspects, the choice of the FDT should be reconsidered. Aspects lying in the range of expressiveness can be omitted deliberately whenever they are considered unessential. Forced abstraction, as explained above, usually concerns quantitative aspects, but can also include qualitative properties such as absence of divergence, or liveness requirements.

1.2.3 Formality

In the theory of computer science, a language is called "*formal*" if rules to generate or recognize the sentences of the language are defined. This notion of formality covers the syntactical aspects of a language. Formality in the context of FDTs must also include the semantical aspects. There exist different ways to define the meaning of specifications. They have in common that - given an FDT - an underlying model structure is chosen. In some cases, the semantics of a specification is then defined by a well-defined subset of all models with this structure. In other cases, rules by which a particular model can be constructed from the specification are given.

It is evident that formality with respect to syntactical and semantical aspects is necessary to attain unambiguous, intelligible, and consistent specifications. Moreover, formality plays an important role when specifications are validated. First of all, it provides the necessary basis for the precise definition of notions such as deadlock, divergence, or unspecified reception, and of relationships between different specifications such as reduction, extension, or conformance. Furthermore, the theoretical results, proof theories, and tools that exist for the underlying mathematical model can be profitably applied and be further developed independently of the FDT.

1.2.4 Explicitness and implicitness

FDTs for open distributed systems have the common intention to describe systems by their ability to interact with their environment. This means that only externally visible behaviour is relevant, but not any internal mechanism to describe that behaviour. There are two basic approaches to the specification of external behaviour. One approach defines the possible orderings of events, i.e., the behaviour, explicitly. This is, for instance, done in Estelle ([ISO89]), and in LOTOS ([ISO88c]). The other approach defines properties that - taken together - restrict possible orderings of events, which defines the behaviour implicitly. This is done in logic-based formalisms such as temporal logic ([Pnu86]), interval logic ([ScMeVo83]), and trace logic ([Hoa85]).

In general, *explicit approaches* are constructive in the sense that they can be executed[4]. This has the advantage that specifications can be used for rapid prototyping or for the derivation of reference implementations, which can be used for test purposes ([BoBe89]). A disadvantage is that the properties of a system "generally are not expressible in constructive techniques. Consequently, they must be verified as implicit properties of descriptions" ([Bri88a]). However, it is difficult to incorporate all and only the essential properties of the system in a constructive specification. If non-essential properties or too specific properties are included, that will result in correct solutions being missed. If on the other hand some essential properties are not included, incorrect solutions are possible. Moreover, it is difficult to discover the essential properties when reading a constructive specification.

With *implicit approaches*, the properties of a system are expressed directly. This has the advantage that each property can be considered and understood separately, which makes it easier to decide whether it is essential or not. Also, implicit approaches are preferable for formal reasoning and verification purposes. A disadvantage is that it is generally not easy to decide whether a specification is complete in the sense that *all* essential properties are captured.

It should be clear that both kinds of approaches are needed in the design of open distributed systems. From the previous discussion it follows that they are orthogonal: implicit approaches are capable of defining properties explicitly; with explicit approaches, properties can be expressed implicitly. However, to verify implicit properties of a constructive specification, these properties have to be stated explicitly. Therefore, even if a property-oriented specification is not complete, it delivers a basic set of requirements which a constructive specification must satisfy.

1.2.5 Compositionality

An FDT is called "*compositional*" if the specification of a system can be obtained by composing the specification of its constituents[5]. If a set of separately specified entities is composed, the behaviour of the system is completely determined by their joint behaviour. Compositionality leaves no space for unexpected system behaviour. Other approaches are the composition of functional units or properties.

---

[4] Note that there are also implicit approaches which are executable and therefore constructive (for instance, see [Mos86]).

From the previous discussion it is clear that the notions of compositionality and modularity are closely related. A compositional FDT supports the modularity of specifications, and a modular specification has certainly been written in a compositional FDT. Also, compositionality improves the modifiability of a specification.

1.3 Synthesis and analysis activities

During the design of open distributed systems, a number of synthesis and analysis activities are performed with the aim of finally leading to a correct implementation. *Synthesis* in a broader sense denotes the process of building a structure from a number of predefined components. This can be done according to a fixed set of rules determining how components may be put together to form the structure. Ideally, the structure possesses certain desired properties by construction. With respect to software engineering, the purpose of synthesis activities is the construction of less abstract descriptions that are free of errors. *Analysis* means decomposition of an already existing structure and examination of its components and their relationships. The purpose of analysis activities is the detection of errors.

To define and perform synthesis and analysis activities of the system design process rigorously, they have to be based on formal description techniques with a precise syntax and semantics. Only then will the structures to be synthesized or analyzed have a well-defined meaning. A well-defined semantics is a necessary condition for the formal definition of such desirable properties as consistency, absence of deadlock, and conformance. Moreover, only then can synthesis rules and analysis techniques be formally defined, and thereby can be proven to yield correct results.

Formal synthesis and analysis techniques have been developed for and applied to many different areas of computer science, among them sequential programs, data base relations, and communication protocols. Analysis of a sequential program is mostly understood as a formal proof that the program meets its requirements, i.e., is correct with respect to its input/output assertions ([Hoa69]). Synthesis, on the other hand, starts from these assertions and constructs the correct program by stepwise insertion of intermediate assertions and program statements ([Dij76]). Analysis of data base relations is used to discover the presence of undesired properties such as insertion,

---

5 The notion of compositionality is further discussed in [HoRo89].

deletion, and update anomalies ([Dat81]). Synthesis starts from basic relations and avoids the anomalies by construction ([BeBe79]).

In the area of communication protocols, analysis techniques have been developed and applied to detect design errors such as deadlocks, unspecified receptions, nonexecutable interactions, state ambiguities ([Zaf80]), and non-conformance with the service specification. The best-known approach here seems to be reachability analysis, usually based on the specification of protocol entities as finite state automata ([Boc78], [RuWe82]). Because the analysis of a sufficiently complex protocol specification usually reveals some of the above design errors, the specification has to be revised and the analysis to be repeated until no more errors are found. With protocol synthesis, these design errors can be avoided a priori (for instance, see [GoYu84], [BoGo86], [GoBo90]).

From a systematical point of view, a proper formal synthesis can make analysis obsolete. If all design errors are provably avoided by construction, an analysis of the synthesized structure will not detect any errors. In practice, however, a synthesis activity can not always be formalized, and if it is formally defined, it usually does not guarantee that all desired properties hold. This means that a synthesis activity has to be complemented by formal analysis activities.

2 Requirement specification of open distributed systems

The *requirement specification* serves as a vehicle for the system designer to convey the essential ideas about a given problem[6]. It supports the process of clarification and design and should therefore be easy to comprehend in the first place. Moreover, it forms the basis for the development and check of problem solutions. We can subdivide the requirement specification into two basic constituents. Firstly, there is the *conceptual system architecture,* which addresses static aspects. We will need basic architectural concepts to define it. Secondly, there is the *system behaviour*[7], which addresses dynamic aspects. We will need a formal language with a suitable execution model to characterize it precisely. This characterization will refer to the conceptual system architecture, which in turn is required for the understanding of the system behaviour. In other words, a requirement specification will only be complete with the definition of the conceptual system architecture and the description of the system behaviour. However, both constituents may be comprised into a single description.

Generally, the requirement specification can go beyond the characterization of a system as perceived from the environment. It could, for instance, be an aspect of the problem[8] to decompose a system into a number of smaller parts, to define an internal system architecture and a form of cooperation among system parts. The external appearance of the system is then determined by the composition of these parts (cf. Chapter 1.2.5).

2.1 Basic architectural concepts

From the development and standardization of open distributed systems, a variety of architectural concepts have resulted. Some of them can be considered as basic, general concepts that are common to all kinds of open distributed systems. Others are more specific to a particular area of application. Furthermore, basic concepts can have a less general meaning (and often different names) when used in a particular context. We will now identify a small number of basic architectural concepts and introduce them informally. In Chapters 2.4 and 2.5, we discuss how these concepts can be related to

6 A requirement specification may also contain information about reliability, efficiency, feasibility, machine environment, etc.

7 The distinction into architectural and behavioural aspects is further discussed in [COS87].

8 Often, such a decomposition is made only to obtain behaviour descriptions that are easier to understand, not due to the problem itself.

architectural concepts of OSI, and address their representation in formal specifications. A formal treatment of some of the basic concepts - together with appropriate references - can be found in subsequent chapters.

Intuitively, we perceive an open distributed system as a number of active components performing local actions and interacting with their environment. To conceptually model active components, we use the notion of *agent*[9] and define:

- An *agent* is an active component.

The agent is the structural unit to which we will later ascribe knowledge: an agent can have knowledge about itself and knowledge about other agents. We will address this important topic in Chapters 6 and 7.

- An *event* is a local action.

An agent can perform only local actions. However, these actions can have an influence on other agents, if certain preconditions are fulfilled.

- An *interaction* is an action which is common to two or more agents.

It is by means of interaction that agents can mutually influence each other. This influence consists of exchange of information[10]. An interaction can be decomposed into a set of events, which together form the interaction. In other words, the event is the portion one agent has in an interaction.

- An *interaction point* is a pervious boundary between an agent and its environment.

Interaction points model conceptual locations where interactions take place. Several agents may share the same interaction point, in which case they can interact directly. Depending on the context, it can be necessary to assign different specific meanings to interaction points.

It should be pointed out that the explicit introduction of the interaction point concept has some important consequences. Firstly, we can model the scope of interactions to include precisely those agents sharing the corresponding interaction point. Also, the concept allows considering agents separately from their environment and composing

---

9 The notion of *agent* is also used in DAI (for instance, see [Wer88]).

10 This includes so-called pure synchronization which contains information.

them later on. Furthermore, it can be used as the basis for a class of very general conformance notions (see Chapter 4.6).

2.2 System architectures

With the basic concepts "agent" and "interaction point", it is possible to define more complex structures termed *system architectures*. The concepts "event" and "interaction" will play a role later on when we specify behaviour. In this chapter, we introduce some of the principles and ideas of architectural modeling and reconsider the notions of openness, distribution, and abstraction in this light.

Figure 2.1a shows an architecture consisting of two agents ag_1 and ag_2 that have a common interaction point ip. From this architecture it can be inferred that ag_1 and ag_2 have the capability to interact, however, we can not yet say whether they will actually do so. This can only be derived from the behaviour of the agents and the meaning of the interaction point, which still have to be specified. We require as a rule of architectural composition that an interaction point is introduced explicitly in the system architecture whenever a group of agents has the capability to interact. Depending on the kind of interaction, two or more agents may in general be involved in interactions.

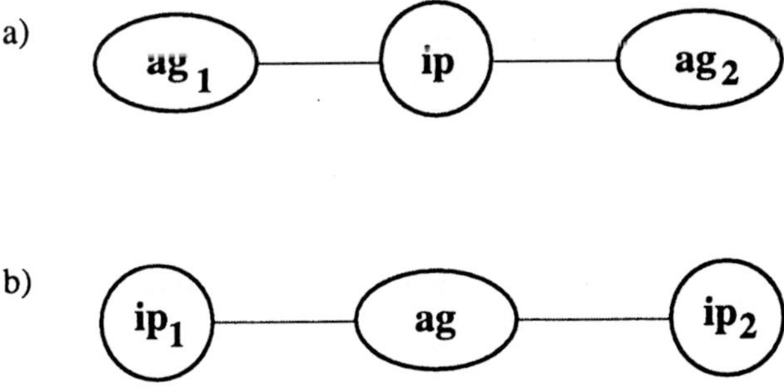

Figure 2.1: System architectures

Figure 2.1b shows an agent ag having two interaction points ip_1 and ip_2. From a global point of view, this architecture is incomplete, because it does not show the agents which have the capability to interact with ag through ip_1 and ip_2. However, such a situation is frequently encountered in the context of open distributed systems, which are incomplete in the same sense: although an open system forms part of a larger system, the environment into which it is embedded later on is not considered from the beginning. In most cases, it is not even known in advance, and it is the task of the design to specify the open system such that it shows the intended behaviour in *every* possible environment. With respect to Figure 2.1b, we can say that the agents not shown in the architecture form the environment of ag. Following our rules of architectural composition, we require that the interaction points an agent has with its environment, termed "*external interaction points*", are introduced explicitly, but we allow that the agents forming the environment may be omitted.

Definition 2.1: A system architecture $\mathcal{Arch}$ is a structure $\langle$ AG,IP,$\mathcal{Archf}$ $\rangle$, where

- AG is a non-empty, finite set of agents,
- IP is a non-empty, finite set of interaction points, and
- $\mathcal{Archf}$: AG $\rightarrow 2^{IP}$ is a total function called "*architecture function*" associating with each agent a set of interaction points. It is required that each element from IP is associated with one or more agents, i.e., IP = $\bigcup_{ag \in AG} \mathcal{Archf}(ag)$.

A set AG* $\subseteq$ AG of agents has one or more interaction points in common if and only if $\bigcap_{ag \in AG^*} \mathcal{Archf}(ag) \neq \{\}$. As pointed out before, the existence of a common interaction point is a necessary condition for direct interactions between a set of agents. Whether such interactions will actually take place is a behavioural aspect that we will address later. Note that if we consider only agents and abstract from interaction points, the system architecture is reduced to a structure $\langle$ AG $\rangle$.

2.3 Refinement and abstraction

The concepts of agent and interaction point naturally lead to the dual notions of architectural refinement and architectural abstraction. In general, it is desirable that the refinement of a single system component has no influence on the other system components. Only then will it be possible to perform incremental system design and modular verification, which is a prerequisite for the development of large systems. By incremental system design, we mean that we can modify or replace a part of the system without affecting the other parts. Modular verification means that only the modified or replaced parts have to be verified, not the entire system. To allow for incremental system design and modular verification, we have to make suitable restrictions with respect to system architecture and system behaviour. Architecturally, we require that agents and interaction points are refined separately. In other words, a single component of the refinement (an agent or interaction point) is uniquely related to a single component of the refined architecture. Also, we require that the number of interaction points an agent is associated with remains the same. These and further architectural constraints are formalized in Definition 2.2[11]. Behavioural constraints will be addressed in Chapter 3.3.9.

Definition 2.2: Let $\mathcal{Arch} = \langle AG, IP, \mathcal{Archf} \rangle$ and $\mathcal{Arch}' = \langle AG', IP', \mathcal{Archf}' \rangle$ be system architectures. $\mathcal{Arch}'$ is an *architectural refinement* of $\mathcal{Arch}$ (written "$\mathcal{Arch}'$ *refines* $\mathcal{Arch}$") if and only if there is a *refinement function* ref: $AG \cup IP \rightarrow 2^{AG' \cup IP'}$ such that the following restrictions hold:

i) Each architectural component of $\mathcal{Arch}$ is refined, i.e., ref is a total function.
ii) The refinement of an agent must include at least one agent: $\forall ag \in AG.\ ref(ag) \cap AG' \neq \{\}$.
iii) The refinement of an interaction point must include at least one interaction point: $\forall ip \in IP.\ ref(ip) \cap IP' \neq \{\}$.
iv) Each agent and each interaction point is refined separately, i.e., the refinement is disjoint: $\forall x,y \in AG \cup IP.\ x \neq y$ implies $ref(x) \cap ref(y) = \{\}$.
v) AG' is the set of exactly those agents resulting from the refinement, i.e., $AG' = (\bigcup_{ag \in AG} ref(ag) \cup \bigcup_{ip \in IP} ref(ip)) \setminus IP'$.
vi) IP' is the set of exactly those interaction points resulting from the refinement, i.e., $IP' = (\bigcup_{ip \in IP} ref(ip) \cup \bigcup_{ag \in AG} ref(ag)) \setminus AG'$.
vii) If an agent $ag \in AG$ is associated with an interaction point $ip \in IP$, then exactly one agent of the refinement of ag must be associated with exactly one interaction point of the refinement of ip. Formally:
$\forall ip \in IP, ag \in AG.\ ip \in \mathcal{Archf}(ag)$ implies

$$(\mid ref(ip) \setminus AG' \cap \bigcup_{ag' \in ref(ag) \setminus IP'} \mathcal{Archf}'(ag') \mid = 1 \text{ and }$$
$$\mid \{ ag' \in ref(ag) \setminus IP' \mid \mathcal{Archf}'(ag') \cap ref(ip) \setminus AG' \neq \{\} \} \mid = 1)$$

Figure 2.2a shows a possible refinement of the interaction point ip (compare Figure 2.1a), which on a lower level of abstraction comprises an agent ag that can interact with ag_1 and ag_2 through ip_1 and ip_2, respectively. It is necessary to introduce interaction points in the refinement, because otherwise the rule of architectural composition about their explicit introduction would be violated. Also, we notice that

11 In [Rei86], a different notion of architectural refinement is introduced, which is based on Petri nets. Here, the refinement of a single component can have an influence on other components. Also, system behaviour can only be introduced on the lowest level of refinement.

the duality between agents and interaction points is nicely carried into the refinement. On the other hand, when moving from the composition of ip_1, ag, and ip_2 to ip, we obtain a useful architectural abstraction.

Figure 2.2b shows a possible refinement of the agent ag (compare Figure 2.1b), which now consists of agents ag_1 and ag_2 with a common interaction point ip. To retain the external appearance as defined for agent ag, subsets of the agents introduced in the refinement are associated with the external interaction points of ag. As before, the duality between agents and interaction points is nicely carried into the refinement.

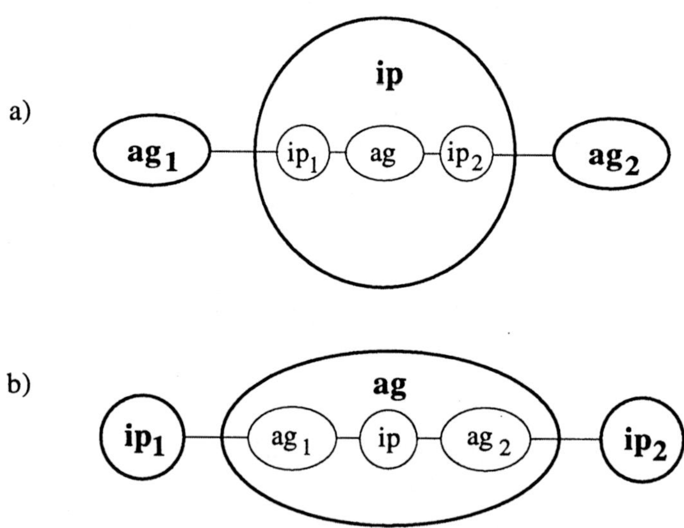

Figure 2.2: Architectural refinement and abstraction

Clearly, the system architectures shown in Figure 2.2a and 2.2b are architectural refinements of those shown in Figures 2.1a and 2.1b, respectively. If only agents are considered, i.e., if the system architecture is reduced to a structure $\langle AG \rangle$, the definition of architectural refinement can be adapted as follows:

__Definition 2.3:__ Let $\mathcal{A}rch = \langle AG \rangle$ and $\mathcal{A}rch' = \langle AG' \rangle$ be system architectures. $\mathcal{A}rch'$ *refines* $\mathcal{A}rch$ if and only if there is a *refinement function* ref: $AG \rightarrow 2^{AG'}$ such that:

i) ref is a total function
ii) $\forall ag \in AG.\ ref(ag) \neq \{\ \}$
iii) $\forall x,y \in AG.\ x \neq y$ implies $ref(x) \cap ref(y) = \{\ \}$
iv) $AG' = \bigcup_{ag \in AG} ref(ag)$

__Definition 2.4:__ Let $\mathcal{A}rch$ and $\mathcal{A}rch'$ be system architectures. $\mathcal{A}rch'$ is an architectural abstraction of $\mathcal{A}rch$ (written "$\mathcal{A}rch'$ *abstracts* $\mathcal{A}rch$") if and only if $\mathcal{A}rch$ *refines* $\mathcal{A}rch'$.

This definition formalizes the duality of architectural abstraction and architectural refinement: *refines* = $abstracts^{-1}$. Note that both relations are reflexive and transitive.

Having introduced basic architectural concepts and some rules how we can use them to define system architectures, let us now reconsider the notion of *open distributed system*. Following [Bri88a], we define:

- A *system* is a collection of interacting agents.

As we have seen, architectural abstraction allows us identifying a collection of agents as a single, abstract agent. Therefore, it is actually not necessary to introduce a new architectural concept. However, as a concession to common practice, we will also use the term "system" where appropriate.

- An *open system* has external interaction points.

It is admittedly tempting to define a system to be open if it has external interaction points. But such a definition would not take the broader meaning of openness in the context of OSI and ODP (see Chapter 0) into account. Therefore, we have constrained ourselves to expressing that the existence of external interaction points is one characteristic of an open system. Indeed, it is the characteristic that we can make precise in our architectural framework.

- A *distributed system* consists of several interacting agents[12].

The notion of distribution does not refer to the external appearance, but to the internal organization of a system. An open system may equally well be distributed as non-

12 We only consider architectural aspects at this point. A behavioural characteristic of a distributed system is its decentralized control.

distributed. Consequently, the notion of openness is orthogonal to the notion of distribution.

The explicit definition of system architectures is of particular relevance in the context of open distributed systems. Other than in the context of, for instance, abstract data types[13], the system architectures of two open distributed systems are usually not identical. Furthermore, the system architecture is often part of the problem and therefore has to be represented in the implementation. On an abstract level, the explicit definition of the system architecture allows us to identify, specify, and reason about each of its parts separately. It also determines how the parts - agents and interaction points - are put together, which leads to a joint behaviour. Ideally, the joint behaviour should be predictable from the specification and composition of the parts.

2.4 The Basic Reference Model of Open Systems Interconnection

The architectural concepts introduced in Chapter 2.1 and applied to the definition of system architectures in Chapter 2.2 are basic for the area of open distributed systems. In a particular context such as OSI, their meaning can be specialized to arrive at corresponding basic concepts. Also, further basic concepts, which are typical in a specific context, can be added. As an example and because of its relevance, we briefly discuss the Basic Reference Model (BRM) of OSI ([ISO81]).

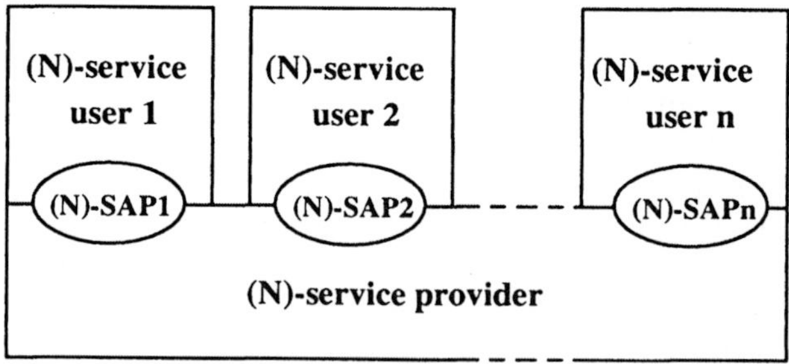

Figure 2.3: Service architecture

[13] Basic concepts here are objects and operations. An abstract data type is a collection of objects and operations.

The BRM introduces a number of basic architectural concepts, among them service, protocol, entity, connection, service access point (SAP), connection end point, and applies these concepts to define a reference architecture for OSI. Basic concepts are defined informally, for instance: "a *service-access-point* is the access means by which a pair of entities in adjacent layers use or provide services", "an (N)-service-access-point is only attached to one (N+1)-entity at a time", and "an (N)-service-access-point may be reattached to the same or another (N+1)-entity" ([ISO81]). Taking current practice into account, we can add that service access points in the context of OSI ought to be reliable in the sense that no interactions are lost, duplicated, corrupted, or created, which is not explicitly stated in the BRM. *Entities* are the carriers of activities, the BRM mentions application entities, protocol entities, relay entities, etc.

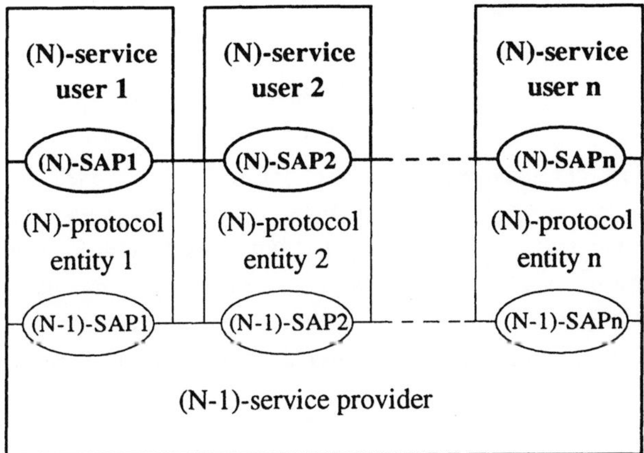

Figure 2.4: Protocol architecture

With the two basic concepts "entity" and "service access point", the service architecture of Figure 2.3 can be defined. The (N)-service users and the (N)-service provider are entities, each service user has a common SAP with the service provider. On a lower level of architectural abstraction, the (N)-service provider can be refined as shown in Figure 2.4. A set of entities termed "(N)-protocol entities" and an (N-1)-service provider are introduced, realizing the external behaviour of the (N)-service provider by their joint behaviour. We will address this important topic in more detail in Chapter 5.

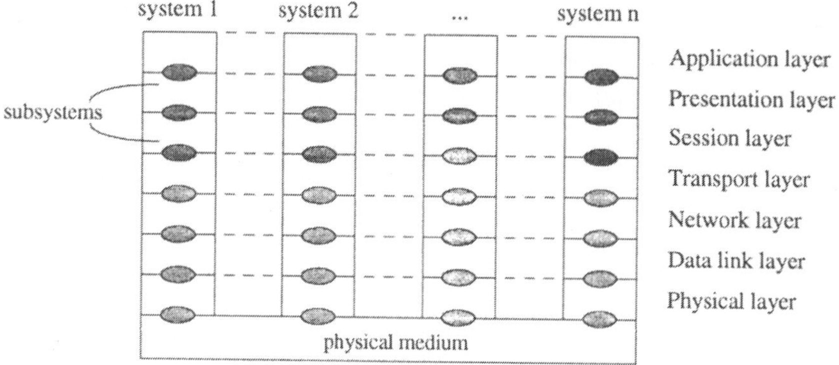

Figure 2.5: OSI Reference Model

Figure 2.5 illustrates some aspects of the OSI Reference Model, which defines a conceptual system architecture for computer networks by vertical and horizontal structuring, and assigns certain functionalities to the resulting parts. The outcome of a vertical structuring is a set of *systems*, horizontal structuring yields *layers*. The intersection of a system and a layer is termed "*subsystem*". Each subsystem can consist of one or more entities that can be attached to SAPs as shown in Figure 2.6.

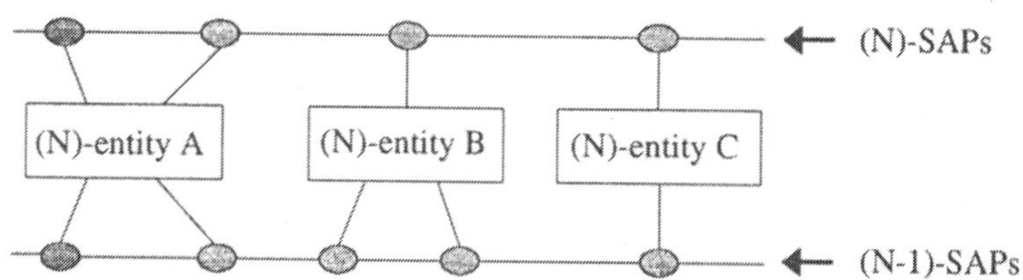

Figure 2.6: Layer N of the Reference Model

It should be evident that the concepts of entity and service access point are closely related to the basic notions of agent and interaction point in Chapter 2.1. In fact, "entity" and "agent" can be used interchangeably, and a SAP can be understood as an interaction point with a more specific meaning. Also, as we have explained earlier, "system" (and "subsystem") can be replaced by "agent". Therefore, the architectural aspects of the BRM of OSI can be regarded as a specialization and extension of the basic concepts and architectures introduced in Chapters 2.1 and 2.2.

Within the framework of the BRM, methodologies for conformance testing are being developed. This work has lead to more specialized basic architectural concepts such as implementation under test (IUT), upper tester, lower tester, point of control and observation (PCO), and to a number of predefined test architectures. In Figure 2.7, the distributed test architecture, which is composed from basic concepts, is shown. An overview on test architectures can be found in [Lin88].

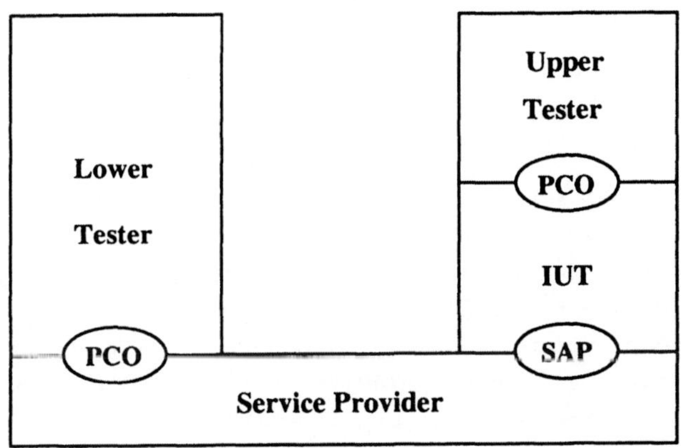

Figure 2.7: Distributed test architecture

The notions of IUT, upper tester, and lower tester are specializations of the OSI concept of entity, which is closely related to the concept of agent in Chapter 2.1. PCO is more specific than SAP ([Bau88]) and can therefore be understood as an interaction point with a more detailed meaning. Therefore, the architectural aspects of conformance testing can again be regarded as a specialization and extension of the basic concepts and architectures introduced in Chapters 2.1 and 2.2.

2.5 Basic concepts of formal description techniques

It is worthwhile investigating whether basic architectural concepts should be represented in formal specifications defining the behaviour of open distributed systems. To what extent is it necessary to carry the conceptual system architecture into the operational specification, and finally into the implementation?

On the different stages of open distributed systems design, "some internal structure and a form of interaction with the environment have to be assumed" in the description of a system. "It seems natural" and straightforward "to carry the ... conceptual architecture" into the specification and physical implementation ([Svo89]). This requires that architectural concepts of the higher level are represented on the lower level. However, for various reasons the internal structure of the lower level is often different. Guidelines for the application of FDTs for open distributed systems, for instance, explicitly state that the internal structure of the specification is not mandatory for the implementation.

It is a controversial issue whether any parts of the conceptual system architecture should be represented on the different levels of description. But there is consensus that for verification purposes, it is necessary to somehow relate formal descriptions of different levels. This is only possible if a mapping between corresponding description units can be found. In general, the description units that are used to establish the mapping need not be related to the conceptual system architecture. In the context of open distributed systems, however, it is desirable to build the mapping upon description units representing basic architectural concepts. This means that portions of the conceptual system architecture have to be identified in the specification. We shortly address this issue with respect to specifications written in the FDTs Estelle ([ISO89]), LOTOS ([ISO88c]), SDL ([CCITT87]), and TTCN ([ISO90]), and consider the concepts of agent and interaction point. More work on this subject can be found in [ISO88d], [Tur87], [BeHoTr88], [Got92d], and in Chapter 4.

Estelle, LOTOS, and SDL are FDTs designed for the specification of distributed, concurrent information processing systems, in particular communication services and protocols of the OSI BRM. Estelle and SDL are based on the model of extended finite state machines, LOTOS is an algebraic approach. Estelle and LOTOS have been developed within ISO and currently have the status of international standards. SDL has been designed and standardized within CCITT.

An Estelle specification describes a hierarchically structured system of nondeterministic, sequential components, called *module instances*. They can perform *interactions* through bidirectional *channels* between their *interaction points*. With each module instance, a finite set of interaction points is associated. Access in and out of the module instance is made through these interaction points. Each interaction point of a module instance has an associated first-in-first-out (FIFO) queue of infinite capacity, which receives and stores interactions sent to that module instance through this interaction point. The module instance may also send interactions to other module instances through its own interaction points.

In general, it would be sufficient to decide on a case to case basis which pieces of an Estelle specification are related to which parts of the conceptual system architecture. Another approach is to represent agents by module instances and conceptual interaction points by Estelle interaction points, which relates basic architectural concepts to FDT concepts directly. Note that although the same names are used, Estelle interaction points are a specialization of conceptual interaction points, they can, for instance, not be refined, and are asynchronous.

A LOTOS specification describes a hierarchically structured system of active components, termed *process instances*. Process instances communicate with their environment through *gates*. With each process instance, a finite set of gates is associated. Several process instances may share the same gate. A communication (or interaction) is a synchronized action between two or more process instances, taking place at a common gate.

As before, it would be sufficient to relate pieces of a given LOTOS specification to parts of the conceptual system architecture. Alternatively, agents and interaction points can be represented by process instances and gates, respectively. Again, this is a specialization of the basic architectural concepts, a gate, for instance, is synchronous and can not be refined.

An SDL specification structures a system into *blocks*, which in turn can be decomposed into further blocks and/or *processes*. Thus one obtains a hierarchical system structure, with processes at the leaves. All activities in the system are performed by processes. They can send and receive *signals* via *signalroutes*, which can be uni- or bi-directional. Blocks can be connected by *channels*, which are extended over block-boundaries by channels or signalroutes.

Agents can be represented in SDL either as blocks or processes. Only blocks can be refined. Interaction points can be represented by SDL input ports, signalroutes, or channels (see [BeHoTr88]). Here, refinement is possible, channels can be substructured into blocks, channels, signalroutes, and processes.

TTCN is a description technique designed for the specification of test suites. It has been developed within ISO and has the status of a draft international standard. No formal semantics has been defined so far. Currently, architectural aspects are expressed informally by relating TTCN descriptions to predefined test architectures ([Lin88]), and PCOs to testers. Interaction points can be represented in TTCN by PCOs. An extension to define test architectures within TTCN in order to cope with multi-party testing is under investigation.

2.6 Some remarks

In this chapter, we have introduced the basic architectural concepts "agent" and "interaction point" in an informal way, and have defined how they can be composed into conceptual system architectures. Both concepts can be decomposed, which naturally leads to dual notions of architectural refinement and architectural abstraction.

The basic concepts that we have chosen are general enough to be applied to all kinds of open distributed systems. They are specific enough to draw meaningful distinctions. Furthermore, it is feasible to adapt the basic concepts to particular contexts by specialization and extension, as it has been shown for OSI.

The meaning of the basic architectural concepts has not been made precise so far. We will address this important issue in subsequent chapters after having introduced a suitable formalism.

3 The design of a temporal logic for open distributed systems

In order to convey the essential ideas about a given problem, the system designer defines a requirement specification, consisting of the conceptual system architecture and the system behaviour. In Chapter 2, we have informally introduced basic architectural concepts and shown how they can be composed to yield system architectures. In this chapter, we will develop semantical models and design a temporal logic for the formal modeling and specification of system architectures and system behaviour. As it will turn out, this formalism can also be used to define the semantics of basic architectural concepts.

Temporal logic ([Pri67], [ReUr71]) has a long history, it has been traced back to the ancient Greeks. The Stoics, Megarians, and Aristotle have been reasoning about time in different ways by making statements about the actual, the possible, and the necessary. After some development during the Middle Ages by medieval Arabic logicians and Thomas Aquinas, since the later 1940's a revival of interest has occurred. The origin of this interest came from the study of historical material, the logical analysis of grammatical tenses, and the analysis of issues in the philosophy of science. It was not until the late 1970's that the interest of computer science manifested itself. At that time, some years after the software crisis, computer scientists were investigating formal techniques for the specification and analysis of concurrent programs. The opinion was advocated that temporal logic is particularly useful for this purpose (for instance, see [Lam83]). Today, temporal logic is a well-established formalism in computer science, and is applied to open distributed systems.

The temporal logic we will introduce in the following belongs to the category of property-oriented approaches. This means that the properties characterizing a problem can be stated explicitly, which is particularly important in the early system design stages. With respect to open distributed systems, a property-oriented specification can serve two major purposes. Firstly, it can be the basis for the development of a physical implementation. Because properties can restrict the possible ordering of events, they define system behaviour implicitly. Secondly, it can define properties that are ascribed to a constructive specification and consequently have to be verified. This improves understanding and increases confidence in the constructive specification, even if the properties do not characterize the legal system behaviour completely.

3.1 Some requirements on expressiveness

In Chapter 1, we have presented a number of requirements for formal description techniques, for instance, expressiveness, abstraction, formality, and compositionality. It was argued that the right degree of expressiveness strongly depends on the area of application. Having introduced an architectural framework for open distributed systems, we can now reconsider expressiveness in order to arrive at more concrete requirements.

system architecture
- agents - interaction points - architectural composition - architectural refinement - architectural abstraction
system behaviour
- event occurrence - interactions - safety and liveness - inevitable and potential behaviour - orderings of event occurrences

Table 3.1: Overview of expressiveness requirements

The purpose of specifying an open distributed system is to define the abstract requirements consisting of system architecture and system behaviour (see Chapter 2). An adequate formal description technique must provide expressiveness with respect to both constituents of the requirement specification. Firstly, it has to cover the static aspects related to the system architecture. In Chapter 2, basic architectural concepts such as agent and interaction point have been introduced informally, and it has been defined how they may be composed to arrive at system architectures. In the formal specification of an open distributed system, this has to be made precise, which requires expressiveness of the FDT with respect to the architectural aspects of the requirement specification.

Secondly, the FDT has to cover the dynamic aspects related to the external system behaviour. The external behaviour of an open distributed system is perceived as a sequence of interactions with its environment occurring at the system boundaries. At the time of specification, the environment is not fixed. Therefore, we can only deal with the readiness of the open system to participate in interactions, which would result in a behaviour when the system is embedded in an environment. Following [Bri88a], we understand an interaction as an activity that is common to two or more active components. It can be decomposed into a set of local actions called "*events*", which together form the interaction (see Chapter 2.1). In other words, the event is the portion that an active component has in an interaction.

Having identified the event as the basic constituent of external behaviour, we conclude that any mathematical formalism for open distributed systems specifications should be capable of modeling and expressing events. We consider the event to be the only basic constituent of system behaviour and exclude, for instance, internal states as irrelevant detail. However, it should be noted that in some techniques, for instance, Estelle ([ISO89]), SDL ([CCITT87]), and Z ([Hay87]), an internal state is used as a vehicle to specifying external behaviour.

Properties characterizing system behaviour can be classified into *safety and liveness properties*[14]. In this context, safety means that nothing bad *can* happen, or - alternatively - if something happens, it is something good. Thus, safety properties state what may or may not happen, which can be expressed by referring to the present and the past. Liveness means that something good *will* happen, so liveness properties determine what must happen, which is an assertion on the future and may depend on events that occur in the present or have occurred in the past. In a specification, safety and liveness properties are often invariant over time.

In the area of open distributed systems, both safety and liveness properties need to be expressed. Consider, for instance, a connection-oriented communication service. A connection indication may only be given to a service user if another service user has previously issued a connection request to the service provider. Moreover, if a service user issues a connection request, then either the addressed service user will get a connection indication, or the service user requesting the connection will obtain a disconnection indication by the service provider.

14 Formal definitions of safety and liveness have been given in [AlSc85] and [LiPnZu85].

Safety and liveness properties have a complementary role for the specification of system behaviour. Safety properties are already satisfied if nothing at all happens. Liveness properties do not exclude illegal behaviour. Therefore, a formalism for the specification of open distributed systems should be capable of expressing both safety and liveness properties. For a property-oriented formalism, this requires expressiveness with respect to past, present, and future (see [LiPnZu85]).

Many open distributed systems are unreliable in the sense that unsuccessful behaviour may occur. In this situation, it is essential to draw a clear distinction between successful and unsuccessful behaviour. Consider again a connection-oriented communication service where a service user has issued a connection request. It should, for instance, be *inevitable* that the service provider shows some reaction on this request, either a connection indication to the addressed service user, or a disconnection indication informing the requesting user that the connection has not been established. Moreover, the requesting user expects that the service provider is principally capable of delivering a connection indication, which amounts to requiring the connection indication being *potential* behaviour. Requiring that it is inevitable would be too strong if we allow that the service provider is unreliable. Not stating that it is potential would not be strong enough, since it would allow that the service provider *always* returns a disconnection indication. Note that the two properties explained above allow for a reliable service provider that *always* delivers a connection indication as a consequence of a connection request. Generally, expressiveness both for potential and for inevitable behaviour is needed, if the essential features of unreliable systems - like a number of communication services - are to be specified. In case of reliable systems, it should suffice to express inevitable behaviour.

Another important aspect of open distributed systems that has not yet been sufficiently covered is the ordering of event occurrences, possibly of event occurrences within a certain context. A simple ordering property of a communication service would be that a connection indication is always preceded by a connection request. A more complex property states that the order of receptions since the last connection establishment shall be the same as the order of transmissions as long as the connection exists. This should be expressable even in the presence of an infinite data domain. Ordering as discussed here seems to be a typical safety requirement, expressiveness therefore concerns sufficient means to refer to present and past.

It should not be forgotten that an open distributed system has to be embedded in an environment. Therefore, it is necessary to model the boundaries with the environment -

which we have termed "interaction points" - and to define their meaning. Making assumptions about interaction points is not necessary as long as the open system is considered separately. But it immediately becomes essential when we want to derive the view of the environment.

The discussion so far could mislead to the conclusion that the formalism that we want to design should be as expressive as possible. However, enhancing the expressiveness of a formalism in general weakens the reasoning capabilities in the following senses: an increase of computational complexity, undecidability results may become a factor, and the possibility of incompleteness of the axiomatic system. Therefore, the expressiveness of a formalism should be customized such that it suits the needs of the area of application in order to preserve as much reasoning power as possible. It is, for instance, a great advantage if the formalism remains decidable or at least semi-decidable, because reasoning can then be automated. But decidability must not be enforced at the cost of sufficient expressiveness. Since the required expressiveness changes with the problem, it would be best to have a formalism that can be adapted to a given situation.

3.2 A survey of temporal logics

Temporal logic is a branch of formal logic that has been of particular interest to the computer science community since the pioneering work by Amir Pnueli in the later 1970's ([Pnu77]). Since then, research concerned with temporal logic has become substantially broader, with many new ideas and results having immediate relevance to computer science.

A variety of temporal logics for the specification and verification of open distributed systems has been introduced in the literature ([ReUr71], [Krö87], [Got92b]). The primary motivation for the design of different temporal logics is the strive for the right degree of expressiveness (see Chapter 1.2.1), another motivation is the improvement of intelligibility (see Chapter 0.3). The following survey reviews some temporal logics. As it turns out, each of these logics can cover only some of the requirements stated in Chapter 3.1.

3.2.1 Traditional temporal logic

By interpreting the basic modal operators L and M expressing *necessity* and *possibility* ([HuCr68], [HuCr84]) over time, a temporal logic can be obtained directly from modal logic ([Pri57]). This logic is referred to as *traditional temporal logic* here. Traditional temporal logic is based on propositional logic. From a temporal point of view, statements about the present can be made by using only propositional logic. Traditional temporal logic provides expressiveness to refer to the future by adding two operators. Let φ be a formula, then

- $\Box\,\varphi$ (read "henceforth φ" or "always φ") means that φ is true now and will always be true in the future;
- $\Diamond\,\varphi$ (read "eventually φ") means that φ is true now or will be true sometimes in the future.

The formal semantics of traditional temporal logic is usually given with respect to *Kripke structures* $\langle W,R,V\rangle$ ([Kri63], [HuCr68]), where the set of *worlds* W is well-ordered with respect to the *seeing-relation* $R \subseteq W \times W$, and $V: \Phi \times W \rightarrow \{0,1\}$ is a *value assignment*. This is the case for a model that is a (possibly infinite) sequence $\sigma = \langle\, \sigma_0\sigma_1 \ldots \sigma_n \ldots\rangle$ of *states* (worlds), where each state is defined by a set of true atomic propositions, and corresponds to a linear, discrete view of time. The semantics of temporal formulas is then defined by a relation $\models$ termed "*satisfaction relation*" between a model, one of its states, and a formula which holds if and only if the formula is true in that situation. For the n-th state of a model σ, the meaning of "henceforth" and "eventually" can be defined as follows:

$$\sigma,n \models \Box\,\varphi \quad \text{iff} \quad \forall m \geq n.\ \sigma,m \models \varphi$$
$$\sigma,n \models \Diamond\,\varphi \quad \text{iff} \quad \exists m \geq n.\ \sigma,m \models \varphi$$

"Henceforth" and "eventually" are dual operators, i.e., each of them can be defined in terms of the other and negation:

$$\Box\,\varphi \quad =_{Df} \quad \neg \Diamond \neg\varphi$$
$$\Diamond\,\varphi \quad =_{Df} \quad \neg \Box \neg\varphi$$

Prefixing a formula φ with the "henceforth" operator expresses that φ is invariant over time. $\Diamond\varphi$ states that φ is guaranteed to hold at some point in time, without giving a precise time value or an upper bound. These are quantitative aspects falling outside the scope of traditional temporal logic (and all other logics considered in the following). It is possible to combine the temporal operators. If time is regarded as infinite, then $\Box\Diamond\varphi$

expresses that φ holds from time to time, or infinitely often. $\Diamond\Box\varphi$ states that there is a point in time from which onward φ remains true.

Traditional temporal logic has been applied to specifying and reasoning about concurrent systems. In [Hai82], it is used to specify safety and liveness properties of communication protocols and operating system components. Implementations of these systems are provided in a concurrent programming language whose temporal semantics is captured by a set of axioms and inference rules, and proved to meet their specifications. In [Lam83] and [Lam83a], traditional temporal logic is used to specify concurrent program modules. In [Vog82], it is applied to specifying and reasoning about the alternating-bit protocol.

Traditional temporal logic provides some expressiveness to refer to the future. If properties are related to the history, i.e., to the past, auxiliary variables recording the relevant part of that history can be introduced at the cost of abstractness (see [Hai82]). Also, contexts can be established with auxiliary variables, which is not possible otherwise, because both "henceforth" and "eventually" refer to the entire future. In [Lam80], it has been shown that potential behaviour can not be expressed in traditional temporal logic. More generally, potential behaviour can not be expressed in any linear time temporal logic[15].

It has already been mentioned that traditional temporal logic is based on propositional logic. This means that atomic formulas can not be decomposed within the logical framework, other than in first-order logic. A decomposition, however, is necessary in order to formally associate architectural meaning with formulas. Consequently, any architectural interpretation that is given to atomic propositions can only be informal[16]. Therefore, traditional temporal logic - just as any other temporal logic based on propositional logic - lacks architectural expressiveness.

3.2.2 Extensions of traditional temporal logic

The expressiveness and intelligibility of traditional temporal logic can be enhanced by adding further temporal operators. Assuming again a linear, discrete view of time, the

15 If linear time operators are supplemented with modal operators expressing possibility, then potential behaviour can be expressed.

16 It is, however, possible to incorporate architectural components into the underlying semantical model and to associate atomic propositions with them (see Chapter 3.3.1).

following operators to refer to the future have been reported in [Boc82], [Krö87], [Lam77], [Lam83], [Pnu77], [ScMe82]. Let φ, φ_1, φ_2 be formulas, then

- φ_1 *atnext* φ_2 means that φ_1 will hold at the next time that φ_2 holds (excluding the present time);
- $\circ\varphi$ (read "next φ") means that φ is true in the next state;
- φ_1 *before* φ_2 means that if φ_2 holds sometime in the future (excluding the present time), then φ_1 holds before;
- $\varphi_1\ W\ \varphi_2$ (read "φ_1 unless φ_2") means that if φ_2 eventually becomes true, φ_1 holds until then, otherwise, φ_1 always holds;
- $\varphi_1\ U\ \varphi_2$ (read "φ_1 until φ_2") means that eventually φ_2 becomes true, and until then, φ_1 holds;
- $\varphi_1 \leadsto \varphi_2$ (read "φ_1 leads to φ_2") means that if φ_1 holds, φ_2 eventually becomes true;
- $\varphi_1 \trianglelefteq \varphi_2$ means that φ_2 remains true at least as long as φ_1;
- φ_1 *while* φ_2 means that if φ_2 is true at present, then φ_1 is true at present and remains true as long as φ_2 remains true;
- φ_1 *until-after* φ_2 means that φ_2 eventually becomes true, and until after then, φ_1 holds;
- φ_1 *latches-until* φ_2 means that φ_2 eventually becomes true, and until then, if φ_1 becomes true, it will remain true until φ_2 becomes true.

For the n-th state of a model σ, the meaning of the operator *atnext* is formally defined to be:

$$\sigma,n \models \varphi_1\ \textit{atnext}\ \varphi_2 \quad \text{iff} \quad \forall m > n.\ \sigma,m \models \neg\varphi_2 \text{ or } \exists m > n.$$
$$(\sigma,m \models \varphi_1 \wedge \varphi_2 \text{ and } \forall k.\ (n < k < m \text{ implies } \sigma,k \models \neg\varphi_2))$$

The other operators can be defined in terms of *atnext* as follows:

$$
\begin{array}{ll}
\circ\,\varphi & =_{Df}\ \varphi\ \textit{atnext true} \\
\varphi_1\ \textit{before}\ \varphi_2 & =_{Df}\ \neg\varphi_2\ \textit{atnext}\ (\varphi_1 \vee \varphi_2) \\
\Box\,\varphi & =_{Df}\ \varphi \wedge \textit{false atnext}\ \neg\varphi \\
\Diamond\,\varphi & =_{Df}\ \neg\Box\neg\varphi \\
\varphi_1\ W\ \varphi_2 & =_{Df}\ \varphi_2 \vee \varphi_1 \wedge \varphi_2\ \textit{atnext}\ (\varphi_1 \supset \varphi_2) \\
\varphi_1\ U\ \varphi_2 & =_{Df}\ \varphi_1\ W\ \varphi_2 \wedge \Diamond\,\varphi_2 \\
\varphi_1 \leadsto \varphi_2 & =_{Df}\ \varphi_1 \supset \Diamond\,\varphi_2 \\
\varphi_1 \trianglelefteq \varphi_2 & =_{Df}\ \varphi_2\ W \neg\varphi_1 \\
\varphi_1\ \textit{while}\ \varphi_2 & =_{Df}\ \varphi_2 \trianglelefteq \varphi_1
\end{array}
$$

φ_1 *until-after* φ_2 $\quad =_{Df} \varphi_1 \, U \, (\varphi_1 \wedge \varphi_2)$
φ_1 *latches-until* φ_2 $\quad =_{Df} (\varphi_1 \supset (\varphi_1 \, U \, \varphi_2)) \, U \, \varphi_2$

By choosing subsets of the operators listed here, a variety of temporal logics that are more expressive than traditional temporal logic can be obtained. For a few of these combinations involving the operators *U* and $\circ$, expressiveness results have been formally proved in [EmHa86].

The "next" operator increases the expressiveness of traditional temporal logic, since it is now possible to detect *stuttering*, i.e., to distinguish between models σ and σ', where σ' is the same as σ except that some subsequence $\langle \sigma_{i-1}\sigma_i \rangle$ of σ is replaced by the stuttering sequence $\langle \sigma_{i-1}\sigma_{i-1}...\sigma_{i-1}\sigma_i \rangle$ in σ' (see [Lam83]). Also, a notion of event can be defined (see Chapter 3.2.6). The "next" operator may only be introduced if the next state is well-defined, which is the case for linear discrete time, but not for dense time.

With the "until" operator, one can make statements about bounded intervals, which is not possible with the operators of traditional temporal logic. Because the operators $\Box$, $\Diamond$, *W*, ~~>, $\unlhd$, *while*, *until-after*, *latches-until* can all be defined in terms of *U*, they do not enhance the expressiveness, but possibly the intelligibility of a temporal logic containing the "until" operator.

Extensions of traditional temporal logic have been applied to specifying and reasoning about concurrent systems. In [Pnu79], the temporal semantics of concurrent programs is defined using a temporal logic with $\Box$ and $\circ$, and it is shown how reasoning can be performed in this framework. Further work on this topic can be found in [Krö87], where the temporal logic is based on *atnext*. A logic with $\Box$, $\circ$ and *while* is applied to the specification of hardware modules in [Boc82]. [ScMe82] provides an alternating-bit protocol specification in a logic with *U* and *latches-until*.

With respect to abstraction and composition, the "next" operator is problematic. Specifying $\circ\varphi$ requires that φ holds in the next moment in time, which could be invalidated when moving to a finer granularity on a lower level of abstraction, where further moments in time could be inserted between the current and the next moment. Furthermore, if two components are combined into one system, it can happen that $\circ\varphi$ is no longer possible due to synchronization constraints. These difficulties make the "next" operator inappropriate for open distributed systems as recognized, for instance, in [Lam83]: "increasing the expressiveness of our temporal logic with a next operator would destroy the entire logical foundation for its use in hierarchical methods". Since the "next" operator can be expressed in terms of *atnext* and *before*, the same concerns apply to these operators.

The "until" operator is an important extension, since it allows specifying bounded intervals. However, it is not possible to specify intervals within intervals by, for instance, nesting several 'until's: for $\sigma,n \models (\varphi_1\ U\ \varphi_2)\ U\ \varphi_3$ to hold, there must be $m \geq n$ such that $\sigma,m \models \varphi_3$, thus establishing the scope of a bounded interval. Within that interval, i.e. for all $n \leq k < m$, $\sigma,k \models \varphi_1\ U\ \varphi_2$ must hold. If $m > n$, then this is only possible if there is $j \geq m\text{-}1$ such that $\sigma,j \models \varphi_2$, which establishes the scope of another bounded interval that can overlap with the first one.

3.2.3 Past time temporal logic

The classical temporal logics (see [Pri67], [ReUr71]) are usually symmetrical, including operators to refer both to future and past. "Resistance to the inclusion of the past operators was based on the strive for minimality and on the observation ... that if we restrict [ourselves to systems] that have a definite start point in time, then the past operators do not add any expressive power" ([LiPnZu85]). However, many requirements arising in specifications are easier to express and therefore better intelligible using past operators. The following past operators are obtained from their counterparts referring to the future. Let φ, φ_1, φ_2 be formulas, then

- $\blacksquare\ \varphi$ (read "always in the past φ") means that φ is true now and has always been true in the past;
- $\blacklozenge\ \varphi$ (read "sometime in the past φ") means that φ is true now or has been true sometime in the past;
- $\bullet\ \varphi$ (read "previously φ") means that φ has been true in the previous state, if that state exists;
- $\varphi_1\ S\ \varphi_2$ (read "φ_1 since φ_2") means that φ_2 has been true sometime in the past, and since then, φ_1 holds.

For the n-th state of a model σ, the meaning of these operators is formally defined to be:

$$\sigma,n \models \blacksquare\ \varphi \quad \text{iff} \quad \forall m.\ (0 \leq m \leq n \text{ implies } \sigma,m \models \varphi)$$

$$\sigma,n \models \blacklozenge\ \varphi \quad \text{iff} \quad \exists m.\ (0 \leq m \leq n \text{ and } \sigma,m \models \varphi)$$

$$\sigma,n \models \bullet\ \varphi \quad \text{iff} \quad (n > 0 \text{ implies } \sigma,n\text{-}1 \models \varphi)$$

$$\sigma,n \models \varphi_1\ S\ \varphi_2 \quad \text{iff} \quad \exists m.\ (0 \leq m \leq n \text{ and } \sigma,m \models \varphi_2 \text{ and } \forall k.\ (m < k \leq n \text{ implies } \sigma,k \models \varphi_1))$$

■ and ◆ are, as the related future operators, dual operators. They can also be defined in terms of *S*:

$$\blacksquare\ \varphi \quad =_{Df} \quad \neg \blacklozenge \neg\varphi$$
$$\blacklozenge\ \varphi \quad =_{Df} \quad \neg \blacksquare \neg\varphi$$
$$\blacklozenge\ \varphi \quad =_{Df} \quad true\ S\ \varphi$$

As shown in [LiPnZu85], a natural classification of formulas into safety and liveness properties is possible in a temporal logic with past and future operators. The syntactical characterization of safety coincides with the semantical definition of safety in [AlSc85], and the class of liveness properties according to [AlSc85] is strictly contained in the class of liveness properties in [LiPnZu85].

With the past fragment of temporal logic, it is possible to state safety properties only. In order to state liveness properties, future operators have to be added. In a temporal logic with future operators, the addition of corresponding past operators does not add any expressive power, if systems having a definite starting point in time are to be specified ([LiPnZu85]). Here, properties referring to the past can be stated by introducing auxiliary variables such as state histories or traces. Alternatively, the use of history variables can be avoided by including past operators. Moreover, the past fragment allows in many cases a more natural and concise specification. Therefore, it furthers abstractness and intelligibility of temporal properties.

Like the "next" operator, the "previous" operator is problematic with respect to abstraction. The property ••φ, for instance, could be invalidated when moving to a finer granularity on a lower level of abstraction. Also, it is not possible to specify intervals within intervals using the "since" operator.

3.2.4 Branching time temporal logic

The temporal logics considered so far have in common that formulas are interpreted over a sequence of states. Therefore, these logics are collectively referred to as *linear time temporal logics*. If the view is taken that at each point in time there exist several alternative futures, then it is straightforward to replace the sequence of states by a tree of states and to interpret formulas on such trees. These logics are referred to as *branching time temporal logics*. The following operators have been introduced in *Computation Tree Logic* (*CTL*, see [ClEmSi86]). Let, φ, φ_1, φ_2 be formulas, then

- AG φ (read "φ is global") means that φ will hold for every sequence at every moment in time;
- AF φ (read "φ is inevitable") means that φ will hold for every sequence at some moment in time;
- EG φ means that φ will hold for some sequence at every moment in time;
- EF φ (read "φ is potential") means that φ will hold for some sequence at some moment in time;
- AX φ (read "next time φ") means that φ holds at every immediate successor state;
- EX φ means that φ holds at some immediate successor state;
- A [φ_1 U φ_2] means that for every sequence, φ_2 will hold at some state, and until then, φ_1 holds;
- E [φ_1 U φ_2] means that for some sequence, φ_2 will hold at some state, and until then, φ_1 holds.

The formal semantics of these operators is defined with respect to *Kripke structures* $\langle W,R,V \rangle$ ([Kri63], [HuCr68]) where the *seeing-relation* $R \subseteq W \times W$ on the set of *worlds* W is reflexive, transitive, antisymmetrical, and backwards linear. This is the case for a model that is a (possibly infinite) state tree. Let π be a state tree and $\sigma = \langle \sigma_0\sigma_1 ... \sigma_n ... \rangle$ be a state sequence. $\sigma \in \pi$ denotes a complete state sequence of the state tree π, $\sigma^{n-} = \langle \sigma_0\sigma_1 ... \sigma_n \rangle$ is the prefix of σ of length n+1. $\sigma^{n-} < \sigma'$ expresses that σ^{n-} is a prefix of σ'. Then the meaning of the branching time operators AX, EX, A[.U.], E[.U.] is defined for the n-th state of the state sequence $\sigma \in \pi$ to be:

$$\pi,\sigma,n \models \text{AX } \varphi \quad \text{iff} \quad \forall \sigma' \in \pi. \, (\sigma^{n-} < \sigma' \text{ implies } \pi,\sigma',n+1 \models \varphi)$$

$$\pi,\sigma,n \models \text{EX } \varphi \quad \text{iff} \quad \exists \sigma' \in \pi. \, (\sigma^{n-} < \sigma' \text{ and } \pi,\sigma',n+1 \models \varphi)$$

$$\pi,\sigma,n \models \text{A } [\varphi_1 \text{ U } \varphi_2] \quad \text{iff} \quad \forall \sigma' \in \pi. \, (\sigma^{n-} < \sigma' \text{ implies } \exists m \geq n. \, (\pi,\sigma',m \models \varphi_2 \text{ and } \forall k. \, (n \leq k < m \text{ implies } \pi,\sigma',k \models \varphi_1)))$$

$$\pi,\sigma,n \models \text{E } [\varphi_1 \text{ U } \varphi_2] \quad \text{iff} \quad \exists \sigma' \in \pi. \, (\sigma^{n-} < \sigma' \text{ and } \exists m \geq n. \, (\pi,\sigma',m \models \varphi_2 \text{ and } \forall k. \, (n \leq k < m \text{ implies } \pi,\sigma',k \models \varphi_1)))$$

The other operators can be defined in terms of A[.U.] and E[.U.]:

$$\text{AF } \varphi \;=_{Df}\; \text{A } [\textit{true} \text{ U } \varphi]$$

$$\text{EF } \varphi \;=_{Df}\; \text{E } [\textit{true} \text{ U } \varphi]$$

$$AG\ \varphi =_{Df} \neg EF \neg\varphi$$
$$EG\ \varphi =_{Df} \neg AF \neg\varphi$$

By choosing subsets of the operators listed here, several branching time temporal logics are obtained. For some of them, expressiveness results can be found in [EmHa86].

With the operators AG and AF, it can be expressed that a property is global and inevitable, which corresponds to the meaning of "henceforth" and "eventually" in the linear framework. Moreover, EF φ states that φ is potential, which goes beyond the expressiveness of linear time temporal logic. The reason that it can be expressed in the branching time version is that existential quantification over the paths of the tree (see semantics of EF) is possible.

Branching time temporal logic has been applied to specifying and reasoning about the mutual exclusion problem and the alternating-bit protocol in [ClEmSi86]. In order to verify properties of finite-state concurrent systems expressed in branching time temporal logic, model-checking can be performed. Here, it suffices to have a finite-state system after a suitable abstraction. Many systems are "in essence" finite-state systems such as protocol systems ([Wol86]) where the control flow is independent of the messages being conveyed.

3.2.5 Interval logic

"A higher-level temporal concept that pervades almost all temporal specifications is that of a property being true for an interval" ([ScMeVo83a]). As outlined in Chapter 3.2.2, the "until" operator provides some expressiveness to refer to bounded intervals. However, this is very rudimentary and quickly leads to unmanageable formulas when the context gets more complex. Also, it is not possible to express intervals within intervals.

Interval logic ([ScMeVo83], [ScMeVo83a], [Mel88]) is a formalism in which bounded intervals can be expressed in a systematical and intelligible way. It provides operators to construct future intervals, thereby extending traditional temporal logic. Interval logic still belongs to the category of linear time temporal logics, since all formulas are interpreted on a state sequence. As before, it is assumed that time is discrete. Formulas of interval logic have the form [I] φ, which informally means: the next time the interval I is found, the formula φ will hold for that interval.

To construct intervals, a notion of *event* is introduced which is captured by the change of the truth value of formulas. This conforms to the view that an event is a detectable change. For instance, let φ be a formula, then $[\varphi]$ denotes the primitive interval consisting of the next sequence of two consecutive states such that $\neg\varphi$ is true for the first state, and φ is true for the second state.

More complex intervals can be constructed with the help of two interval operators $\Rightarrow$ and $\Leftarrow$. Intuitively, the directions of the arrows indicate in which direction and in which order the interval end points are located. The end point of the interval expressed by the interval term at the tail of the arrow is located first, followed by a search in the direction of the arrow for the end point of the interval denoted by the interval term at the head of the arrow. For instance, $[I \Rightarrow J]\ \varphi$ means that the interval I must be located first, and J has to be located in the context starting with the end point of I. The intervals I and J can be primitive intervals as defined by an event interval consisting of two consecutive states, or complex intervals constructed with interval operators $\Rightarrow$ and $\Leftarrow$. The interval defined by $[I \Rightarrow J]$ starts at the end point of I and ends at the end point of J. If it can be constructed, i.e., I and J can be located in the current context in that order, φ must hold for that interval; if it can not be constructed, the formula $[I \Rightarrow J]\ \varphi$ is vacuously true. The formal semantics of interval formulas is given in [ScMeVo83a].

Another complex interval is expressed by $[(I \Rightarrow J) \Leftarrow K]$. Here, the end point of K is located first, followed by a search for I in the backward direction. From there, J is located in the forward direction, and the constructed interval starts at the end point of J and ends at the end point of K. Note that interval formulas are interpreted with respect to the future, so a backward search for an interval can never be extended to the past. Also, when a bounded interval has been established, backward and forward search takes place within these boundaries. This means that for the interval $[(I \Rightarrow J) \Leftarrow K]$ to be constructed, J must be found within $[I \Leftarrow K]$.

Two functions *begin* and *end* are defined on intervals to extract unit intervals. If I is an interval term, then *begin* I (*end* I) denotes the first (last) state of I.

The formula $[I]\ \varphi$ is vacuously true if the interval I can not be constructed. Specifying $[*I]\ \varphi$ requires I to occur. This formula can be rewritten as $[I]\ \varphi \wedge *I$, where $*I =_{Df} \neg [I]\, \mathit{false}$.

In interval logic, it is straightforward to express intervals within intervals. For instance, $[I]\ [J]\ \varphi$ states that φ must hold for the interval J located within I. Thus, the outer interval term establishes the context in which the rest of the formula is interpreted.

Interval logic has been applied to specifying and reasoning about the alternating-bit protocol in [ScMeVo83] and [Mel88].

Because interval logic belongs to the class of linear time temporal logics, it is not possible to express potential behaviour. A classification of formulas into safety and liveness properties is probably difficult, since interval logic provides only future operators. Also, architectural meaning can not be formally associated with formulas within the framework of interval logic, because it is based on propositional logic.

3.2.6 Incorporation of events

In Chapter 2.1, the notion of *event* has been identified as a basic architectural concept of open distributed systems. An event is a local action performed by an agent. A derived concept is the *interaction*, which is decomposable into a set of events associated with different agents. Since events are the basic constituents of behaviour, they should be explicitly expressable in any formalism applied to the specification of open distributed systems.

There are several ways to model and express events in temporal logic. One approach is to interpret atomic formulas as events. If p is an atomic formula, then the event p occurs if p is true, i.e., if $\sigma,n \models p$ holds. This approach has been chosen in [Vog82], where the *event model* is introduced: "The Event-Model EM is a triple (E,σ,Σ) where E is a finite set of interaction events, σ is an infinite sequence of interaction events (past) and Σ is a in general infinite set of sequences of events (future)." Formulas of traditional temporal logic are then interpreted in this model. Since the event model is built from sequences of events, the restriction applies that at each moment in time only one event can occur, i.e., the events of every single event sequence are totally ordered.

In [Pnu86], the temporal language is extended by *event-predicates* of the form $P_E(x)$ denoting the occurrence of event E with data parameter x. Particular event predicates are $\langle \alpha!d \rangle$ interpreted as "The value d is currently written on channel α" and $\langle \alpha?d \rangle$ stating that "The value d is currently read from channel α". Event-predicates are interpreted in an extended model $\sigma = \sigma_0 \rightarrow_{\tau_0} \sigma_1 \rightarrow_{\tau_1} \sigma_2 \rightarrow_{\tau_2} \ldots$ concentrating on transitions τ_i between states σ_i and σ_{i+1} (see also [BaKuPn84]). Several events may occur in the same transition.

Another approach is presented in [HeMi85], where a set of events termed "*types of observation*" is defined. The view is taken that any observation performed by a process p entails some participation by p as well as by the observed environment. Thus, an observation changes the state of the process. To express observations, temporal operators $\langle i \rangle$ and $[i]$ are defined for each i ∈ I of observation types. If φ is a formula, p a process, then $p \models \langle i \rangle \varphi$ is true if and only if p can perform an observation of type i such that afterwards φ is true. $[i]$ is a dual operator which can be defined as $[i]\varphi =_{Df} \neg\langle i \rangle\neg\varphi$.

In [ScMeVo83] (see Chapter 3.2.5), the change of the truth value of a formula is interpreted as an event occurrence. If φ is a formula, then the event φ occurs whenever there are two consecutive states σ_{n-1} and σ_n such that $\sigma,n\text{-}1 \models \neg\varphi$ and $\sigma,n \models \varphi$ hold. This corresponds to the view that an event is a detectable change. Different from the event model, atomic formulas are not interpreted as events. Furthermore, it is not required that at every moment in time only one event can occur. In fact, whenever two consecutive states of a model σ differ, an infinite number of events occurs, because there is an infinite number of formulas changing their truth value. However, in a specification, only a finite number of events are used, therefore, the generality of this approach is not fully exploited.

3.2.7 The impact of validity

In order to define what it means for a system to have a property expressed in temporal logic, the notions of satisfaction and validity are used. A formula φ is said to be *satisfied in a model* σ (written "$\sigma \models \varphi$") if and only if φ is true in some state of σ, i.e., $\exists n \geq 0.\ \sigma,n \models \varphi$. φ is *satisfiable* if such a model exists, otherwise it is called *unsatisfiable*. φ is *valid* (written "$\models \varphi$") if and only if φ is true in all states of all models σ. Note that under these standard definitions, φ is valid if and only if ¬φ is unsatisfiable, and φ is not valid if and only if ¬φ is satisfiable.

In [Pnu86], different notions of satisfaction and validity are given. A formula φ is said to be *initially-satisfied in a model* σ (written "$\sigma \models_i \varphi$") if and only if φ is true in the first state of σ, i.e., $\sigma,0 \models \varphi$. φ is *initially-satisfiable* if such a model exists. φ is *initially-valid*[17] (written "$\models_i \varphi$") if and only if φ is initially-satisfied in all models σ.

The notions of validity and initial validity can be extended to models Σ that are sets of state sequences. Such models are often associated with concurrent systems. A formula φ is said to be *valid for a model* Σ (written "$\Sigma \models \varphi$") if and only if φ is true in all states

17 Initial validity as defined here has been termed "validity" in [Pnu79].

of all sequences of Σ, i.e., $\forall \sigma \in \Sigma.\ \forall n \geq 0.\ \sigma, n \models \varphi$. φ is *initially-valid for a model* Σ (written "$\Sigma \models_i \varphi$") if and only if φ is initially-satisfied for all sequences $\sigma \in \Sigma$. From these definitions, it is clear that for any linear time temporal logic the following holds:

$$\begin{array}{lll} \sigma \models_i \varphi & \text{implies} & \sigma \models \varphi \\ \Sigma \models \varphi & \text{implies} & \Sigma \models_i \varphi \\ \models \varphi & \text{implies} & \models_i \varphi \end{array}$$

Also, under the usual interpretation of $\Box$ and $\Diamond$ (see Chapter 3.2.1), the following can be shown:

$$\begin{array}{lll} \sigma \models \varphi & \text{iff} & \sigma \models_i \Diamond \varphi \\ \Sigma \models \varphi & \text{iff} & \Sigma \models_i \Box \varphi \\ \models \varphi & \text{iff} & \models_i \Box \varphi \end{array}$$

A system is said to have the property φ if and only if φ is initially-valid for the associated model Σ (compare [Pnu79][18], [Hai82], [Pnu86]). Under this definition, it is possible to specify constraints for the initial state of a system, which is exploited, for instance, in [Lam80]: INIT $\supset \Box$ GOOD, i.e., if the system is in a proper initial state, something bad never happens.

Alternatively, we could define that a system has the property φ if and only if φ is valid for the associated model Σ. Under this definition, all properties are *invariant*. Therefore, it is in general not possible to specify restrictions for the initial state only[19]. Furthermore, recall that $\Sigma \models \varphi$ iff $\Sigma \models_i \Box \varphi$. From the latter two observations, it follows that the expressiveness of a temporal logic with respect to models Σ is in general strictly stronger under initial validity than under validity. So, the notion of validity has an impact on the expressiveness of temporal logic.

If we define that a system has the property φ if and only if φ is initially-valid for the associated model Σ, the question arises whether this affects reasoning in temporal logic. Are the decision procedures for validity also applicable to decide initial validity? Certainly, if a formula is valid, then it is initially-valid. However, the converse does not hold in general; but for many temporal logics, validity and initial validity are equivalent:

---

18 Initial validity has been termed "validity" in [Pnu79].

19 If the temporal logic allows defining a formula that is true only for the initial state, such as $\bullet$ *false*, it is possible.

Proposition: There are temporal logics where $\models_i \varphi$ does not imply $\models \varphi$.

Proof: Let $\sigma,n \models \bullet\ \varphi$ iff $n > 0$ implies $\sigma,n\text{-}1 \models \varphi$. Then the formula $\bullet$ *false* is initially-valid, but not valid.

Proposition: For temporal logics without operators to refer to the past, $\models_i \varphi$ implies $\models \varphi$.

Proof: Assume this is not the case. Then there must be a model $\sigma = \langle\, \sigma_0\sigma_1...\sigma_n... \,\rangle$ such that $\sigma,0 \models \varphi$ and $\exists n \geq 0.\ \sigma,n \not\models \varphi$. Now take the model σ^{n+} that is obtained from σ by removing the sequence $\langle\, \sigma_0\sigma_1...\sigma_{n-1} \,\rangle$. Because due to our assumption φ is initially-valid, $\sigma^{n+},0 \models \varphi$ holds. However, $\sigma^{n+},0 \models \varphi$ implies $\sigma,n \models \varphi$, which contradicts the assumption.

It follows that for temporal logics without operators to refer to the past, validity and initial validity are equivalent. Therefore, the decision procedures for validity can be applied to decide initial validity in these cases. However, they can not be applied to decide initial validity in general, as the first proposition shows.

For the specification of open distributed systems, it is often required to define properties holding in the initial state. In these cases, the definition that a system has the property expressed by a formula φ if and only if φ is initially-valid for the associated model Σ has to be chosen unless a property which is initially-valid, but not valid is expressable.

3.3 A modular temporal logic for open distributed systems

The previous survey has shown that each of the temporal logics can cover only some of the requirements that have been studied in Chapter 3.1. For instance, potential behaviour can be expressed in branching time temporal logic, complex contexts can be established using interval logic, architectural meaning can be associated with formulas of first-order logic, etc. However, just throwing these different kinds of logics together is certainly not the right approach for obtaining a suitable formalism. Like any other formalism, a temporal logic for a particular area of application should be designed very carefully.

One important criterion for the design of a temporal logic is its degree of expressiveness. The more expressive a formalism is, the more can be specified. However, there is a reciprocal effect between the expressive power and the reasoning power of a formalism, namely increasing expressiveness can render the decision problem more complex or even unsolvable. Therefore, the degree of expressiveness should be chosen with great care. We have made the experience that the necessary expressiveness can vary considerably within the same problem area. For instance, open systems can be reliable or unreliable, they can involve finite or infinite data domains, etc. It follows that any formalism will be too expressive for some problems and/or not expressive enough for other problems.

In order to escape this intrinsic difficulty, we will introduce a so-called "*modular*" temporal logic, i.e., a temporal logic that is formed as a set of building blocks, each consisting of a class of atomic formulas or a group of logical operators. From this modular temporal logic, different temporal logics can be obtained by combining subsets of these building blocks. The advantage of this approach is that the temporal logic can be customized according to the needed expressiveness with the consequence that as much reasoning power as possible is preserved.

3.3.1 Semantical models

Formulas of propositional modal logic are interpreted in semantical models $\langle W,R,V \rangle$, termed "*Kripke structures*" ([Kri63], [HuCr68]), where W is a set of *worlds*, $R \subseteq W \times W$ is a *seeing-relation* on the set of worlds, and $V: \Phi \times W \rightarrow \{0,1\}$ is a *value assignment* determining the truth value of every atomic proposition in every world. Since temporal logics belong to the category of modal logics, temporal formulas can be interpreted in Kripke structures. However, to take the nature of time into account, certain restrictions on the seeing-relation R have to be imposed. Usually, time is conceived as linear, which can be formally captured by demanding R to be a total order. On occasion, time is conceived as branching, i.e., at each point in time, there exist several alternative futures, which is formally expressed by R being a partial order with backward linearity. In both cases time can have a starting point, and it is either dense or discrete, which can be captured by further constraints on R (see [HuCr68], [HuCr84]).

We will follow current practice in computer science and interpret temporal formulas on state sequences and state trees rather than referring to Kripke structures. However, note that the corresponding Kripke structure can be directly obtained from state sequences or state trees, and vice versa. Here, each element of the state sequence or state tree corresponds to a different world of the related Kripke structure. This means that different occurrences of the same state correspond to different worlds. We assume that time is discrete and has a starting point.

The temporal logics introduced in the following can be based on propositional logic as well as first-order logic. First-order logic is more expressive, but undecidable, whereas a temporal logic that is based on propositional logic is often decidable. In the propositional framework, a state is defined by a set of true atomic propositions; in the first-order framework, it is given by a set of functions and relations.

To interpret temporal formulas in these different frameworks, the following types of semantical models will be used:

- $\mathcal{M}_{PL}$ model of propositional linear time temporal logic
- $\mathcal{M}_{PB}$ model of propositional branching time temporal logic
- $\mathcal{M}_{FL}$ model of many-sorted first-order linear time temporal logic
- $\mathcal{M}_{FB}$ model of many-sorted first-order branching time temporal logic

When only a distinction between linear and branching time is to be drawn, we write $\mathcal{M}_L$ and $\mathcal{M}_B$, respectively. Similarly, $\mathcal{M}_P$ and $\mathcal{M}_F$ abstract from the nature of time and refer to the propositional and first-order frameworks, respectively.

To define the structure of these model types and the semantics of temporal formulas, some notational conventions are useful. σ and σ' denote infinite state sequences, σ_i is the (i+1)th element of the state sequence σ. $\sigma^{i,j}$ denotes the subsequence $\langle \sigma_i ... \sigma_j \rangle$, $\sigma^{0,j} < \sigma'$ expresses that $\sigma^{0,j}$ is a prefix of σ'. π and π' are infinite state trees, $r(\pi)$ is the root state of π. $\sigma \in \pi$ means that σ is a branch of π, so from $\sigma \in \pi$ it follows that $\sigma_0 = r(\pi)$.

__Definition 3.1:__ A model $\mathcal{M}_{PL}$ of propositional linear time temporal logic is a structure $\langle AG, S, S_0, \Sigma, \Phi, lp \rangle$, where

- AG is a non-empty, finite set of objects termed "*agents*";
- S is a set of states, where each state is defined by a set of true atomic propositions;
- $S_0 \subseteq S$ is a non-empty set of initial states;
- $\Sigma \subseteq S^{\omega}$ is a set of infinite state sequences $\sigma = \langle \sigma_0 \sigma_1 ... \sigma_n ... \rangle$ with initial states from S_0, i.e., $\sigma_0 \in S_0$ for all $\sigma \in \Sigma$;
- Φ is a finite set of atomic propositions;
- lp: $AG \rightarrow 2^{\Phi}$ is a function associating with each agent the set of its local atomic propositions; an atomic proposition can only be local to one agent,

therefore, it is required that $ag, ag' \in AG$ and $ag \neq ag'$ implies $lp(ag) \cap lp(ag') = \{\}$.

Definition 3.2: A model $\mathcal{M}_{PB}$ of propositional branching time temporal logic is a structure $\langle AG, S, S_0, \Pi, \Phi, lp \rangle$, where

- AG, S, S_0, Φ, and lp are defined as for $\mathcal{M}_{PL}$ (see Definition 3.1);
- Π is a set of infinite state trees with root states from S_0, i.e., $r(\pi) \in S_0$ for all $\pi \in \Pi$; furthermore, it is required that for all $\pi, \pi' \in \Pi$, $r(\pi) = r(\pi')$ implies $\pi = \pi'$ (or, $\pi \neq \pi'$ implies $r(\pi) \neq r(\pi')$).

Definition 3.3: A model $\mathcal{M}_{FL}$ of many-sorted first-order linear time temporal logic is a structure $\langle AG, IP, E, \mathcal{A}rchf, S, S_0, \Sigma \rangle$, where

- AG is a non-empty, finite set of objects termed "*agents*";
- IP is a non-empty, finite set of objects termed "*interaction points*";
- $E = (E_1, \ldots, E_n)$ is a family of sets of objects;
- $\mathcal{A}rchf$: $AG \rightarrow 2^{IP}$ is a total function called "*architecture function*" associating with each agent a set of interaction points; it is required that each element from IP is associated with one or more agents, i.e., $IP = \bigcup_{ag \in AG} \mathcal{A}rchf(ag)$.
- S is a set of states, where each state is given by the function $\mathcal{A}rchf$, a set $\mathcal{F}$ of functions, and a set $\mathcal{R}$ of relations on E, AG, and IP;
- S_0 and Σ are defined as for $\mathcal{M}_{PL}$ (see Definition 3.1).

Definition 3.4: A model $\mathcal{M}_{FB}$ of many-sorted first-order branching time temporal logic is a structure $\langle AG, IP, E, \mathcal{A}rchf, S, S_0, \Pi \rangle$, where

- AG, IP, E, $\mathcal{A}rchf$, S, and S_0 are defined as for $\mathcal{M}_{FL}$ (see Definition 3.3);
- Π is defined as for $\mathcal{M}_{PB}$ (see Definition 3.2).

Associating architectural meaning with atomic formulas is straightforward in many-sorted first-order temporal logic, and has been taken into account by the explicit introduction of a set AG of agents and a set IP of interaction points in $\mathcal{M}_{FL}$ and $\mathcal{M}_{FB}$. Moreover, an architecture function $\mathcal{A}rchf$ associating with each agent a set of interaction points is defined. Thus, system architectures $\mathcal{A}rch$ (see Definition 2.1) can be completely modeled. A set $\{ag_1, \ldots, ag_n\}$ of $n > 1$ agents has one or more common interaction points if and only if the intersection of $\mathcal{A}rchf(ag_i)$ for i from 1 to n is not empty. As outlined in Chapter 2.1, the existence of a common interaction point is a necessary condition for a direct interaction between a set of $n > 1$ agents. Note that $\mathcal{A}rchf$ is a static function, i.e., the architecture does not change between states. $\mathcal{A}rchf$ could also be a dynamic function, however, these aspects are not treated in this work.

Atomic formulas are not decomposable within the framework of propositional temporal logic. This renders their architectural interpretation more difficult. To make propositional temporal logic applicable to the specification of distributed systems, we have extended the semantical model by introducing a set AG of agents and a function lp associating with each agent the set of its local atomic propositions. Atomic propositions which are not in the range of lp are called "*non-local*". Incorporation of further architectural concepts, for instance, interaction points, requires a modification of this semantical model.

In the following chapters, the semantics of temporal formulas with respect to the satisfaction relation $\models$ will be given. For models of type $\mathcal{M}_{PL}$, $\models$ is a relation between $\mathcal{M}_{PL}$, a sequence $\sigma \in \Sigma$, positions i, j, and a formula φ (written "$\mathcal{M}_{PL},(\sigma,i,j) \models \varphi$"). For models of type $\mathcal{M}_{FL}$, it is a relation between $\mathcal{M}_{FL}$, σ, i, j, φ as before and a *variable valuation* h (written "$\mathcal{M}_{FL},(\sigma,i,j,h) \models \varphi$" or "$\mathcal{M}_{FL},(\sigma,i,j) \models \varphi$" for short). For models of type $\mathcal{M}_{PB}$, $\models$ is a relation between $\mathcal{M}_{PB}$, a tree $\pi \in \Pi$, a sequence $\sigma \in \pi$, positions i, j, and a formula φ (written "$\mathcal{M}_{PB},(\pi,\sigma,i,j) \models \varphi$"). For models of type $\mathcal{M}_{FB}$, it is a relation between $\mathcal{M}_{FB}$, π, σ, i, j, φ as before and a variable valuation h (written "$\mathcal{M}_{FB},(\pi,\sigma,i,j,h) \models \varphi$" or "$\mathcal{M}_{FB},(\pi,\sigma,i,j) \models \varphi$" for short). Given this relation, several derived notions (see Chapter 3.2.7) can be defined:

Definition 3.5: For models of linear time temporal logic, the notions of satisfaction and validity of a formula φ are defined to be:

- φ is *L-satisfied in a model* $\mathcal{M}_L$ for a state sequence $\sigma \in \Sigma$ (written "$\mathcal{M}_L,\sigma \models \varphi$") if $\mathcal{M}_L,(\sigma,0,j) \models \varphi$ holds for some $j \geq 0$;
- φ is *L-valid in a model* $\mathcal{M}_L$ (written "$\mathcal{M}_L \models \varphi$") if $\mathcal{M}_L,(\sigma,0,j) \models \varphi$ holds for all $\sigma \in \Sigma$ and all $j \geq 0$;
- φ is *L-valid* (written "$\models_L \varphi$") if $\mathcal{M}_L \models \varphi$ for every model $\mathcal{M}_L$;
- φ is *L-initially-satisfied in a model* $\mathcal{M}_L$ for a state sequence $\sigma \in \Sigma$ (written "$\mathcal{M}_L,\sigma \models_i \varphi$") if $\mathcal{M}_L,(\sigma,0,0) \models \varphi$ holds;
- φ is *L-initially-valid in a model* $\mathcal{M}_L$ (written "$\mathcal{M}_L \models_i \varphi$") if $\mathcal{M}_L,\sigma \models_i \varphi$ holds for all $\sigma \in \Sigma$;
- φ is *L-initially-valid* (written "$\models_{iL} \varphi$") if $\mathcal{M}_L \models_i \varphi$ for every model $\mathcal{M}_L$.

Definition 3.6: For models of branching time temporal logic, the notions of satisfaction and validity of a formula φ are defined to be:

- φ is *B-satisfied in a model* $\mathcal{M}_B$ for a state tree π (written "$\mathcal{M}_B,\pi \models \varphi$") if $\mathcal{M}_B,(\pi,\sigma,0,j) \models \varphi$ holds for some $\sigma \in \pi$ and some $j \geq 0$;

- φ is *B-valid in a model* $\mathcal{M}_B$ (written "$\mathcal{M}_B \models \varphi$") if $\mathcal{M}_B,(\pi,\sigma,0,j) \models \varphi$ holds for all $\pi \in \Pi$, all $\sigma \in \pi$ and all $j \geq 0$;
- φ is *B-valid* (written "$\models_B \varphi$") if $\mathcal{M}_B \models \varphi$ for every model $\mathcal{M}_B$;
- φ is *B-initially-satisfied in a model* $\mathcal{M}_B$ for a state tree π (written "$\mathcal{M}_B,\pi \models_i \varphi$") if $\mathcal{M}_B,(\pi,\sigma,0,0) \models \varphi$ holds for some $\sigma \in \pi$;
- φ is *B-initially-valid in a model* $\mathcal{M}_B$ (written "$\mathcal{M}_B \models_i \varphi$") if $\mathcal{M}_B,\pi \models_i \varphi$ holds for all $\pi \in \Pi$;
- φ is *B-initially-valid* (written "$\models_{iB} \varphi$") if $\mathcal{M}_B \models_i \varphi$ for every model $\mathcal{M}_B$.

Corollary 3.1: From these definitions, it follows directly that

i) $\mathcal{M}_L,\sigma \models_i \varphi$ implies $\mathcal{M}_L,\sigma \models \varphi$
ii) $\mathcal{M}_L \models \varphi$ implies $\mathcal{M}_L \models_i \varphi$
iii) $\models_L \varphi$ implies $\models_{iL} \varphi$
iv) $\mathcal{M}_B,\pi \models_i \varphi$ implies $\mathcal{M}_B,\pi \models \varphi$
v) $\mathcal{M}_B \models \varphi$ implies $\mathcal{M}_B \models_i \varphi$
vi) $\models_B \varphi$ implies $\models_{iB} \varphi$

When the nature of time is clear from the context, the prefixes and subscripts L and B will be omitted.

3.3.2 Atomic formulas and non-temporal operators

In this and the following chapters, a so-called "*modular*" temporal logic is introduced. It is formed as a set of building blocks, each consisting of a class of atomic formulas or a group of logical operators. For each of these building blocks, formation rules defining the syntactically correct formulas are presented. Then, the semantics of these formulas when interpreted in the models $\mathcal{M}_{PL}$, $\mathcal{M}_{PB}$, $\mathcal{M}_{FL}$, and $\mathcal{M}_{FB}$ (see Chapter 3.3.1) is recursively defined. If available, an axiomatic basis is provided for each group of logical operators. In the appendix, selections of theorems and valid formulas are listed.

To begin with, the non-temporal aspects of the logic are briefly summarized. We can distinguish between atomic formulas of propositional logic, atomic formulas of many-sorted first-order logic, propositional operators, and quantifiers, which leads to four building blocks referred to as At_P, At_F, Pr, and Q.

In propositional temporal logic, formulas are formed starting from a set Φ of atomic propositions, i.e., propositions which can not be decomposed within the logical framework. Syntax and semantics of atomic formulas can be defined as follows:

Syntax At_P

i) Let $p \in \Phi$, then p is a formula.

Semantics At_P

Let $p \in \Phi$, then

i) $\mathcal{M}_{PL}, (\sigma,i,j) \models p$ iff $p \in \sigma_j$

ii) $\mathcal{M}_{PB}, (\pi,\sigma,i,j) \models p$ iff $p \in \sigma_j$

In many-sorted first-order temporal logic, atomic formulas are formed starting from the following sets of symbols:

- a denumerable list $\mathcal{S}$ of symbols called *sorts*;
- a denumerable list $\mathcal{V}$ of symbols called *individual variables*; each $x \in \mathcal{V}$ is attached to a sort $s \in \mathcal{S}$, which is expressed by writing x^s;
- for each integer $n \geq 0$, a denumerable set $\mathcal{F}^{(n)}$ of *n-ary function symbols*; each $f \in \mathcal{F}^{(n)}$ is associated with sorts $s, s_1, \ldots, s_n \in \mathcal{S}$ (written "$f_{s,s_1,\ldots,s_n}$");
- for each integer $n \geq 0$, a denumerable set $\mathcal{R}^{(n)}$ of *n-ary relation symbols* (also called "*predicate symbols*"); each $r \in \mathcal{R}^{(n)}$ is associated with sorts $s_1, \ldots, s_n \in \mathcal{S}$ (written "$r_{s_1,\ldots,s_n}$").

With these preparations, the syntax of atomic formulas can be defined as follows:

Syntax At_F

i) For all $x^s \in \mathcal{V}$: x^s is a term of sort s.

ii) For all $n \geq 0$, $f_{s,s_1,\ldots,s_n} \in \mathcal{F}^{(n)}$, and terms $t_1,\ldots,t_n$ of sorts $s_1,\ldots,s_n$: $f_{s,s_1,\ldots,s_n}(t_1,\ldots,t_n)$ is a term of sort s.

iii) For all $n \geq 0$, $r_{s_1,\ldots,s_n} \in \mathcal{R}^{(n)}$, and terms $t_1,\ldots,t_n$ of sorts $s_1,\ldots,s_n$: $r_{s_1,\ldots,s_n}(t_1,\ldots,t_n)$ is a formula.

Formulas of many-sorted first-order logic are interpreted in a model of type $\mathcal{M}_F$ by associating *for each state* $\sigma_j \in S$ sort symbols with sets of objects, function symbols with functions, relation symbols with relations as follows:

- to every sort symbol $s \in \mathcal{S}$, a set $D^s \in \{AG, IP, E_1, \ldots, E_n\}$ is attached; for notational convenience, we will use the same identifiers as sort symbols and to refer to the attached object sets, i.e.: $AG, IP, E_i \in \mathcal{S}$ and $D^{AG} = AG$, $D^{IP} = IP$, $D^{E_i} = E_i$;
- for each integer $n \geq 0$: to each n-ary function symbol $f_{s,s_1,\ldots,s_n} \in \mathcal{F}^{(n)}$, a function $f: D^{s_1} \times \ldots \times D^{s_n} \rightarrow D^s$ is attached;
- for each integer $n \geq 0$: to each n-ary relation symbol $r_{s_1,\ldots,s_n} \in \mathcal{R}^{(n)}$, a relation $r \subseteq D^{s_1} \times \ldots \times D^{s_n}$ is attached.

Semantics At_F

Let $t_1,...,t_n$ be terms of sorts $s_1,...,s_n$, x^s be an individual variable, $f_{s,s_1,...,s_n} \in \mathcal{F}^{(n)}$ be a function symbol, $r_{s_1,...,s_n} \in \mathcal{R}^{(n)}$ be a relation symbol. Let h be a *variable valuation*, i.e., a function mapping each individual variable x^s to a value $v \in D^s$:

i) $\mathcal{M}_{FL},(\sigma,i,j,h) \models x^s =_{Df} h(x^s)$

ii) $\mathcal{M}_{FB},(\pi,\sigma,i,j,h) \models x^s =_{Df} h(x^s)$

iii) $\mathcal{M}_{FL},(\sigma,i,j,h) \models f_{s,s_1,...,s_n}(t_1,...,t_n) =_{Df} f(\mathcal{M}_{FL},(\sigma,i,j,h) \models t_1,..., \mathcal{M}_{FL},(\sigma,i,j,h) \models t_n)$ in state σ_j

iv) $\mathcal{M}_{FB},(\pi,\sigma,i,j,h) \models f_{s,s_1,...,s_n}(t_1,...,t_n) =_{Df} f(\mathcal{M}_{FB},(\pi,\sigma,i,j,h) \models t_1,..., \mathcal{M}_{FB},(\pi,\sigma,i,j,h) \models t_n)$ in state σ_j

v) $\mathcal{M}_{FL},(\sigma,i,j,h) \models r_{s_1,...,s_n}(t_1,...,t_n)$ iff $(\mathcal{M}_{FL},(\sigma,i,j,h) \models t_1,..., \mathcal{M}_{FL},(\sigma,i,j,h) \models t_n) \in r$ in state σ_j

vi) $\mathcal{M}_{FB},(\pi,\sigma,i,j,h) \models r_{s_1,...,s_n}(t_1,...,t_n)$ iff $(\mathcal{M}_{FB},(\pi,\sigma,i,j,h) \models t_1,..., \mathcal{M}_{FB},(\pi,\sigma,i,j,h) \models t_n) \in r$ in state σ_j

Other than in propositional temporal logic, it is straightforward to formally associate architectural meaning with formulas of many-sorted first-order temporal logic. For this purpose, a set AG of agents, a set IP of interaction points, and an architecture function $\mathcal{Arch}$: AG $\rightarrow 2^{IP}$ have been introduced (see Chapter 3.3.1).

The next building block consists of a group of non-temporal operators termed "*propositional operators*", which are negation ($\neg$), conjunction ($\wedge$), disjunction ($\vee$), implication ($\supset$), and equivalence ($\equiv$):

Syntax Pr

i) Let φ be a formula, then $\neg\varphi$ is a formula.

ii) Let φ_1, φ_2 be formulas, then $(\varphi_1 \wedge \varphi_2)$, $(\varphi_1 \vee \varphi_2)$, $(\varphi_1 \supset \varphi_2)$, $(\varphi_1 \equiv \varphi_2)$ are formulas.

Semantics Pr

Let φ, φ_1, φ_2 be formulas, then

i) $\mathcal{M}_L,(\sigma,i,j) \models \neg\varphi$ iff $\mathcal{M}_L,(\sigma,i,j) \not\models \varphi$

ii) $\mathcal{M}_L,(\sigma,i,j) \models (\varphi_1 \wedge \varphi_2)$ iff $\mathcal{M}_L,(\sigma,i,j) \models \varphi_1$ and $\mathcal{M}_L,(\sigma,i,j) \models \varphi_2$

iii) $\mathcal{M}_B,(\pi,\sigma,i,j) \models \neg\varphi$ iff $\mathcal{M}_B,(\pi,\sigma,i,j) \not\models \varphi$

iv) $\mathcal{M}_B,(\pi,\sigma,i,j) \models (\varphi_1 \wedge \varphi_2)$ iff $\mathcal{M}_B,(\pi,\sigma,i,j) \models \varphi_1$ and $\mathcal{M}_B,(\pi,\sigma,i,j) \models \varphi_2$

v) $(\varphi_1 \vee \varphi_2) =_{Df} \neg(\neg\varphi_1 \wedge \neg\varphi_2)$

vi) $(\varphi_1 \supset \varphi_2) =_{Df} \neg\varphi_1 \vee \varphi_2$

vii) $(\varphi_1 \equiv \varphi_2) =_{Df} (\varphi_1 \supset \varphi_2) \wedge (\varphi_2 \supset \varphi_1)$

Formulas with operators for disjunction, implication, and equivalence can be replaced by semantically equivalent formulas with propositional operators for negation and conjunction only.

Axiomatic basis *Pr*

Let φ, φ_1, φ_2 be formulas:

A1: $(\varphi \vee \varphi) \supset \varphi$

A2: $\varphi_2 \supset (\varphi_1 \vee \varphi_2)$

A3: $(\varphi_1 \vee \varphi_2) \supset (\varphi_2 \vee \varphi_1)$

A4: $(\varphi_1 \supset \varphi_2) \supset ((\varphi_3 \vee \varphi_1) \supset (\varphi_3 \vee \varphi_2))$

Tr1: $\vdash \varphi_1$ and $\vdash (\varphi_1 \supset \varphi_2)$ implies $\vdash \varphi_2$ (rule of modus ponens)

The axiomatic basis *Pr*, consisting of axiom schemata and transformation rules derives from Whitehead and Russell's *Principia Mathematica* ([WhRu10]). It is correct, i.e., $\vdash \varphi$ implies $\models \varphi$, and complete, i.e., $\models \varphi$ implies $\vdash \varphi$. A selection of theorems that can be proved using the axiomatic basis *Pr* is given in Appendix A.1.

The building block *Q* consists of a group of non-temporal operators termed "*quantifiers*", which are universal quantification ($\forall$) and existential quantification ($\exists$):

Syntax *Q*

i) Let φ be a formula of many-sorted first-order temporal logic, x^s be an individual variable, then $\forall x^s.\varphi$ and $\exists x^s.\varphi$ are formulas.

Semantics *Q*

Let φ be a formula, h be a variable valuation mapping each variable x^s to a value $v \in D^s$. Let $h[v/x^s]$ be the function mapping x^s to v and otherwise being identical with h:

i) $\mathcal{M}_{FL}, (\sigma,i,j,h) \models \forall x^s.\varphi$ iff for all $v \in D^s$, $\mathcal{M}_{FL}, (\sigma,i,j,h[v/x^s]) \models \varphi$

ii) $\mathcal{M}_{FB}, (\pi,\sigma,i,j,h) \models \forall x^s.\varphi$ iff for all $v \in D^s$, $\mathcal{M}_{FB}, (\pi,\sigma,i,j,h[v/x^s]) \models \varphi$

iii) $\exists x^s.\varphi =_{Df} \neg\forall x^s.\neg\varphi$

In specifications, only closed formulas, i.e., formulas where all variable occurences are within the scope of a quantification, will be meaningful.

Axiomatic basis *Q*

Let φ_1 be a closed formula, φ_2 be a formula where x^s is the only free variable, $f_s \in \mathcal{F}^{(0)}$ be a function symbol, and $\varphi_2[f_s/x^s]$ be the formula φ_2 where f_s is substituted for all free occurrences of x^s:

A5: $\forall x^s. (\varphi_1 \supset \varphi_2) \supset (\varphi_1 \supset \forall x^s.\varphi_2)$

A6: $\forall x^s. (\varphi_2 \supset \varphi_1) \supset (\exists x^s.\varphi_2 \supset \varphi_1)$

A7: $(\varphi_1 \supset \exists x^s.\varphi_2) \supset \exists x^s. (\varphi_1 \supset \varphi_2)$

A8: $\varphi_2[f_s/x^s] \supset \exists x^s.\varphi_2$

Tr2: $\vdash \varphi_2[f_s/x^s]$ implies $\vdash \forall x^s.\varphi_2$

If the axiomatic basis *Pr* and *Q* are joined together, they yield a correct and complete axiomatic basis for many-sorted first-order logic.

This ends the synopsis of non-temporal aspects of the modular temporal logic. So far, only few combinations of building blocks are useful, namely At_P and *Pr* yielding propositional logic, At_F and *Pr*, and At_F, *Pr* and *Q* yielding many-sorted first-order logic.

3.3.3 Operators to refer to the future

Operators to refer to the future are needed to express invariance (under initial validity, see Chapter 3.2.7) and liveness. As these are typical properties of open distributed systems, future operators are an essential constituent of a temporal logic for their specification. The survey in Chapter 3.2 has revealed numerous candidates, however, only very few of them will be selected. It is our intention to keep the future fragment of the logic as simple as possible, while adding more expressive power to refer to the past.

In accordance with the decision to have two views of time, namely linear and branching, we will introduce two building blocks F_L and F_B of future operators. Their semantics is independent of the non-temporal aspects, so they can be used both in the propositional and the first-order frameworks. The future operators for linear time are the same as in traditional temporal logic (Chapter 3.2.1):

Syntax F_L

i) Let φ be a formula, then □ φ and ◊ φ are formulas.

Semantics F_L

Let φ be a formula, then

i) $\mathcal{M}_L,(\sigma,i,j) \models \Box\,\varphi$ iff $\forall k \geq j.\ \mathcal{M}_L,(\sigma,i,k) \models \varphi$

ii) $\Diamond\,\varphi =_{Df} \neg\,\Box\,\neg\varphi$

As usual, □ can be read as "henceforth" or "always", and ◊ as "eventually". With these operators, it is possible to state invariance and guarantee. □◊ φ expresses that φ holds from time to time, or infinitely often. ◊□ φ states that from some point in time, φ remains true.

We renounce further future operators for reasons which have been explained in Chapter 3.2. In particular, the "next" operator is rejected because it violates the principles of abstraction and composition, and the "until" operator is not suitable to establish more complex contexts.

Axiomatic basis F_L

Let φ, φ_1, φ_2 be a formulas:

A9:	$\Box\,\varphi \supset \varphi$	(reflexivity)
A10:	$\Box\,(\varphi_1 \supset \varphi_2) \supset (\Box\,\varphi_1 \supset \Box\,\varphi_2)$	(consequence closure)
A11:	$\Box\,\varphi \supset \Box\,\Box\,\varphi$	(transitivity)
A12:	$\Box\,(\Box\,\varphi_1 \supset \Box\,\varphi_2) \vee \Box\,(\Box\,\varphi_2 \supset \Box\,\varphi_1)$	(linearity)
A13:	$\Box\,(\Box\,(\varphi \supset \Box\,\varphi) \supset \varphi) \supset (\Diamond\,\Box\,\varphi \supset \varphi)$	(discreteness)
Tr3:	$\vdash \varphi$ implies $\vdash \Box\,\varphi$	(rule of generalization)

The axiomatic basis F_L can be partially related to constraints imposed on the seeing-relation R (cf. Chapter 3.3.1). Axioms A9 and A11 can be related to reflexivity and transitivity of R, respectively. A12 is valid if R is a total order, and A13 enforces discreteness, i.e. between every pair of states, there is only a finite number of states. The fact that there is a starting point in time (R is well-ordered) can not be captured, because the operators of F_L all refer to the future. The axiomatic basis F_L is a basis for the modal system S4.3.1 ([HuCr68]).

The linear time operators are suitable for specifying liveness properties of reliable systems. If unreliable systems are to be characterized, they are not sufficiently expressive, because it is not possible to specify potential behaviour (see [Lam80]). To cover this, we introduce another building block F_B with future operators for branching time (see Chapter 3.2.4):

<u>Syntax F_B</u>

i) Let φ be a formula, then AG φ, AF φ, EF φ, EG φ are formulas.

<u>Semantics F_B</u>

Let φ be a formula, then

i) $\mathcal{M}_B,(\pi,\sigma,i,j) \models AG\ \varphi$ iff $\forall\sigma' \in \pi.\ \sigma^{0,j} < \sigma'$ implies $\forall k \geq j.\ \mathcal{M}_B,(\pi,\sigma',i,k) \models \varphi$

ii) $\mathcal{M}_B,(\pi,\sigma,i,j) \models AF\ \varphi$ iff $\forall\sigma' \in \pi.\ \sigma^{0,j} < \sigma'$ implies $\exists k \geq j.\ \mathcal{M}_B,(\pi,\sigma',i,k) \models \varphi$

iii) $EF\ \varphi =_{Df} \neg AG \neg \varphi$

iv) $EG\ \varphi =_{Df} \neg AF \neg \varphi$

As usual, AG φ, AF φ, and EF φ express that φ is global, inevitable, and potential, respectively. Note that AG and AF are related to $\Box$ and $\Diamond$ with respect to their interpretations, but are <u>not</u> dual operators. Again, we renounce further operators such as AX and A[.U.].

<u>Axiomatic basis F_B</u>

Let φ, φ_1, φ_2 be a formulas:

A14:	$AG\ \varphi \supset \varphi$	(reflexivity)
A15:	$AG\ (\varphi_1 \supset \varphi_2) \supset (AG\ \varphi_1 \supset AG\ \varphi_2)$	(consequence closure)
A16:	$AG\ \varphi \supset AG\ AG\ \varphi$	(transitivity)
A17:	$AG\ (AG\ (\varphi \supset AG\ \varphi) \supset \varphi) \supset (EF\ AG\ \varphi \supset \varphi)$	(discreteness)
A18:	$\varphi \supset AF\ \varphi$	(reflexivity)
A19:	$AF\ AF\ \varphi \supset AF\ \varphi$	(transitivity)
A20:	$EG\ (EG\ (\varphi \supset EG\ \varphi) \supset \varphi) \supset (AF\ EG\ \varphi \supset \varphi)$	(discreteness)
Tr4:	$\vdash \varphi$ implies $\vdash AG\ \varphi$	(rule of generalization)

Axioms A14, A18 and A16, A19 can be related to reflexivity and transitivity of the seeing-relation R, respectively, A17 and A20 enforce discreteness. Interestingly, the backward linearity of R can not be captured by an extra axiom. The reason is that the operators of F_B are future operators, whereas backward linearity is a property of the past. Therefore, it can be captured in the axiomatic basis P (Chapter 3.3.4). The formulas listed in Appendix A.1, which are valid according to the semantics F_B and Pr, should be provable to be theorems. However, as we could not find syntactical proofs for all of them, we believe that the axiomatic basis F_B is incomplete. We leave this topic for further study.

3.3.4 Operators to refer to the past

For systems having a definite starting point in time, properties referring to the past can be specified by introducing auxiliary variables recording the relevant part of the past ([OwGr76], [LiPnZu85]). A specification may then refer to the values of these variables. Examples of auxiliary variables are *history variables* ([Hai82]) recording a sequence of selected values which some variables assumed in the past, and *traces* ([Hoa85]) recording the sequence of observable events. The alternative and - in the framework of temporal logic - also cleaner approach is the inclusion of temporal operators to refer to the past. In Chapters 3.3.4 through 3.3.6, several groups of past operators will be introduced, starting here with building block P. The operators of P are obtained from their counterparts of traditional temporal logic, defined in F_L (see Chapter 3.3.3):

Syntax P

i) Let φ be a formula, then $\blacksquare\, \varphi$ and $\blacklozenge\, \varphi$ are formulas.

Semantics P

Let φ be a formula, then

i) $\mathcal{M}_L,(\sigma,i,j) \models \blacksquare\, \varphi$ iff $\forall k.\ (i \leq k \leq j$ implies $\mathcal{M}_L,(\sigma,i,k) \models \varphi)$

ii) $\mathcal{M}_B,(\pi,\sigma,i,j) \models \blacksquare\, \varphi$ iff $\forall k.\ (i \leq k \leq j$ implies $\mathcal{M}_B,(\pi,\sigma,i,k) \models \varphi)$

iii) $\blacklozenge\, \varphi =_{Df} \neg \blacksquare \neg\varphi$

Since the past is linear both in $\mathcal{M}_L$ and $\mathcal{M}_B$, no distinction between linear and branching time as it was necessary for the future operators is made. Note that the semantics covers the general case that a limited context in the past has been established: the meaning of $\blacksquare$ and $\blacklozenge$ is defined with respect to a sequence $\langle \sigma_i...\sigma_j \rangle$, where $i,j \geq 0$. In order to establish such a context, further past operators are required (see Chapter 3.3.6). It should be pointed out that - in terms of Kripke structures (see Chapter 3.3.1) -

the semantics of past operators can only be given at the cost of another seeing-relation $R' = R^{-1}$.

Axiomatic basis *P*

Let φ, φ_1, φ_2 be formulas:

A21:	$\blacksquare\, \varphi \supset \varphi$	(reflexivity)
A22:	$\blacksquare\, (\varphi_1 \supset \varphi_2) \supset (\blacksquare\, \varphi_1 \supset \blacksquare\, \varphi_2)$	(consequence closure)
A23:	$\blacksquare\, \varphi \supset \blacksquare\, \blacksquare\, \varphi$	(transitivity)
A24:	$\blacksquare\, (\blacksquare\, \varphi_1 \supset \blacksquare\, \varphi_2) \vee \blacksquare\, (\blacksquare\, \varphi_2 \supset \blacksquare\, \varphi_1)$	(linearity)
A25:	$\blacksquare\, (\blacksquare\, (\varphi \supset \blacksquare\, \varphi) \supset \varphi) \supset (\blacklozenge\, \blacksquare\, \varphi \supset \varphi)$	(discreteness)
A26:	$\blacklozenge\, (\blacksquare\, \varphi \vee \blacksquare\, \neg\, \varphi)$	(boundedness)
Tr5:	$\vdash \varphi$ implies $\vdash \blacksquare\, \varphi$	(rule of generalization)

In analogy to F_L, the axiomatic basis *P* is a basis for the modal system S4.3.1. In addition, the boundedness of the model is captured by the extra axiom A26.

3.3.5 Operators for event occurrence

There is broad consensus that open distributed systems should be characterized by their ability to interact with their environment, i.e., by their external behaviour. In Chapter 2.1, the notion of *event*, which denotes a local action performed by an agent, has been identified as a basic constituent of behaviour. A derived concept is the interaction, which consists of a set of events associated with different agents sharing a common interaction point according to the architecture function $\mathcal{Archf}$.

In Chapter 3.2.6, we have surveyed several approaches to express events in temporal logic. We follow the approach in [ScMeVo83] and interpret the change of the truth value of a formula as an event occurrence. However, unlike [ScMeVo83], we introduce an operator for event occurrence and another operator to express the number of event occurrences up to the current point in time. Also, we associate with every event occurrence a single point in time, not two consecutive states.

The operator for event occurrence (or "event operator" for short) can be defined informally and formally as follows:

- $[\varphi]$ (read "event occurrence φ") means that φ has just become true, the event φ has just occurred.

Syntax E_P

i) Let φ be a formula, then $[\varphi]$ is a formula.

Semantics E_P

Let φ be a formula, then

i) $\mathcal{M}_L,(\sigma,i,j) \models [\varphi]$ iff $\mathcal{M}_L,(\sigma,i,j) \models \varphi$ and ($j>0$ implies $\mathcal{M}_L,(\sigma,i,j-1) \not\models \varphi$)

ii) $\mathcal{M}_B,(\pi,\sigma,i,j) \models [\varphi]$ iff $\mathcal{M}_B,(\pi,\sigma,i,j) \models \varphi$ and ($j>0$ implies $\mathcal{M}_B,(\pi,\sigma,i,j-1) \not\models \varphi$)

We have taken the view that an event occurrence is a change which can only be detected a posteriori. Therefore, the event operator does not refer to the future, but to the present and the past. It should be pointed out that the event operator presents less problems with respect to abstraction and composition, as compared to "next" and "previous" (see Chapters 3.2.2 and 3.2.3). The reason is that with [.], references to concecutive moments in time are restricted[20]. In terms of $\bullet$ (see Chapter 3.2.3), $[\varphi]$ could be expressed as $\varphi \wedge \bullet\neg\varphi$. But $\bullet$ cannot be expressed in terms of [.]. Also, with [.] it is not possible to refer to more than two consecutive moments in time, as in $\bullet\bullet\varphi$ or $\circ\circ\varphi$.

Possible candidates for an axiomatic basis of E_P have not been studied so far. Therefore, a list of valid formulas is provided (see Appendix A.1).

The operator for the number of event occurrences can be defined informally and formally as follows:

- $\#[\varphi]$ (read "number of event occurrences φ") denotes the number of occurrences of the event φ in the past up to and including the current moment in time.

Syntax E_F

i) Let φ be a formula, then $\#[\varphi]$ is a term of sort $\mathbb{N}_0$.

20 Even with these restricted possibilities to refer to concecutive moments in time, problems with respect to abstraction exist. For instance, the formula $\varphi \equiv [\varphi] \wedge \neg\varphi \equiv [\neg\varphi]$ requires that φ and $\neg\varphi$ hold alternately. However, such problems will not occur in the following applications.

Semantics E_F

$$\text{i) } \mathcal{M}_{FL'}(\sigma,i,j) \models \#[\varphi] =_{Df} \begin{cases} 0 & j = i \text{ and not } \mathcal{M}_{FL'}(\sigma,i,j) \models [\varphi] \\ 1 & j = i \text{ and } \mathcal{M}_{FL'}(\sigma,i,j) \models [\varphi] \\ \mathcal{M}_{FL'}(\sigma,i,j\text{-}1) \models \#[\varphi] & j > i \text{ and not } \mathcal{M}_{FL'}(\sigma,i,j) \models [\varphi] \\ \mathcal{M}_{FL'}(\sigma,i,j\text{-}1) \models \#[\varphi]+1 & j > i \text{ and } \mathcal{M}_{FL'}(\sigma,i,j) \models [\varphi] \end{cases} \text{ if}$$

$$\text{ii) } \mathcal{M}_{FB'}(\pi,\sigma,i,j) \models \#[\varphi] =_{Df} \begin{cases} 0 & j = i \text{ and not } \mathcal{M}_{FB'}(\pi,\sigma,i,j) \models [\varphi] \\ 1 & j = i \text{ and } \mathcal{M}_{FB'}(\pi,\sigma,i,j) \models [\varphi] \\ \mathcal{M}_{FB'}(\pi,\sigma,i,j\text{-}1) \models \#[\varphi] & j > i \text{ and not } \mathcal{M}_{FB'}(\pi,\sigma,i,j) \models [\varphi] \\ \mathcal{M}_{FB'}(\pi,\sigma,i,j\text{-}1) \models \#[\varphi]+1 & j > i \text{ and } \mathcal{M}_{FB'}(\pi,\sigma,i,j) \models [\varphi] \end{cases} \text{ if}$$

#[.] is a temporal function from the past into the set of natural numbers. Therefore, it can not be used in a temporal logic based on propositional logic. The number of event occurrences is uniquely defined for each moment in time and each context, and increases monotonically over time.

Temporal formulas involving #[.] can be replaced by formulas with counter variables. However, just as history variables and traces, counter variables are auxiliary variables, which we have rejected (see Chapter 3.3.4). #[.] provides an alternative and equally powerful approach to refer to the past.

3.3.6 Operators for interval construction

The past fragment of the temporal logic can be extended by adding operators for interval construction. Intervals have been identified as a high-level temporal concept in [ScMeVo83a], where an interval logic with future operators is introduced (see Chapter 3.2.5). The interval fragment we are proposing in this chapter follows the main ideas of [ScMeVo83a], but also differs in some respects. To some degree, this is a consequence of our requirements on the design of the temporal formalism.

The most important difference is that the interval operators introduced subsequently refer to the past instead of the future, i.e., contexts can only be established in the past. There are several arguments in favour of this design decision. Firstly, many requirements arising in specifications are easier to express and therefore better understandable using past operators ([LiPnZu85], Chapters 4 and 5). Secondly, the enhancement of expressiveness allows for purely temporal specifications in many cases where otherwise auxiliary variables (see Chapter 3.3.4) would have to be introduced. Thirdly, a natural classification of formulas into safety and liveness properties (see [LiPnZu85]) is possible. Another argument of more technical nature is that it is difficult to define a branching time semantics for interval logic. The design decision to define intervals in the past - which is linear and bounded - is also in line with our intention to keep the future fragment of the logic as simple as possible.

To construct intervals, the notion of event as introduced in Chapter 3.3.5 is used. With an event occurrence, an atomic interval, i.e., a single point in time, is associated. As in [ScMeVo83a], complex intervals can be constructed with the help of two interval operators $\Rightarrow$ and $\Leftarrow$. Intuitively, the directions of the arrows indicate in which direction and in which order the interval end points are located. The end point of the interval expressed by the interval term at the tail of the arrow is located first, followed by a search, in the direction of arrow, for the end point of the interval denoted by the interval term at the head of the arrow. An explicit operator to refer to the next/last but one event occurrence is introduced. Informally, the interval extension for the past can be interpreted as follows:

- $\langle \beta \rangle \varphi$ (read "φ restricted on the context β") means that φ holds in the context established by the interval term β. It is vacuously true if the context does not exist.
- $\bullet\, \alpha$ (read "the last but one event occurrence α" and "the next but one event occurrence α", respectively) means that if the search direction is backward, $\bullet\, \alpha$ refers to the last but one event occurrence α; if it is forward, $\bullet\, \alpha$ denotes the next but one event occurrence α.
- *begin* δ and *end* δ denote atomic intervals consisting of the first and the last state of the interval δ, respectively.
- $\delta_1 \Rightarrow \delta_2$ denotes the interval commencing at the end of δ_1 and ending at the end of δ_2, where δ_1 is located first, and δ_2 is searched within the current context in the forward direction, starting with the end of δ_1.
- $\delta_1 \Leftarrow \delta_2$ denotes the interval commencing at the end of δ_1 and ending at the end of δ_2, where δ_2 is located first, and δ_1 is searched within the current context in the backward direction, starting with the end of δ_2.

Another obvious class of operators can be directly obtained by defining $\bullet^n \alpha =_{Df} \bullet\bullet ... \bullet\, \alpha$ (n-times "$\bullet$", $n > 0$). Unlike the "previous" operator (cf. Chapter 3.2.3), $\bullet^n$ is not problematic with respect to abstraction, because it does not refer to consecutive moments in time.

Syntax I

i) Let φ be a formula, α be an event term, then $[\varphi]$, $\bullet\ \alpha$ are event terms.

ii) Let α be an event term, β be an interval term, then α, (β) are interval expressions.

iii) Let δ, δ_1, δ_2 be interval expressions, then $\delta \Rightarrow$, $\delta \Leftarrow$, $\Rightarrow \delta$, $\Leftarrow \delta$, $\delta_1 \Rightarrow \delta_2$, $\delta_1 \Leftarrow \delta_2$, *begin* δ, *end* δ are interval terms.

iv) Let φ be a formula, β be an interval term, then $\langle \beta \rangle\ \varphi$ is a formula.

Semantics I

Let φ be a formula, β be an interval term, δ, δ_1, δ_2 be interval expressions, and α be an event term:

i) $\mathcal{M}_L,(\sigma,i,j) \models \langle \beta \rangle\ \varphi$ iff $\theta(\beta,\mathcal{M}_L,(\sigma,i,j),b) \neq$ undefined implies $\mathcal{M}_L,(\sigma,\theta(\beta,\mathcal{M}_L,(\sigma,i,j),b)) \models \varphi$

ii) $\theta(\delta \Rightarrow,\mathcal{M}_L,(\sigma,i,j),d) =_{Df}$ last$(\theta(\delta,\mathcal{M}_L,(\sigma,i,j),d))$,j

iii) $\theta(\delta \Leftarrow,\mathcal{M}_L,(\sigma,i,j),d) =_{Df}$ last$(\theta(\delta,\mathcal{M}_L,(\sigma,i,j),b))$,j

iv) $\theta(\Rightarrow \delta,\mathcal{M}_L,(\sigma,i,j),d) =_{Df}$ i,last$(\theta(\delta,\mathcal{M}_L,(\sigma,i,j),f))$

v) $\theta(\Leftarrow \delta,\mathcal{M}_L,(\sigma,i,j),d) =_{Df}$ i,last$(\theta(\delta,\mathcal{M}_L,(\sigma,i,j),d))$

vi) $\theta(\delta_1 \Rightarrow \delta_2,\mathcal{M}_L,(\sigma,i,j),d) =_{Df} \theta(\Rightarrow \delta_2,\mathcal{M}_L,(\sigma,\theta(\delta_1 \Rightarrow,\mathcal{M}_L,(\sigma,i,j),d)),f)$

vii) $\theta(\delta_1 \Leftarrow \delta_2,\mathcal{M}_L,(\sigma,i,j),d) =_{Df} \theta(\delta_1 \Leftarrow,\mathcal{M}_L,(\sigma,\theta(\Leftarrow \delta_2,\mathcal{M}_L,(\sigma,i,j),d)),b)$

viii) $\theta(\text{begin } \delta,\mathcal{M}_L,(\sigma,i,j),d) =_{Df}$ first$(\theta(\delta,\mathcal{M}_L,(\sigma,i,j),d))$,first$(\theta(\delta,\mathcal{M}_L,(\sigma,i,j),d))$

ix) $\theta(\text{end } \delta,\mathcal{M}_L,(\sigma,i,j),d) =_{Df}$ last$(\theta(\delta,\mathcal{M}_L,(\sigma,i,j),d))$,last$(\theta(\delta,\mathcal{M}_L,(\sigma,i,j),d))$

x) $\theta((\delta),\mathcal{M}_L,(\sigma,i,j),d) =_{Df} \theta(\delta,\mathcal{M}_L,(\sigma,i,j),d)$

xi) $\theta(\alpha,\mathcal{M}_L,(\sigma,i,j),f) =_{Df}$ min(event_set$(\alpha,\mathcal{M}_L,(\sigma,i,j),f)$)

xii) $\theta(\alpha,\mathcal{M}_L,(\sigma,i,j),b) =_{Df}$ max(event_set$(\alpha,\mathcal{M}_L,(\sigma,i,j),b)$)

xiii) event_set$(\bullet\ \alpha,\mathcal{M}_L,(\sigma,i,j),f) =_{Df}$ event_set$(\alpha,\mathcal{M}_L,(\sigma,i,j),f)$ - min(event_set$(\alpha,\mathcal{M}_L,(\sigma,i,j),f)$)

xiv) event_set$(\bullet\ \alpha,\mathcal{M}_L,(\sigma,i,j),b) =_{Df}$ event_set$(\alpha,\mathcal{M}_L,(\sigma,i,j),b)$ - max(event_set$(\alpha,\mathcal{M}_L,(\sigma,i,j),b)$)

xv) event_set$([\varphi],\mathcal{M}_L,(\sigma,i,j),d) =_{Df}$ if i,j $\neq$ undefined
then $\{k \mid i \leq k \leq j \text{ and } \mathcal{M}_L,(\sigma,i,k) \models [\varphi]\}$
else $\{\}$

xvi) min$(\{\}) =_{Df}$ max$(\{\}) =_{Df}$ undefined

xvii) first(i,j) $=_{Df}$ first(i) $=_{Df}$ i

xviii) last(i,j) $=_{Df}$ last(j) $=_{Df}$ j

To define the semantics of the interval extension, a function θ which takes as arguments an interval formula, a model $\mathcal{M}_L$, a state sequence σ, positions i,j, and a direction of search is used. The search is limited to the subsequence $\langle \sigma_i ... \sigma_j \rangle$, starting with σ_i (σ_j), if the direction of search is forward (backward). Rules with the parameter d apply to both directions, d can be replaced uniformly by f or b. If the interval can be located within $\langle \sigma_i ... \sigma_j \rangle$, θ yields the bounding positions k, l, where $i \le k \le l \le j$; otherwise, θ yields "undefined".

The semantics of interval formulas is given for models $\mathcal{M}_L$. For models $\mathcal{M}_B$, it can be defined analogously by replacing $\mathcal{M}_L$ and (σ,i,j) by $\mathcal{M}_B$ and (π,σ,i,j), respectively. This is possible, because in both model types, the past is linear and bounded.

Possible candidates for an axiomatic basis of *I* have not been investigated so far. Therefore, we provide a list of valid formulas (see Appendix A.1).

3.3.7 Customizing temporal logics

In the previous chapters, several building blocks which together form the modular temporal logic have been introduced. For a given problem, a subset of these building blocks can be selected and combined, i.e., the formation rules, semantics, and axiomatic bases are joined together, in order to customize the appropriate temporal logic. A few obvious restrictions apply to the combination of building blocks:

- exactly one of the building blocks At_P and At_F must be selected;
- selection of *Pr* is mandatory;
- only one of the building blocks F_L and F_B may be selected;
- E_F may not be combined with At_P;
- if *I* is chosen, E_P must also be selected.

The combination of several groups of temporal operators yields a so-called *mixed* temporal logic. While the formation rules and semantics of a mixed logic obtained by joining together the formation rules and semantics of the selected building blocks are complete, the axiomatic basis needs supplement. However, there is little work on that topic, therefore, we will provide lists of valid formulas for pairs or triples of building blocks instead (see Appendix A.1). It is assumed that the above restrictions are observed.

When customizing a temporal logic, the following heuristics are helpful to make an adequate choice:

- select At_F, if architectural aspects have to be expressed in formulas;
- select Q for quantification over infinite value domains;
- select F_L to express invariance and liveness for reliable systems;
- select F_B to express invariance and liveness for *un*reliable systems;
- select P to avoid history variables;
- select E_P to express events;
- select E_F to count event occurrences without introducing history variables;
- select I to express contexts in the past and thus to avoid history variables.

Example "mutual exclusion"

To specify the mutual exclusion problem for a finite set of processes ([ClEmSi86]), a propositional linear time temporal logic, consisting of At_P, Pr, and F_L is adequate[21]. After a suitable abstraction step, three primitive propositions are left for each process (agent):

N_i: process i is in the non-critical region
T_i: process i is in the trying region
C_i: process i is in the critical region

This determines the sets Φ and AG as well as the function lp associating with each agent a set of primitive propositions (see Definition 2.1). For two processes, the mutual exclusion problem can then be characterized by the following properties:

(1)	$\neg \Diamond (C_1 \wedge C_2)$	mutual exclusion
(2a)	$\Box (T_1 \supset \Diamond C_1)$	absence of starvation for process 1
(2b)	$\Box (T_2 \supset \Diamond C_2)$	absence of starvation for process 2

Example "drink server"

A drink server DS takes orders for tea and coffee from customers. For each tea order, one cup of tea is served. For each coffee order, one cup of coffee is served.

21 For technical reasons, a temporal logic consisting of At_P, Pr, and F_B has been used in [ClEmSi86].

The system architecture of DS is shown in Figure 3.1. Its internal structure is not revealed.

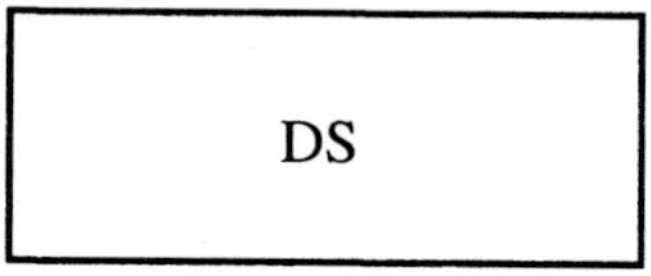

DS

Figure 3.1: Simplified system architecture of a drink server

When the behaviour of DS is specified, no assumptions about the environment are to be made. This means that only the *readiness* of DS to take orders and to serve drinks can be described. Whether orders will be taken when DS is placed into some environment depends on whether they are actually given, and whether drinks will actually be served depends on the readiness of the environment to accept them. We abstract from limitations of resources, i.e., tea and coffee are always available, and from failures.

To specify the drink server, a logic consisting of the building blocks At_P, Pr, and F_L is used, formulas are interpreted in a model $\mathcal{M}_{PL}$ (see Definition 3.1). The drink server is described as a single agent, i.e., AG = {DS}. The set $\Phi = \Phi_{DS}$ consists of the following primitive propositions:

tea_order:	one or more unsatisfied orders for tea
coffee_order:	one or more unsatisfied orders for coffee
ready_to_take_order:	DS is ready to take an order
ready_to_serve_tea:	DS is ready to serve tea
ready_to_serve_coffee:	DS is ready to serve coffee

All primitive propositions are local to DS, i.e., $lp(DS) = \Phi$. The desired behaviour of DS can be captured by the properties listed in Table 3.2. Property DS1 expresses that DS is ready to take an order from time to time. DS2 states that if there is an unsatisfied tea order, DS will eventually be ready to serve tea. DS3 covers the complementary situations, where it is required that DS is not ready to serve tea. DS4 and DS5 state analogous behaviour in case of coffee orders. The behaviour of DS is then given by the logical conjunction of these properties, i.e., $\mathcal{B}ehav_{DS} = \bigwedge_{1 \leq i \leq 5} DSi$.

DS1.	$\Box \Diamond$ ready_to_take_order
DS2.	$\Box$ (tea_order $\supset \Diamond$ ready_to_serve_tea)
DS3.	$\Box$ ($\neg$ tea_order $\supset \neg$ ready_to_serve_tea)
DS4.	$\Box$ (coffee_order $\supset \Diamond$ ready_to_serve_coffee)
DS5.	$\Box$ ($\neg$ coffee_order $\supset \neg$ ready_to_serve_coffee)

Table 3.2: Specification of DS

The fact that the primitive propositions in DS2 and DS4 are local to DS can not be expressed in the specification itself. The reason is that atomic formulas can not be decomposed in the framework of propositional logic, and therefore, locality can not be *specified*. However, it has been *modeled* by the function lp.

Further logics will be customized in the following chapters. To specify interaction point properties, a temporal logic consisting of At_F, Pr, Q, F_L, P, E_P, and E_F will be used in Chapter 4. For the specification of unreliable communication services, a temporal logic consisting of At_F, Pr, Q, F_B, P, E_P, E_F, and I will be applied in Chapter 5.

3.3.8 Composition of behavioural specifications

An FDT is called "*compositional*" if the specification of a system can be obtained by composing the specification of its constituents (see Chapter 1.2.5). Architectural composition has been treated in Chapter 2.2. In order to introduce behavioural composition, we assume that the behaviour of each system component has been specified. In the following, $\mathcal{Behav}_{ag}$ denotes the behavioural specification of agent ag $\in$ AG (see, for instance, Chapter 3.3.7). $\mathcal{Seman}_{ip}$ denotes the semantics of interaction point ip $\in$ IP (for details, see Chapter 4). Behavioural composition is defined in terms of logical conjunction:

Definition 3.7: Let $\mathcal{Arch} = \langle$ AG,IP,$\mathcal{Archf} \rangle$ be a system architecture, $\mathcal{Behav}_{ag}$ be the behavioural specifications of agents ag $\in$ AG, and $\mathcal{Seman}_{ip}$ be the semantics of interaction points ip $\in$ IP. Then the *system behaviour* $\mathcal{Behav}$ is given as the conjunction $\bigwedge_{ag \in AG} \mathcal{Behav}_{ag} \wedge \bigwedge_{ip \in IP} \mathcal{Seman}_{ip}$.

If only agents are considered, the system architecture is reduced to a structure $\langle$ AG $\rangle$. In this case, the system behaviour $\mathcal{Behav}$ is defined to be $\bigwedge_{ag \in AG} \mathcal{Behav}_{ag}$. Based on Definitions 2.1 and 3.7, the notion of requirement specification (see Chapter 2) can be formalized as follows:

Definition 3.8: A *requirement specification* $\mathcal{RS}$ of an open distributed system is a structure $\langle \mathcal{Arch}, \mathcal{Behav} \rangle$, where $\mathcal{Arch}$ is a system architecture, and $\mathcal{Behav}$ is a system behaviour.

Example "drink server" (continued)

The requirement specification $\mathcal{RS} = \langle \mathcal{Arch}, \mathcal{Behav} \rangle$ of the drink server (see Chapter 3.3.7) is given by the simplified system architecture $\mathcal{Arch} = \langle$ DS $\rangle$ and the system behaviour $\mathcal{Behav} = \mathcal{Behav}_{DS}$.

In a subsequent design step, the drink server DS can be decomposed into a waiter W, a tea girl TG, and a coffee boy CB (see Figure 3.2). Informally, the waiter takes orders for tea and coffee from customers. If tea is ordered, the waiter asks the tea girl to serve tea, who will then eventually do so. The same pattern applies to the coffee boy.

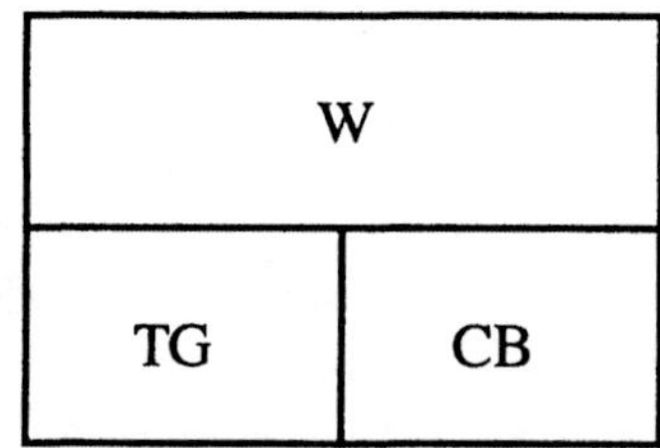

Figure 3.2: Refined system architecture of the drink server

To specify the waiter, the tea girl, and the coffee boy, a logic consisting of the building blocks At_P, Pr, and F_L is used. Formulas are interpreted in a model $\mathcal{M}_{PL}$ with AG = {W,TG,CB}, $\Phi = \Phi_W \cup \Phi_{TG} \cup \Phi_{CB}$, and lp(W) = Φ_W, lp(TG) = Φ_{TG}, lp(CB) = Φ_{CB}. The set Φ_W consists of the following primitive propositions, the desired behaviour of W is captured by the properties in Table 3.3:

tea_to_request:	one or more orders for tea to be passed on
coffee_to_request:	one or more orders for coffee to be passed on

ready_to_take_order:	W is ready to take an order
ready_to_request_tea:	W is ready to ask for tea
ready_to_request_coffee:	W is ready to ask for coffee

W1. $\Box \Diamond$ ready_to_take_order
W2. $\Box$ (tea_to_request $\supset \Diamond$ ready_to_request_tea)
W3. $\Box$ ($\neg$ tea_to_request $\supset \neg$ ready_to_request_tea)
W4. $\Box$ (coffee_to_request $\supset \Diamond$ ready_to_request_coffee)
W5. $\Box$ ($\neg$ coffee_to_request $\supset \neg$ ready_to_request_coffee)

Table 3.3: Specification of W

The set Φ_{TG} consists of the following primitive propositions, the specification of TG is listed in Table 3.4:

tea_to_serve:	one or more unsatisfied requests for tea
ready_to_take_tea_request:	TG is ready to take a tea request
ready_to_serve_tea:	TG is ready to serve tea

TG1. $\Box \Diamond$ ready_to_take_tea_request
TG2. $\Box$ (tea_to_serve $\supset \Diamond$ ready_to_serve_tea)
TG3. $\Box$ ($\neg$ tea_to_serve $\supset \neg$ ready_to_serve_tea)

Table 3.4: Specification of TG

The set Φ_{CB} consists of the following primitive propositions, the specification of CB is listed in Table 3.5:

coffee_to_serve:	one or more unsatisfied requests for coffee
ready_to_take_coffee_request:	CB is ready to take a coffee request
ready_to_serve_coffee:	CB is ready to serve coffee

CB1. $\Box \Diamond$ ready_to_take_coffee_request
CB2. $\Box$ (K'_{CB} coffee_to_serve $\supset \Diamond$ ready_to_serve_coffee)
CB3. $\Box$ ($\neg K'_{CB}$ coffee_to_serve $\supset \neg$ ready_to_serve_coffee)

Table 3.5: Specification of CB

The specifications of W, TG, and CB are very similar to the specification of DS, which has been explained in Chapter 3.3.7. The requirement specification $\mathcal{RS}' = \langle \mathcal{Arch}', \mathcal{Behav}' \rangle$ of the drink server refinement is given by the system architecture $\mathcal{Arch}' = \langle \{W,TG,CB\} \rangle$ and the system behaviour $\mathcal{Behav}' = \bigwedge_{ag \in \{W,TG,CB\}} \mathcal{Behav}'_{ag}$, where $\mathcal{Behav}'_W = \bigwedge_{1 \leq i \leq 5} Wi$, $\mathcal{Behav}'_{TG} = \bigwedge_{1 \leq i \leq 3} TGi$, and $\mathcal{Behav}'_{CB} = \bigwedge_{1 \leq i \leq 3} CBi$.

In general, properties defining the behaviour of an agent may refer to local and non-local aspects of that agent. For instance, to exhibit a certain behaviour, an agent may rely on certain properties of its environment. In turn, the environment may rely on some properties guaranteed by the agent. As long as these properties are not violated, modifications of the agent's specification have no influence on the environment. Otherwise, the environment would be affected by the modifications in the sense that the properties which it has to guarantee or which it can rely on are changed.

Behavioural specifications referring to non-local aspects are problematic in later design stages, because they can not be directly implemented. In an implementation, it is only possible to refer to local aspects, for instance, the local state or local actions. Therefore, specifications referring to local aspects only have to be developed such that their behavioural composition satisfies the non-local properties. In a distributed system, this can require the explicit introduction of suitable interactions between system components, which leads to less abstract specifications. In the description of an open system, some assumptions about the environment may remain, since the description of its environment is not known in advance.

If the behavioural specification of an agent refers to aspects which are local to this agent only, we say that it is *syntactically-local*, otherwise, it is called "*non-local*". If it can be implemented independently of its environment, it is called "*semantically-local*" or "*self-contained*". Syntactical locality is a necessary condition for semantical locality. However, it is possible that a syntactically-local specification is not self-contained. The definitions in this paragraph also apply to properties that form part of a specification, and to the semantics of interaction points (see Chapter 4).

For semantical models $\mathcal{M}_P$, the notion of syntactical locality can be made precise as follows:

Definition 3.9: In the propositional framework, the behavioural specification of an agent ag is called "*syntactically-local*" if and only if all primitive propositions Φ_{ag} occurring in the specification are local to ag according to lp, i.e., $\Phi_{ag} \subseteq lp(ag)$.

According to this definition, the behavioural specifications of DS, W, TG, and CB in the example "drink server" are syntactically-local.

For semantical models $\mathcal{M}_F$, syntactical locality can not be defined in such a general way. However, it can be made precise with respect to a particular system architecture and a given set of atomic formulas (for instance, see Chapter 7.2.4).

If syntactically-local specifications of agents and interaction points are composed by logical conjunction, the question arises whether this results in a description of their joint behaviour. The crucial idea here is the explicit introduction of interaction points as connection links between agents. By this basic architectural concept, sets of local events forming interactions can be related. How they are related depends on the system architecture and the semantics of the interaction points, which will be treated formally in Chapter 4. Behavioural composition is illustrated in Chapters 5 and 7.

3.3.9 A notion of conformance

In order to prove open distributed systems correct, a formal notion of conformance relating requirement specifications of different abstraction levels is required. Let $\mathcal{RS} = \langle \mathcal{Arch}, \mathcal{Behav} \rangle$ and $\mathcal{RS}' = \langle \mathcal{Arch}', \mathcal{Behav}' \rangle$ be requirement specifications, then intuitively, $\mathcal{RS}'$ conforms to $\mathcal{RS}$, if $\mathcal{RS}'$ is "*more specific*" than $\mathcal{RS}$. With respect to the system architecture, this is the case if all agents and interaction points of $\mathcal{RS}$ are represented in $\mathcal{RS}'$, and if their composition is maintained in $\mathcal{RS}'$. We can use the notion of architectural refinement (see Definition 2.2) to formally capture this conception. Concerning the system behaviour, $\mathcal{RS}'$ is more specific than $\mathcal{RS}$, if the behaviour of $\mathcal{RS}'$ with respect to the system architecture of $\mathcal{RS}$ is not in conflict with the behaviour of $\mathcal{RS}$. The difficulty here is to derive this abstract behaviour of $\mathcal{RS}'$ from the behaviour obtained by composition of the parts of $\mathcal{RS}'$.

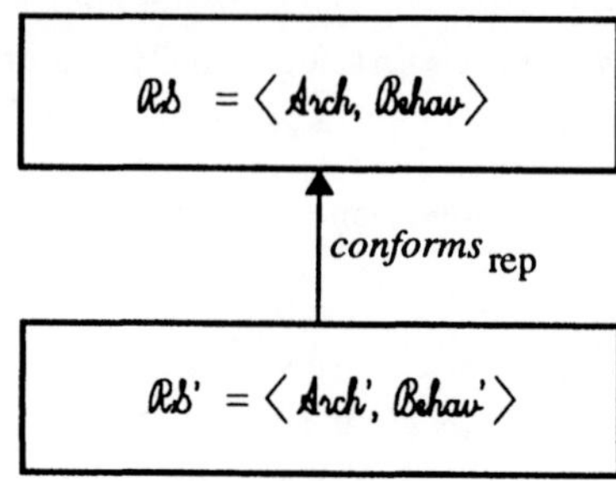

Figure 3.3: Conformance relation between requirement specifications

In operational formalisms such as CSP ([Hoa85]) or LOTOS ([ISO88c]), behavioural abstraction is achieved by considering certain events as *internal*. This is expressed by particular operators (termed "concealment" or "hiding") and yields a well-defined abstract behaviour. This behaviour can then be directly related to another specification. In property-oriented formalisms such as temporal logic, abstraction could be achieved by considering some atomic formulas as *internal*. However, it is not clear how properties characterizing the abstract behaviour of the system could be derived after such an abstraction step, and how they should be related to another specification with different atomic formulas.

An alternative approach is to define a *representation function* mapping the system behaviour $\mathcal{Behav}$ to a formula on the abstraction level of $\mathcal{RS}'$. It is then sufficient to show that the result of this mapping is logically implied by the system behaviour $\mathcal{Behav}'$, which leads to the following notion of conformance:

Definition 3.10: Let $\mathcal{RS} = \langle \mathcal{Arch}, \mathcal{Behav} \rangle$ and $\mathcal{RS}' = \langle \mathcal{Arch}', \mathcal{Behav}' \rangle$ be requirement specifications. $\mathcal{RS}'$ *conforms to* $\mathcal{RS}$ *under the representation function* rep (written "$\mathcal{RS}'$ $conforms_{rep}$ $\mathcal{RS}$ ") if and only if the following holds:

i) $\mathcal{Arch}'$ *refines* $\mathcal{Arch}$
ii) $\models_i \mathcal{Behav}' \supset \text{rep}(\mathcal{Behav})$

Note that this definition of conformance incorporates both system architecture and system behaviour. This differs from other notions of conformance or correctness, where architecture or system structure has no formal meaning (for instance, see [Mil80], [BrScSt86], [Hoa85]).

The representation function rep can be defined recursively, following the formation rules of the selected building blocks. In particular, each atomic formula of the logic applied to $\mathcal{RS}$ is mapped to a formula of the logic applied to $\mathcal{RS}'$. Defining rep is a crucial step in the verification process, because it can cause bad results, therefore, rep should be kept simple.

Example "drink server"

Let $\mathcal{RS}$ and $\mathcal{RS}'$ be the requirement specifications of the drink server (Chapter 3.3.7) and the drink server refinement (Chapter 3.3.8). To show $\mathcal{RS}'$ *conforms*$_{rep}$ $\mathcal{RS}$, $\mathcal{Arch}'$ *refines* $\mathcal{Arch}$ (see Definition 2.3) must hold, which is the case for the refinement function ref: AG $\rightarrow 2^{AG'}$ with ref(DS) = {W,TG,CB}.

rep (tea_order)	= tea_to_request $\vee$ tea_to_serve
rep (coffee_order)	= coffee_to_request $\vee$ coffee_to_serve
rep (ready_to_take_order)	= ready_to_take_order
rep (ready_to_serve_tea)	= ready_to_serve_tea
rep (ready_to_serve_coffee)	= ready_to_serve_coffee
rep $(\neg\varphi)$	= $\neg$ rep (φ)
rep $(\varphi_1 \wedge \varphi_2)$	= rep $(\varphi_1) \wedge$ rep (φ_2)
rep $(\Box\, \varphi)$	= $\Box$ rep (φ)

Table 3.6: The representation function rep

I1. $\Box$ (ready_to_request_tea $\wedge \Diamond$ ready_to_take_tea_request
$\supset \Diamond$ tea_to_serve)

I2. $\Box$ (ready_to_request_coffee $\wedge \Diamond$ ready_to_take_coffee_request
$\supset \Diamond$ coffee_to_serve)

Table 3.7: Interaction properties

To prove $\models_i \mathcal{Behav}' \supset$ rep($\mathcal{Behav}$), we define a representation function rep by mapping formulas of the more abstract description level to corresponding formulas of the lower level as shown in Table 3.6. Each primitive proposition of Φ_{DS} is mapped to a formula of the lower level description.

It turns out that to conduct a formal proof of $\models_i \mathcal{B}ehav' \supset \mathrm{rep}(\mathcal{B}ehav)$, further assumptions are necessary. The reason is that in order to exhibit the behaviour of the drink server, the agents W, TG, and CB have to interact. The properties of these interactions are listed in Table 3.7 and are in fact rather obvious. Together with I1 and I2, conformance between $\mathcal{RS}'$ and $\mathcal{RS}$ is straightforward to prove.

Definition 3.10 formally captures the conception that $\mathcal{RS}'$ is more specific than $\mathcal{RS}$ by relating their *entire* system architectures and their *entire* system behaviours. Therefore, it seems that this definition does not support incremental system design and modular verification, as addressed in Chapter 2.3. So, if we modify or replace a part of the system, do we have to verify the entire system?

Sufficient *architectural* restrictions for modular verification have been introduced in Chapter 2.3 and are taken into account in condition i) of Definition 3.10. Modular verification with respect to system *behaviour* means that for each component ag and ip of $\mathcal{RS}$, the behaviour obtained by composing components of $\mathcal{RS}'$ that refine ag and ip implies the behaviour of ag and the semantics of ip when mapped to the abstraction level of $\mathcal{RS}'$. Formally, we have

$$\text{ii')} \models_i \bigwedge_{ag\in AG} \big(\bigwedge_{ag'\in ref(ag)} \mathcal{B}ehav'_{ag'} \wedge \bigwedge_{ip'\in ref(ag)} \mathcal{S}eman'_{ip'} \supset \mathrm{rep}(\mathcal{B}ehav_{ag})\big) \wedge$$
$$\bigwedge_{ip\in IP} \big(\bigwedge_{ip'\in ref(ip)} \mathcal{S}eman'_{ip'} \wedge \bigwedge_{ag'\in ref(ip)} \mathcal{B}ehav'_{ag'} \supset \mathrm{rep}(\mathcal{S}eman_{ip})\big)$$

Condition ii') implies condition ii) from Definition 3.10, provided $\mathrm{rep}(\varphi_1 \wedge \varphi_2) = \mathrm{rep}(\varphi_1) \wedge \mathrm{rep}(\varphi_2)$, and, together with condition i), is sufficient to prove conformance. Conditions ii) and ii') are equivalent if the behaviour of each agent and the semantics of each interaction point of $\mathcal{RS}$ and $\mathcal{RS}'$ are semantically-local (see Chapter 3.3.8). Syntactical locality is not sufficient, because to prove the refinement of a given component correct, some constraints may have to be placed on its environment. This will, for instance, be the case in the InRes service in Chapter 5.

Note that in general, condition ii) of Definition 3.10 is equivalent to

$$\text{ii")} \models_i \bigwedge_{ag\in AG} (\mathcal{B}ehav' \supset \mathrm{rep}(\mathcal{B}ehav_{ag})) \wedge \bigwedge_{ip\in IP} (\mathcal{B}ehav' \supset \mathrm{rep}(\mathcal{S}eman_{ip})),$$

provided $\mathrm{rep}(\varphi_1 \wedge \varphi_2) = \mathrm{rep}(\varphi_1) \wedge \mathrm{rep}(\varphi_2)$. This allows us to split the conformance proof into smaller fragments, but is not sufficient for modular verification as explained in Chapter 2.3.

4 The interaction point concept

After the introduction of a suitable formalism, we will now readdress the important issue of architectural concepts. In Chapter 2, we have informally characterized a small number of basic and derived concepts, among them the interaction point which is a key concept of open distributed systems design. It is used to conceptually model the boundaries between the system and its environment as well as between the system's agents. These boundaries are pervious in the sense that components on different sides can mutually influence each other in a well-defined way. The existence of *external* interaction points (between the system and its environment) is a characteristic of *open* systems. *Internal* interaction points (between the system's agents) are a characteristic of *distributed* systems.

In this chapter, we will list and formally define a number of generic properties an interaction point can have. The properties constrain the way how agents sharing a common interaction point can mutually influence each other, and assert under which conditions they can expect progress[22]. Some interdependencies between the interaction point properties will be pointed out and proved.

Subsets of the properties can be composed to yield the meaning of the interaction point concept in a particular application area. A specialization within an application area or with respect to a given problem can be achieved by adding further properties. Furthermore, a number of interaction point representations in the operational FDTs Estelle, LOTOS, and SDL (see Chapter 2.5) are investigated. Their meaning is, to some extent, captured by subsets of the listed properties. Finally, conformance between abstraction levels via the interaction point concept is investigated.

4.1 The role of interaction points

From a systematical point of view, it is natural and straightforward to carry the requirement specification including agents, interaction points, and events (see Chapter 2) into the operational specification and physical implementation, according to the principles of step-wise refinement. This can either be achieved on a case to case basis by relating single architectural components to pieces of lower level specification, or more generally by defining how basic architectural concepts are represented in

22 Bi-directional and multi-directional interactions as well as interaction points with a varying number of interacting agents are not treated. (A bi-directional (multi-directional) interaction is an interaction where an exchange of values in two (several) directions occurs.)

operational FDTs and implementation languages. The apparent advantage is that descriptions on different levels of abstraction are clearly related and therefore better intelligible with respect to the conceptual design.

On the other hand, the structure of existing lower level descriptions may differ from the requirement specification. "The OSI Reference Model prescribes *functional* layering, but does not prescribe that individual layer entities must be distinct modules in the implementation, and that a clean service interface be provided for each layer" ([Svo89]). Guidelines for the application of FDTs for open distributed systems explicitly state that the internal structure of the specification is not mandatory for the implementation.

It has already been mentioned in Chapter 2.5 that it is a controversial issue whether the conceptual system architecture should be (partially) represented on the different levels of abstraction. While this would have advantages with respect to intelligibility, a different structure could allow for a more efficient implementation (cf. [Svo89]). Thus the question arises whether any parts of a conceptual system architecture *must* be carried into the lower level descriptions.

In order to prove open distributed systems correct, a formal notion of conformance relating descriptions of different abstraction levels is required. Any definition of conformance, however, supposes that a mapping between corresponding description units can be found. In general, these description units need not be related to the conceptual system architecture. But there are important arguments in favour of such a relationship. Generally, FDTs for open distributed systems have the common intention to describe systems by their ability to interact with their environment. Consequently, only externally visible behaviour is mandatory for the implementation, but not any internal structure or mechanism used to describe that behaviour. Since externally visible behaviour conceptually occurs at external interaction points of a system, it is straightforward to base the notion of conformance on the interaction point concept:

Definition 4.1: A description S1 of an open system is called *conforming* with respect to a description S2 (written "S1 *conf* S2") iff for all environments E, the following holds: every behaviour of S1 in E occurring at the external interaction point representations of S1 is possible at the corresponding interaction point representations of S2, when placing S2 into the same environment E.

It suffices then to find on each abstraction level units representing the external interaction points, and to identify and map visible events occurring on the lower level onto corresponding events of the higher level. Further high-level concepts need not be carried into lower level descriptions.

As one of the key concepts of open distributed systems design and as the basis for the above notion of conformance, the interaction point concept needs a precise definition. A clear semantics is a prerequisite for the understanding of the systems' design. Also, the meaning of the interaction point has a strong impact on the joint behaviour of the system and its environment. Furthermore, it can be the basis for a notion of conformance relating a pair of formal descriptions independently of their environment. We will address this important issue in Chapter 4.6 after the formal treatment of the interaction point concept.

4.2 A list of possible interaction point properties

The interaction point is an architectural concept of open distributed systems design to model the boundaries between the system and its environment. It is associated with two or more agents and can be understood as the means for these agents to mutually influence each other. This influence consists of the exchange of information[23]. In the following, we model an interaction as consisting of offer and acceptance(s), occurring between an arbitrary finite, but fixed number of agents at an interaction point.

The semantics of the interaction point concept depends on the area of application. And even within the same area, different meanings are possible. What we can do in this situation is to identify and formally define a number of generic properties an interaction point *could* have, and leave the choice of which properties are essential in a particular context open. The advantage of this approach is that the semantics of an interaction point (and other architectural concepts) can be customized according to its meaning in a particular domain (such as OSI or ODP) by selecting and composing the essential properties. Moreover, different interaction point representations can be compared, if their essential properties can be expressed in the same formalism.

The following list introduces some possible features of interaction points in an informal way. Most of these properties will be formalized in Chapter 4.3, and some interdependencies will be pointed out and proved in Chapter 4.4.

23 This includes so-called pure synchronization, which contains information.

i) Reliability

An interaction point can be reliable, meaning that interactions can not be lost, duplicated, corrupted or created. This does not impose any restriction on the strategy used to deliver interactions after they have been offered. But it ensures that interactions can be delivered only if they have been previously or are currently offered.

ii) Mode of interaction

An interaction is called *synchronous* if its offer and acceptance(s) take place (= terminate) simultaneously; otherwise, it is called *asynchronous*. In the synchronous case, a distinction between offering and accepting agents may not always be possible. These so-called bi-directional or multi-directional interactions are not treated here. An interaction point is termed "*synchronous*" if only synchronous interactions can occur, it is *asynchronous* if only asynchronous interactions are possible; otherwise, the mode of interaction is *undetermined*.

iii) Distinctness of interactions

We assume that an interaction is identified by the interaction point where it occurs, the agent offering/accepting the interaction, the interaction type[24], and the interaction parameters.[25] Uniqueness of interactions can - if necessary - be achieved by using a suitable parameter (for instance, a sequence number or a time-stamp), but is not considered essential in our treatment.

iv) Progress

Progress can be defined with respect to the readiness of agents to offer or accept an interaction. For example, if one agent is prepared to offer an interaction, and all others sharing the same interaction point are ready to accept, all agents will progress. Or, if more interactions have been offered than have been accepted by a particular agent, and that agent is prepared to accept, then it will progress.

v) Strategies

Restrictions may be imposed on the order in which interactions must be delivered. A strategy is called *fair* if each asynchronous interaction will be

24 Also called "*service primitive*" ([Boc83c]).

25 The distinction between interaction type and interaction parameters is also made in Estelle and SDL; however, it is not mandatory and is, for example, not made in LOTOS.

accepted sometime (i.e., starvation = infinite delay of interactions is prohibited). For synchronous interactions, there is no choice of strategy, because offer and acceptance(s) occur simultaneously.

vi) Capacity
If interactions may occur asynchronously, then more interactions could be offered than are accepted, in other words, interactions are kept until they are accepted. The number of interactions which can be kept is called *capacity* of the interaction point. It is possible to define a minimum and a maximum capacity. Between these boundaries, the capacity may vary dynamically. Note that for asynchronous interactions, the capacity must at least be one, because otherwise, no interaction can be offered. If the capacity is zero, only synchronous interactions can occur.

vii) Context independence
The properties of an interaction point should not depend on the specification of the agents interacting at this point.

viii) Selection of interactions
The choice of the next interaction may depend on constraints concerning its type or parameter values.

ix) Inspection of interactions
Inspection of the next interaction of an interaction point has no effect on the "state" of that interaction point, the interaction is not yet accepted.

x) Typing of interactions
The set of possible interaction types can be restricted.

4.3 Formal specification of interaction point properties

4.3.1 Context and limitations

An interaction point is the (abstract) means for two or more agents to mutually influence each other. This influence consists of the exchange of information. We model an interaction as consisting of offer and acceptance(s), occurring between agents at an interaction point. In general, there may be one offer and several acceptances, depending on the number of interacting agents. Also, each of the agents may offer interactions. In the following, we consider the simplified context shown in Figure 4.1, consisting of two agents ag1 and ag2, which can interact at interaction point ip. With respect to system architectures $\mathcal{Arch} = \langle AG, IP, \mathcal{Archf} \rangle$ (see Chapter 2.2) and semantical models $\mathcal{M}_F$ (see Chapter 3.3.1), this means that ag1, ag2 $\in$ AG, ip $\in$ IP, ip $\in \mathcal{Archf}(ag1) \cap \mathcal{Archf}(ag2)$, and for all ag $\in$ AG different from ag1, ag2, ip $\notin \mathcal{Archf}(ag)$. It is assumed that if an agent is ready to interact, it will remain so until the interaction occurs[26]. We formally define a number of properties the interaction point ip can have. Table 4.2 in Chapter 4.3.6 shows how the formal properties are related to informal properties in Chapter 4.2.

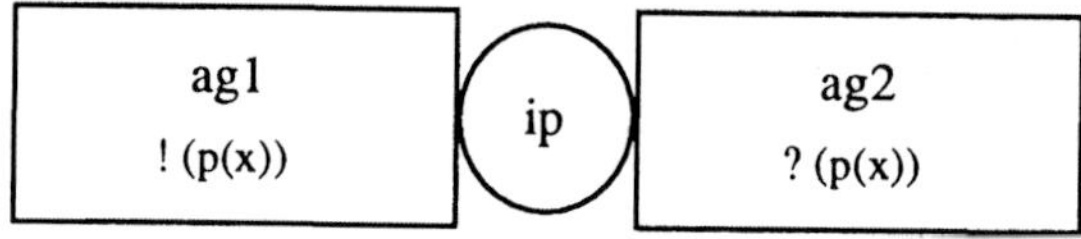

Figure 4.1: Context of the interaction point ip

Each of the properties defined in this chapter can be generalized to a context with an arbitrary finite, but fixed number of agents. Also, the properties we give here refer to one direction only, but can be easily reversed to yield symmetrical properties for the opposite direction. As mentioned before, our treatment does not cover bi-directional and multi-directional interactions as well as interaction points with a dynamically varying number of interacting agents.

4.3.2 Customizing an appropriate temporal logic

Additional notation is used to specify interaction point properties. To model interactions between two or more agents, we use abstract operations ! and ?, denoting the offering and acceptance(s) of an interaction. We write "ag.ip.!(p(x))" to denote that the agent ag offers an interaction of type p with parameter vector x at interaction point ip. Similarly, "ag.ip.?(p(x))" denotes that ag accepts an interaction, where p and x will have values of an interaction that has been previously offered. In most FDTs, the

26 This assumption simplifies the treatment of liveness, but is not used with respect to safety conditions.

distinction between offering and accepting an interaction is only made implicitly, yielding for example ag.ip.send(x), or ip.send(x), if ag is clear from the context[27].

Concerning abstract operations, the situations where an agent is *at* the beginning and immediately *after* the operation are distinguished. The atomic formula at ag.ip.!(p(x)) holds when the agent ag is ready to offer an interaction of type p with parameter vector x at interaction point ip. after ag.ip.!(p(x)) holds immediately after completion of !. The formulas at ag.ip.! and after ag.ip.! hold when ag is at the beginning of and immediately after offering some interaction at ip, respectively. The formula at ag.ip.? holds when ag is prepared to accept an interaction at ip, after ag.ip.?(p(x)) holds just after ag has accepted p(x) at ip. The formula after ag.ip.? holds just after ag has accepted some interaction at ip.

The above notation is related to atomic formulas of many-sorted first-order logic (Chapter 3.3.2) in the following way:

- ag, ag1, ag2 are constants of sort AG with ag1 $\neq$ ag2;
- ip is a constant of sort IP;
- ! and ? are constants of sort OP;
- p, p1, p2 and x, x1, x2 are individual variables of sorts P and X, respectively;
- n, n1, n2, m are individual variables of sort $\mathbb{N}_0$;
- at and after are relation symbols of arity 5, associated with sorts AG, IP, OP, P, X; we overload at and after to be also relation symbols of arity 3 and 4, associated with sorts AG, IP, OP and AG, IP, OP, P, respectively.

The above notation can easily be translated into atomic formulas with a syntax according to the formation rules in Chapter 3.3.2.

With these preparations, we are now ready to customize an appropriate temporal logic for specifying interaction point properties. The logic consists of the building blocks At_F, *Pr*, *Q*, F_L, *P*, E_P, and E_F (see Chapter 3.3). At_F is selected because atomic formulas can then be decomposed, which makes it possible to associate architectural meaning with them. *Q* is selected because it allows quantification over infinite value domains. Since we restrict attention to reliable interaction points, F_L is chosen to refer to the future.

---

27 for instance, see Estelle, and SDL, Chapter 4.5

Some further restrictions apply to the relations at and after. We require that at ag.ip.! and after ag.ip.! do not hold at the same time. For each event after ag.ip.!(p(x)), there must be a corresponding preceding event at ag.ip.!(p(x)), and for two subsequent events at ag.ip.!, there is an event after ag.ip.! in between. Similar constraints apply with respect to the abstract operation ?. Within the logical framework which we have customized to specify interaction point properties, the restrictions can be made precise as follows:

O1.	$\Box\, \forall p,x.\ (\text{at ag.ip.!}(p(x)) \supset \text{at ag.ip.!})$
O2.	$\Box\, \forall p,x.\ (\text{after ag.ip.!}(p(x)) \supset \text{after ag.ip.!})$
O3.	$\Box\, (\text{at ag.ip.!} \supset \neg\ \text{after ag.ip.!})$
O4.	$\Box\, \forall p,x.\ (\#[\text{at ag.ip.!}(p(x))] \geq \#[\text{after ag.ip.!}(p(x))])$
O5.	$\Box\, (\#[\text{at ag.ip.!}] \leq \#[\text{after ag.ip.!}] + 1)$
O6.	$\Box\, \forall p,x.\ (\text{after ag.ip.?}(p(x)) \supset \text{after ag.ip.?})$
O7.	$\Box\, (\text{at ag.ip.?} \supset \neg\ \text{after ag.ip.?})$
O8.	$\Box\, (\#[\text{at ag.ip.?}] \geq \#[\text{after ag.ip.?}])$
O9.	$\Box\, (\#[\text{at ag.ip.?}] \leq \#[\text{after ag.ip.?}] + 1)$

Table 4.1: Properties of the relations at and after

Note that from these restrictions, the following properties can be proved:

$$\Box\, \forall p,x.\ (\text{at ag.ip.!}(p(x)) \supset \neg\ \text{after ag.ip.!}(p(x)))$$

$$\Box\, \forall p,x.\ ([\text{after ag.ip.!}(p(x))] \supset \blacklozenge\ [\text{at ag.ip.!}(p(x))])$$

$$\Box\, \forall p,x.\ (\#[\text{at ag.ip.!}(p(x))] \leq \#[\text{after ag.ip.!}(p(x))] + 1)$$

4.3.3 General properties

The following properties do not impose restrictions on the mode of interaction. Therefore, we refer to them as *general properties*.

P1. $\Box\, \forall p,x.\ (\#[\text{after ag1.ip.!}(p(x))] \geq \#[\text{after ag2.ip.?}(p(x))])$

This is a safety property requiring that interactions delivered to ag2 must have been previously offered by ag1[28]. Since p and x are individual variables of sorts P and X, respectively, an interpretation of P1 will lead to quantification over all objects of D^P and D^X. P1 prevents duplication, corruption, and creation of interactions (*functional correctness*). It does not prevent loss or starvation of interactions (but see P6 and P7, respectively).

In conventional temporal logic, functional correctness can only be stated if all interactions are distinct (see [Pnu86]). "In practice we can always impose the assumption of distinct messages by considering (not necessarily implementing) a unique sequence number or time-stamp associated with each message. The different sequence numbers ensure distinction even when the messages themselves are identical" ([Pnu86]). Clearly, this contradicts the idea that the specification is the implementation instruction, since it is explicitly permitted that a portion of the specification needs not be implemented. Moreover, the assumption of distinct messages or interactions can cause serious problems when more than one channel or interaction point requiring independent sequence numbering is involved. When the assumption is made, it is for technical reasons only, since without it, specifications of channels in conventional temporal logic as given in [Pnu86] would be incorrect. In property P1, the use of the temporal function #[.] allowed us dropping the assumption of distinct messages. Therefore, it does not matter whether several interactions between ag1 and ag2 at interaction point ip have the same type and the same parameter values and thus are indistinguishable.

P2. $\square\,\forall$p1,p2,x1,x2,n1,n2. (#[after ag2.ip.?(p1(x1))] = n1 $\wedge$
#[after ag2.ip.?(p2(x2))] = n2
$\supset$ ◆ (#[after ag1.ip.!(p1(x1))] = n1 $\wedge$
#[after ag1.ip.!(p2(x2))] = n2))

This safety property is provably equivalent (the proof is given in Chapter 4.4, Theorems 4.1 and 4.2) to the FIFO strategy (FIFO without loss): for all possible combinations of interaction types p1, p2, and parameter vectors x1, x2, if at some point in time the interactions p1(x1) and p2(x2) have been accepted n1 times and n2 times at interaction point ip, respectively, then there must be some previous point in

28 P1 implies the weaker property $\square\,\forall$p,x.([after ag2.ip.?(p(x))] $\supset$ ◆[after ag1.ip.!(p(x))]). These properties are equivalent only if all interactions are distinct.

time where p1(x1) and p2(x2) have been offered n1 times and n2 times, respectively. This property is always satisfied, if we consider synchronous interaction points (see below): here, the previous point in time is the current point in time (compare semantics of $\blacklozenge$, Chapter 3.3.4).

P3. $\Box$ (#[after ag1.ip.!] $\leq$ #[after ag2.ip.?] + m)

Safety property P3 constrains the maximum capacity of ip to be m interactions.

P4. $\Box$ $\forall$p,x. (#[at ag2.ip.?(p)] $\geq$ #[after ag2.ip.?(p(x))])

P4 is a safety property requiring that a condition concerning the type is imposed on accepted interactions: for an acceptance of p(x) to occur, ag2 must be prepared to accept an interaction of type p; ag2 thus influences the choice of the next interaction.

P5. $\Box$ (at ag1.ip.! $\wedge$ at ag2.ip.? $\supset$ $\Diamond$ [after ag1.ip.!] $\wedge$ $\Diamond$ [after ag2.ip.?])

This is a liveness property, requiring that if ag1 is prepared to offer and ag2 is prepared to accept an interaction, then both agents may eventually proceed (progress). P5 leaves open whether communication is synchronous or asynchronous. In fact, all properties P1 through P8 allow for both modes of interaction. When considering asynchronous communication, this property should be augmented by P11, P12, or P13 such that ag1 will proceed also if ag2 is not ready to accept.

P6. $\Box$ (at ag2.ip.? $\wedge$ #[after ag1.ip.!] > #[after ag2.ip.?] $\supset$ $\Diamond$ [after ag2.ip.?])

If more interactions have been offered than accepted, and ag2 is prepared to accept, then it will eventually proceed (progress). The precondition of this property can only be satisfied if not all interactions happen synchronously. Thus it supplements the property P5. Moreover, P1, P5 and P6 together prevent loss of interactions: if an interaction would be lost, this would violate P1, because to satisfy P5 and P6 an interaction would have to be created. Thus, P1, P5 and P6 are sufficient to specify reliability as characterized in Chapter 4.2. However, they do not prevent starvation = infinite delay of interactions.

P7. $\Box$ $\forall$p,x. ($\Box\Diamond$ at ag2.ip.? $\wedge$ #[after ag1.ip.!(p(x))] > #[after ag2.ip.?(p(x))]
$\supset$ $\Diamond$ [after ag2.ip.?(p(x))])

P7 is a fairness requirement (*non-starvation property*), stating that if ag2 is prepared to accept from time to time, and interactions p(x) have been offered more often than accepted, then p(x) will eventually be accepted by ag2. It prevents starvation of interactions (fair strategy). Note that absence of starvation should only be demanded if ag2 is prepared to accept from time to time. It can be shown that P2 and P6 together imply P7; that means that an interaction point satisfying P2 and P6 prevents infinite delay of interactions. This is intuitive, because if interactions are accepted from time to time, and they are accepted in the order in which they have been offered, each interaction will eventually be accepted.

P8. $\Box\, \forall p1,p2,x1,x2,n1,n2.\ (\Box\Diamond \text{ at ag2.ip.?} \wedge \#[\text{after ag1.ip.!}(p1(x1))] = n1 \wedge$
$\#[\text{after ag1.ip.!}(p2(x2))] = n2$
$\supset \Diamond\, (\#[\text{after ag2.ip.?}(p1(x1))] = n1 \wedge$
$\#[\text{after ag2.ip.?}(p2(x2))] = n2)\ )$

This is a liveness property specifying a fair FIFO strategy, i.e., a FIFO strategy where interactions are not infinitely delayed, if ag2 is prepared to accept from time to time. It can be shown (as the reader might have already suspected) that P8 implies P7. This is appealing, because it supports our intuition.

Let us emphasize again that a restriction of the mode of interaction has not been made so far: each property can be satisfied both by synchronous and asynchronous interaction points as well as by interaction points where the mode of interaction is not determined.

4.3.4 Mode of interaction

By adding further requirements, we can restrict the mode of interaction to be synchronous or asynchronous. In the synchronous case, this will make some of the requirements obsolete, though they remain satisfied. It is, for instance, not possible that the number of offered interactions exceeds the number of accepted interactions, which is part of the antecedent of P6. Let us first consider the asynchronous case. The following properties can be added:

P9. $\Box\, ([\text{after ag1.ip.!}] \wedge [\text{after ag2.ip.?}] \supset \#[\text{after ag1.ip.!}] > \#[\text{after ag2.ip.?}])$

If an offer- and an accept-event occur simultaneously, then they belong to different interactions. This is not implied by P9 alone, but, for instance, by P9 in conjunction with the FIFO property P2. P9 is a necessary property for the asynchronous mode.

P10. $\Box$([after ag1.ip.!] $\supset \neg$ [after ag2.ip.?])

This property explicitly excludes any offer- and accept-events to occur simultaneously. It is sufficient to express the asynchronous mode, but not necessary: it disallows unrelated offer- and accept-events to occur simultaneously. It is clear that P10 implies P9.

P11. $\Box$(at ag1.ip.! $\wedge$ #[after ag1.ip.!] = #[after ag2.ip.?] $\supset \Diamond$ [after ag1.ip.!])

If the number of offered interactions equals the number of accepted interactions, and ag1 is prepared to offer, then it may eventually proceed. This requires the capacity of the interaction point to be at least one. P11 can be easily adapted to require a minimum capacity of n interactions, as shown in P12:

P12. $\Box$(at ag1.ip.! $\wedge$ #[after ag1.ip.!] < #[after ag2.ip.?] + n $\supset \Diamond$ [after ag1.ip.!])

P13. $\Box$(at ag1.ip.! $\supset \Diamond$ [after ag1.ip.!])

If ag1 is prepared to offer, it may eventually proceed. There is no additional premise as in properties P11 and P12, permitting the interaction point to have a limited capacity. An interaction point fulfilling this liveness property must have infinite capacity.

The synchronous interaction mode can be enforced by constraining the capacity of the interaction point to be zero:

P14. $\Box$(#[after ag1.ip.!] = #[after ag2.ip.?])

P14 requires that accept- and offer-events occur simultaneously. Together with P1 and P5, this should be sufficient to define the essential properties of synchronous interaction points for a pair of entities. We have reliability and fairness, and no loss of interactions can occur. Note that we do not have a choice of strategy, because the capacity is zero.

4.3.5 Inspection

In some cases it can be necessary to inspect the next interaction without accepting it already. To model this, we introduce an abstract operation § (in addition to the already defined ! and ?). We write "ag.ip.§(p(x))" to denote that the agent ag inspects the next interaction at interaction point ip, where p and x will have the values of this interaction. The interaction is not removed from ip. From a conceptual point of view, it would be preferable to avoid the inspection. However, as we need it to capture the semantics of Estelle interaction points (see Chapter 4.5.1), we define it here. The problem that arises is that an interaction which is not yet accepted is not characterized as an interaction, so the properties related to inspection rather fit to interaction point representations than to a conceptual definition. In the following, we list six (context-independent) properties, which we consider as essential concerning inspection.

P15. $\Box\, \forall p,x.\ ([\text{after ag2.ip.§}(p(x))] \wedge p \neq \text{nil}$
$\qquad \supset \#[\text{after ag1.ip.!}(p(x))] > \#[\text{after ag2.ip.?}(p(x))])$

Each interaction which has just been inspected must have been previously offered, but is not yet accepted.

P16. $\Box\, \forall p,x.\ ([\text{after ag2.ip.§}(p(x))] \wedge \#[\text{after ag1.ip.!}] = \#[\text{after ag2.ip.?}] \supset p = \text{nil})$

If all offered interactions have already been accepted, then the inspection will result in p having a distinguished nil-value.

P17. $\Box\, ([\text{at ag2.ip.§}] \supset \Diamond\, [\text{after ag2.ip.§}])$

Inspection of interactions can always proceed, without any preconditions.

P18. $\Box\, ([\text{after ag2.ip.?}] \supset \neg\, [\text{after ag2.ip.§}])$

Inspection and acceptance of interactions may not happen simultaneously. Otherwise, it would not be clear whether the inspection would yield the interaction just accepted or the following interaction.

P19. $\square \forall p1,p2,x1,x2,n.\ ([\text{after ag2.ip.§}(p1(x1))] \wedge \#[\text{after ag2.ip.?}] = n \wedge$
$\blacklozenge\ ([\text{after ag2.ip.§}(p2(x2))] \wedge$
$\#[\text{after ag2.ip.?}] = n \wedge p2 \neq \text{nil})$
$\supset p1 = p2 \wedge x1 = x2)$

Subsequent inspections yield the same results, if no intermediate acceptance has taken place. This property constrains the strategy: once an interaction is the next one, it remains the next one (see also P20).

P20. $\square \forall p1,p2,x1,x2,n.\ ([\text{after ag2.ip.?}(p1(x1))] \wedge \#[\text{after ag2.ip.?}] = n \wedge$
$\blacklozenge\ ([\text{after ag2.ip.§}(p2(x2))] \wedge$
$\#[\text{after ag2.ip.?}] = n\text{-}1 \wedge p2 \neq \text{nil})$
$\supset p1 = p2 \wedge x1 = x2)$

If a previous inspection has yielded an interaction p2(x2), then the next acceptance must yield the same interaction. Together with P19, this property makes sure that once an interaction is the next interaction, it remains the next one. P19 and P20 are fulfilled if the FIFO strategy is applied, but a strategy such as last-in-first-out is ruled out.

4.3.6 Summary

In Chapter 4.3, we have formally specified a number of generic properties an interaction point can have. Some of them are essential for a given application area such as OSI, others are optional. It has proved to be feasible to leave the mode of interaction undetermined. However, restricting the mode of interaction to be synchronous and asynchronous, respectively, is possible by simply adding further properties.

The temporal interaction point properties in Chapter 4.3 are related to the informal properties in Chapter 4.2 as shown in Table 4.2. Subsets of these properties can be composed by logical conjunction to yield the meaning $\mathcal{S}eman_{ip}$ of the interaction point concept in a particular application area. A specialization within an application area or with respect to a given problem can be achieved by adding further properties. Here, the restriction applies that the composition must result in a consistent formula. Some consistent combinations can be found in Chapter 4.5. To see that a temporal formula is consistent, it suffices to show that there is a model in which it is satisfied.

Features[29]	Related properties
i) reliability	P1
ii) mode of interaction	P9, P10, P14
iv) progress	P5, P6
v) strategies	P2, P7, P8
vi) capacity	P3, P11, P12, P13, P14
viii) selection of interactions	P4
ix) inspection of interactions	P15, P16, P17, P18, P19, P20

Table 4.2: Relationship between informal and formal interaction point properties

Interestingly, it turned out to be difficult to capture the property "no loss of interactions can occur". The reason is that loss is an internal notion and can therefore not be expressed in the specification of external behaviour. All we can do here - and this is entirely adequate - is to consider an interaction as lost when it is never delivered, although it may remain forever in the interaction point (see also [Koy87]).

Another consequence originates from the specification of interaction point capacity. Requiring a capacity of exactly k interactions amounts to composing P3 and P12 with $m - n = k$. It is interesting to notice that P3 is a safety property, and P12 is a liveness property.

4.4 Formal reasoning about interaction points

Once a number of properties are formally defined, it is feasible to examine interdependencies which may or may not exist between them. This is an important benefit, because for a given interaction point representation, it suffices to verify some properties in order to infer others. Also, it serves an implementation independent study of the interaction point concept which leads to a better understanding. The following interdependencies and properties can be proved. Some proofs are given subsequently, proofs not listed here can be found in [Got89].

29 An informal explanation has been given in Chapter 4.2.

V1.	P2 is equivalent to the FIFO property
V2.	$P2 \supset P1$
V3.	$P2 \wedge P6 \supset P7$
V4.	$P2 \wedge P6 \supset P8$
V5.	$P2 \wedge P7 \supset P8$
V6.	$P1 \wedge P6 \wedge P13 \supset P5$
V7.	$P8 \wedge \Box\Diamond$ at ag2.ip.? $\supset P2$
V8.	$P8 \supset P7$
V9.	$P10 \supset P9$
V10.	$P13 \supset P11$
V11.	$P13 \supset \forall n \geq 0.\ P12$

Table 4.3: Valid formulas

Theorem 4.1: P2 implies the FIFO property (FIFO without loss).

Proof: Assume that P2 does not imply the FIFO discipline. Then there must be a point in time where an interaction is accepted before all interactions offered earlier have been accepted, and P2 holds.

Recall that interactions are distinguished by the interaction point where they take place, the entities offering/accepting them, the interaction types and the parameter values. Since we allow interactions with the same type and identical parameter values, different interactions may be indistinguishable. So, if two indistinguishable interactions change their order, this will not be observable (and in fact does not matter).

Without loss of generality, we can consider the first observable violation of the FIFO discipline. It suffices to look at all interactions p1(x1) and p2(x2), where $p1(x1) \neq p2(x2)$, occurring between ag1 and ag2 at interaction point ip. Then the first observable violation of the FIFO discipline manifests itself in the following situation:

t1 t2

t1	t2
[after ag1.ip.! (p1(x1))]	[after ag1.ip.? (p1(x1))]
#[after ag1.ip.! (p1(x1))] = n1	#[after ag1.ip.? (p1(x1))] = n1
#[after ag1.ip.! (p2(x2))] = n2>0	#[after ag1.ip.?(p2(x2))] = m2<n2

Let t2 be the current point in time. At t2, the interaction p1(x1) is accepted for the n1-th time. Assume P2 holds, then it follows that p1(x1) must have been previously offered n1 times. Let $t1 \leq t2$ be the point in time where the n1-th offer of p1(x1) has occurred. Up to t1, the interaction p2(x2) has been offered $n2 > 0$ times. If in this situation the FIFO discipline is violated, then p2(x2) is accepted $m2 < n2$ times up to t2, the point where p1(x1) is accepted the n1-th time. Now consider P2 for p1(x1), p2(x2) and t2:

$$\#[\text{after ag2.ip.?(p1(x1))}] = n1 \wedge \#[\text{after ag2.ip.?(p2(x2))}] = m2$$
$$\supset \blacklozenge(\#[\text{after ag1.ip.!(p1(x1))}] = n1 \wedge \#[\text{after ag1.ip.!(p2(x2))}] = m2)$$

The antecedents are satisfied for t2. The time interval where #[after ag1.ip.!(p1(x1))] = n1 of the consequence is satisfied starts at t1. But at t1, #[after ag1.ip.!(p2(x2))] = m2 is not satisfied, because $m2 < n2$, and will not be satisfied later, because #[after ag1.ip.!(p2(x2))] increases monotonically over time. That contradicts the assumption that P2 does not imply the FIFO property.

q.e.d.

Theorem 4.2: The FIFO property implies P2 (FIFO without loss).

Proof: Assume that the FIFO discipline does not imply P2. Then there must be interactions p1(x1) and p2(x2), occurring between ag1 and ag2 at interaction point ip, integers n1, n2 and a point in time t such that the following holds:

(i) $\#[\text{after ag2.ip.? (p1(x1))}] = n1 \wedge \#[\text{after ag2.ip.? (p2(x2))}] = n2 \wedge$
$\blacksquare\,(\#[\text{after ag1.ip.! (p1(x1))}] \neq n1 \vee \#[\text{after ag1.ip.! (p2(x2))}] \neq n2)$

If $p1(x1) = p2(x2)$, the FIFO property is violated, because interactions which have not yet been offered are accepted. For $p1(x1) \neq p2(x2)$, we get the following situation:

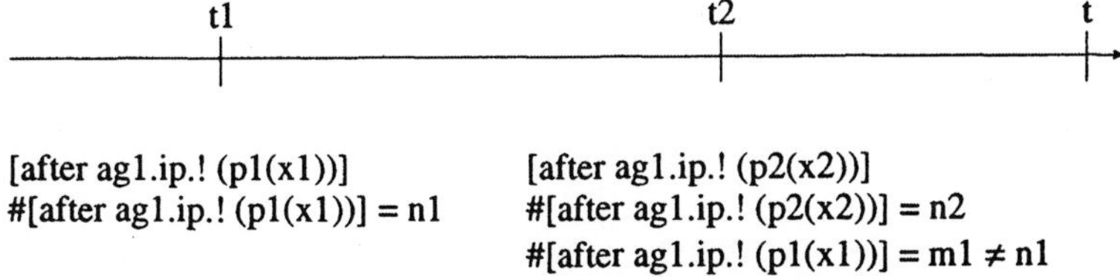

Because according to the FIFO discipline, all interactions accepted until time t must have been previously offered, there are points in time $t1 \leq t$ and $t2 \leq t$

where the n1-st and n2-nd interaction p1(x1) and p2(x2) have been offered, respectively. Without loss of generality, let t1 < t2. Also, because (i) holds by assumption at time t, we have m1 offers of p1(x1) with m1 ≠ n1 at time t2. Since #[.] increases monotonically over time, m1 > n1. This means that m1 interactions p1(x1) have been offered before the n2-nd interaction p2(x2) is offered at time t2. However, at time t, n2 interactions p2(x2) and only n1 interactions p1(x1) have been accepted. It follows that the n2-nd interaction p2(x2) has been accepted before m1 interactions p1(x1) have been accepted. This violates the FIFO property and thus contradicts the initial assumption.

q.e.d.

Theorem 4.3: P2 ∧ P6 ⊃ P7

Proof: Assume that the proposition does not hold. Then there must be an interaction with properties P2, P6 and ¬P7. If P7 is violated, there must be a point in time t where an interaction p(x) that has been offered by ag1 and not yet been accepted by ag2 will starve, although ag2 is prepared to accept from time to time:

(i) ∃p,x. ◊ (□◊ at ag2.ip.? ∧
#[after ag1.ip.!(p(x))] > #[after ag2.ip.?(p(x))] ∧
¬ ◊ [after ag2.ip.?(p(x))])

Without loss of generality, we can consider the first such point in time t. Let p(x) be an interaction for which (i) holds. Then the situation is as follows:

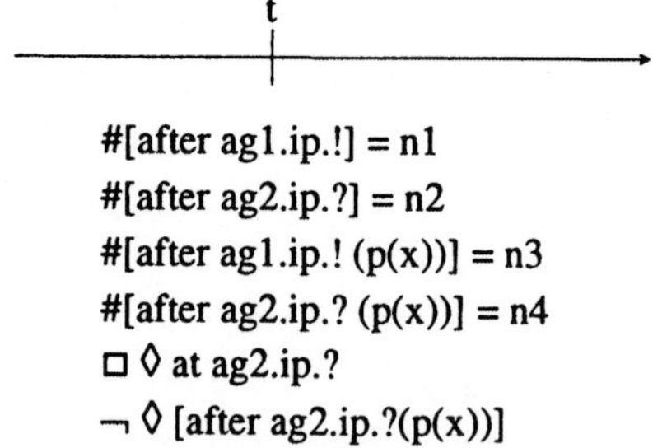

Recall that for an arbitrary formula φ, #[φ] is uniquely defined for each moment in time, so, for instance, for φ = after ag1.ip.!, we obtain

(ii) □ ∃ n1. (#[after ag1.ip.!] = n1)

At t, n1 ≥ 0 interactions have been offered, and n2 interactions have been accepted. Because P2 implies P1 which in turn implies □ (#[after ag1.ip.!] ≥ #[after ag2.ip.?]), n1 ≥ n2.

At t, (n1-n2) interactions that have been offered are not yet accepted. Among these are (n3-n4) interactions with type p and parameter value x. Because we consider a point in time where P7 is violated, n3 must be greater than n4. It is clear that n1 > n2 as long as n3 > n4.

Now ag2 is prepared to accept from time to time, and since n1 > n2 at point t, ag2 will eventually accept and be prepared to accept again. However, ag2 cannot accept interactions that have been offered <u>after</u> t before those offered <u>until</u> t, since this would violate the FIFO property P2. Also, by assumption ag2 cannot accept interactions p(x).

If P2 and P6 hold, and ag2 is prepared to accept from time to time, then eventually the interaction to be accepted next will be an interaction p(x), because n3 > n4 at time t, and consequently n1 > n2. Also, ag2 will be ready to accept, so the antecedent of P6 is satisfied. However, by assumption ag2 cannot accept interactions p(x). This contradicts P2 and P6, because according to P6, ag2 must eventually accept, and according to P2, if ag2 accepts, it can only accept an interaction p(x).

q.e.d.

4.5 Interaction point representations in operational FDTs

Interaction points can be represented by concepts of formal description techniques (FDTs) or even by a piece of a formal description. In the following, representations in Estelle, LOTOS, and SDL, which are FDTs specifically designed for the specification of open distributed systems (see [Tur92] for an introduction), are studied. The semantics of each of these representations is to some extent and with some restrictions captured by subsets of the listed properties. This makes a limited comparison between them feasible. The investigation of interaction point representations is not formalized, however, some indications are given how a formal relationship between FDT semantics and a model in which logical formulas can be interpreted can be established. An entirely formal treatment of these issues is outside the scope of this work. Similar studies concerning representations in the FDTs CRS ([MaNe87], [Sch92]) and Z ([Spi89]) as well as in implementation languages can be found in [Got89] and

[Got90a]. Another important issue is the study of the point of control and observation (PCO) in the context of conformance testing ([Lin88], [Bau88]).

4.5.1 Interaction points in Estelle

Estelle ([ISO89], [Dia89]) is an FDT designed for the specification of distributed, concurrent information processing systems, in particular communication services and protocols of the OSI BRM. Estelle is based on the model of extended finite state machines (as SDL, see Chapter 4.5.3). It has been developed and standardized within ISO (International Standardization Organisation). Estelle has been used to define communication services and protocols in the context of OSI (for instance, see [ISO86a], [ISO86b]), and a proposal exists for how to represent OSI concepts in Estelle ([ISO88d]).

An Estelle specification describes a hierarchically structured system of nondeterministic, sequential components, called "*instances of modules*" or "*modules*" for short. They can perform *interactions* through bidirectional *channels* between their *interaction points*. An example of an Estelle system architecture is shown in Figure 4.2.

With each module instance, a finite set of interaction points is associated. Access in and out of the module instance is made through these interaction points. Each interaction point of a module instance has an associated first-in-first-out (FIFO) queue of infinite capacity, which receives and stores interactions sent to that module through this interaction point. The module instance may also send interactions to other modules through its own interaction points.

Interactions in Estelle have an interaction type. Additionally, they may have a list of parameter values. The sending of an interaction is part of a transition and denoted by OUTPUT ip.p(x), where p is the type, x the parameter vector, and ip is the name of the interaction point through which the interaction is sent. The sender is clear from the context, the receiver is uniquely defined by the communication structure (see Figure 4.2) and not known to the sending module. The reception of an interaction is implicitly included in the execution of a transition, the interaction to be received is defined by WHEN ip.p, which is part of the enabling condition.

The situation in Estelle is slightly more complicated in that there is not just a single interaction point between two module instances, but *two* interaction points to be dynamically connected by a channel (see Figure 4.2). So each interaction point is statically associated with a module instance and may be dynamically associated with a channel, which in turn is associated with the interaction point of the recipient.

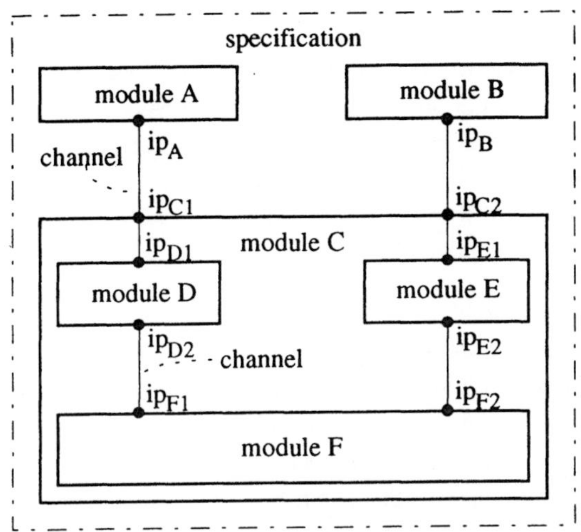

Figure 4.2: An Estelle system architecture

The observations made so far lead to the conclusion that conceptual interaction points can be represented by Estelle interaction points. In order to investigate which properties can be ascribed to an Estelle interaction point, we need a model in which the logical formulas of Chapter 4.3 can be interpreted. This model has to be derived from the Estelle execution model. We are interested in the predicates at ag.ip.op(p(x)) and after ag.ip.op(p(x)), where op $\in$ {!,?}. at ag.ip.!(p(x)) holds when the module instance ag is due to execute the statement OUTPUT ip.p(x) in one of its transitions, after ag.ip.!(p(x)) holds immediately after the execution. Acceptance of interactions is linked to the WHEN-clause: at ag.ip.?(p) holds when the module instance ag has selected a transition with the enabling condition WHEN ip.p for execution, after ag.ip.?(p(x)) holds immediately after ag has started to execute this transition.

The semantics of interaction points with an individual queue can be captured by the properties P2, P6, P9 and P13: $\mathcal{S}eman_{ip\_Estelle} =_{Df}$ P2 $\wedge$ P6 $\wedge$ P9 $\wedge$ P13 (see Chapters 4.3 and 4.4; recall that this implies P1, P5, P7, P8, P11, and P12). P2, P9 and P13 hold because an interaction point has an associated FIFO queue of infinite capacity, and the mode of interaction is asynchronous. To see that P6 is satisfied, we have to take into account that a transition is selected for execution only if its enabling condition including the WHEN-clause is fulfilled.

To see that the conjunction of P2, P6, P9, and P13 is consistent, it suffices to show that there is a model in which it is satisfied. Consider, for instance, a model in which an arbitrary sequence of interactions between ag1 and ag2 is expressed such that the order of offers is identical to the order of acceptances, interactions occur asynchronously, and all offered interactions are accepted. Clearly, such a model exists and satisfies P2, P6, P9, and P13. And since P1, P5, P7, P8, P11, and P12 are implied by the conjunction of P2, P6, P9, and P13 (see Chapter 4.4), they are also satisfied in this model.

The Estelle execution model determines that a module instance selects transitions for execution autonomously. Whether a transition may be executed depends on the enabling condition, in particular on the WHEN- and PROVIDED-clauses. To evaluate these conditions, the module instance must have access to the *next* interaction of each of its interaction points, i.e., to the interaction's type and parameter values. Only then can it determine whether a transition is currently enabled, and can later on choose one of the enabled transitions for execution (see [ISO89]). Note that in general several interaction points have to be inspected, but only one transition of the module instance can be executed, so the inspection may not lead to an acceptance of interactions. Acceptance only takes place during the execution of a transition. To model access to the next interaction, we have introduced the abstract operation § in Chapter 4.3.5. We require it to have the properties P15 to P20. Note that in Estelle, inspection of interactions does not appear explicitly in the specification, but is used in the execution model.

To completely cover the situation depicted in Figure 4.2, we would have to define the component "channel" between two interaction points. This could be done, for example, by giving a property-oriented specification of an agent "channel" relating, for instance, ip_A and ip_{C1}. Moreover, we have not dealt with the set of interactions which may validly be sent and received through a particular interaction point (*typing*). This can easily be incorporated by a restriction of the set of constants of sort P.

A complication arises if several interaction points share a common queue. In that case, the properties of an interaction point can no longer be specified independently of its context. One has to describe all interaction points sharing the same queue in common. Also, the possibility of attaching interaction points has not been taken into account.

Another representation of conceptual interaction points is the composition of a channel and the interaction points which it links. A channel can be described in the same formalism, which leads to properties corresponding to P2, P6, P9 and P13. The composition results in an interaction point representation with the same properties, even if the channel has a limited capacity (property P3).

4.5.2 Interaction points in LOTOS

LOTOS (Language of Temporal Ordering Specification) ([ISO88c]) is an FDT designed for the specification of distributed, concurrent information processing systems, in particular communication services and protocols of the OSI BRM. LOTOS is an algebraic approach. It has been developed and standardized within ISO. LOTOS has been used to define communication services and protocols in the context of OSI (for instance, see [ISO90a], [ISO90b]), and a proposal exists for how to represent OSI concepts in LOTOS ([Tur87]).

A LOTOS specification describes a hierarchically structured system of active components, called "*instances of processes*" or "*processes*" for short. Processes communicate with their environment through *gates*. An example of a LOTOS system architecture is shown in Figure 4.3, where g1 to g4 are gates.

With each process, a finite set of gates is associated. Several processes may share the same gate. A communication is a synchronized action. It takes place between two or more processes at a common gate and is called an "*event*" (or "*interaction*"). In contrast to Estelle and SDL, communication at LOTOS gates is synchronous and allows *multi-way synchronization*.

An event offer in LOTOS has the syntax *<gate_name> <attribute_list>*, where *gate_name* identifies a gate, and *attribute_list* is a finite number of value declarations and/or variable declarations. A value declaration is given by a ! followed by an expression defining the value. A variable declaration is given by a ? followed by a variable identifier and its associated type. An interaction can take place if all concerned processes simultaneously offer matching events at a common gate. Depending on the attribute list, the interaction leads to value matching, value passing, and/or value generation (see [ISO88c]).

It is straightforward to represent conceptual interaction points by LOTOS gates. As before, we have to derive a model in which the logical formulas of Chapter 4.3 can be interpreted before we can investigate which properties can be ascribed to the chosen representation. From the interaction sorts possible in LOTOS, we consider only uni-directional value passing between two agents. We say that a process is *offering* an interaction if the attribute list consists only of value declarations, it is *accepting* an interaction if the attribute list consists only of variable declarations. As outlined in Chapter 4.3, this treatment can be generalized to interactions between an arbitrary finite, but fixed number of agents. However, value matching and value creation, bi-directional and multi-directional interactions, and interaction points with a dynamically varying number of interacting agents, which can be expressed in LOTOS, are not covered.

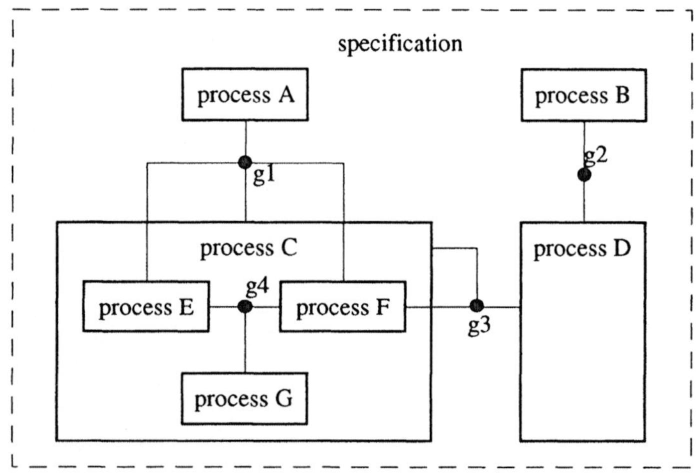

Figure 4.3: A LOTOS system architecture

We determine that the predicate after ag.ip.!(p(x)) holds when the event ip <p> <x> has just occurred, and the process instance ag engaging in this event has previously offered ip !p !x (interaction offer). after ag.ip.?(p(x)) holds when ip <p> <x> has just occurred and ag has offered ip ?p:i_type ?x:i_values (interaction acceptance). Analogously, we can determine that at ag.ip.!(p(x)) (at ag.ip.?) holds when ag is prepared to engage in the event ip !p !x (ip ?p:i_type ?x:i_values). However, care is necessary here, because the readiness of a process to engage in an event does not always imply that this event will take place. If, for instance, a number of events are offered alternatively and one of them occurs, then the other event offers are immediately withdrawn. Since in Chapter 4.3 it was assumed that if an agent is prepared to offer/accept, it remains prepared until the offer/acceptance takes place, we can ascribe properties using "at" predicates (i.e., liveness properties) only to gates where event offers are not withdrawn. This depends on the definitions of the processes sharing that gate.

```
type i_queue_type is boolean, interaction
    sorts i_queue
    opns  new_queue : → i_queue
          add :       i_queue, interaction → i_queue
          remove :    i_queue → i_queue
          first :     i_queue → interaction
          empty :     i_queue → bool
    eqns  forall q:i_queue, i,j:interaction
          ofsort bool
          empty(new_queue) = true
          empty(add(q,i)) = false
          ofsort i_queue
          remove(add(new_queue,i)) = new_queue
          remove(add(add(q,i),j)) = add(remove(add(q,i)),j)
          ofsort interaction
          first(add(new_queue,i)) = i
          first(add(add(q,i),j)) = first(add(q,i))
    endtype
process ip'[in1,in2,out1,out2](q1:i_queue,q2:i_queue):noexit :=
        in1 ?y:interaction; ip'[in1,in2,out1,out2](add(q1,y),q2)
    []  in2 ?y:interaction; ip'[in1,in2,out1,out2](q1,add(q2,y))
    []  [not(empty(q1))] → out1 !first(q1); ip'[in1,in2,out1,out2](remove(q1),q2)
    []  [not(empty(q2))] → out2 !first(q2); ip'[in1,in2,out1,out2](q1,remove(q2))
    endproc
```

Figure 4.4: Abstract data type i_queue and LOTOS process ip'[30]

The semantics of gates in a context as discussed in the previous paragraph can be captured by the safety properties P1 and P14: $\mathcal{S}eman_{ip\_LOTOS} =_{Df} P1 \wedge P14$. Recall that P14 constrains the capacity to be zero, which leads to the synchronous interaction mode. P1 prevents duplication, corruption, and creation of interactions, and taking P1

30 For the sake of simplicity, error cases such as first(new_queue) are omitted. Work on error handling can, for instance, be found in [Poi88].

and P14 together, no loss can occur. Also, under the above reservations, we can ascribe the liveness property P5 to a gate. Inspection as defined in Chapter 4.3.5 cannot be derived from the execution model, because any "inspection" leads to an acceptance and thus to an interaction to occur. Again, to see that the conjunction of P1 and P14 is consistent, it suffices to show that there is a model in which it is satisfied. A possible candidate is a model in which an arbitrary sequence of synchronous interactions between ag1 and ag2 is expressed.

A slightly different interaction point representation has been chosen in [Tur87] for the context of OSI. Here, a service access point is represented by a gate together with a value declaration denoting the address of the service access point. It is then possible to use only one gate for an arbitrary number of distinct service access points.

So far, we have represented architectural concepts by FDT concepts. This is not the only possible choice, an architectural concept can also be represented by a piece of a specification. We can, for instance, represent an asynchronous interaction point in LOTOS by the LOTOS process ip' shown in Figure 4.4. It has two gates and an internal state of sort i_queue for each direction. When ip' is instantiated with q1 = q2 = new_queue, we can ascribe the properties P2, P6, P10 and P13 to this representation: $\mathcal{S}eman_{ip'\_LOTOS} =_{Df} P2 \wedge P6 \wedge P10 \wedge P13$. With respect to P6, we have to repeat the reservations concerning the context (LOTOS event offers are sometimes withdrawn). Another representation is obtained by replacing the sort i_queue by a sort i_bag (bag of interactions). Here, P1 can be ascribed, but P2 no longer holds. Thus, using a LOTOS process can lead to a variety of interaction point representations.

4.5.3 Interaction points in SDL

SDL (Specification and Description Language) ([CCITT87]) is an FDT designed for the specification of the behaviour of real time interactive systems. SDL is based on the model of extended finite state machines (as Estelle). It has been developed and standardized within CCITT (The International Telegraph and Telephone Consultative Committee). SDL has been used to define communication services and protocols in the context of OSI (for instance, see [Hog88], [Hog88a]), and a proposal exists for how to represent OSI concepts in SDL ([BeHoTr88]).

SDL possesses a number of architectural concepts, which allow specifying the internal structure of a system as the result of a design decision: a system can be structured into *blocks*, which in turn can be decomposed into further blocks and/or *processes*. Thus one obtains a hierarchical system structure, with processes at the leaves. Note that the use of SDL architectural concepts does not necessarily imply a design decision about the internal structure as mandatory for the implementation. SDL concepts can also be applied just for decomposition of the specification to cope with complexity and to achieve better understandability; in this case, only the visible behaviour of the structured parts is important, not the internal architecture. This comment also applies to Estelle and LOTOS.

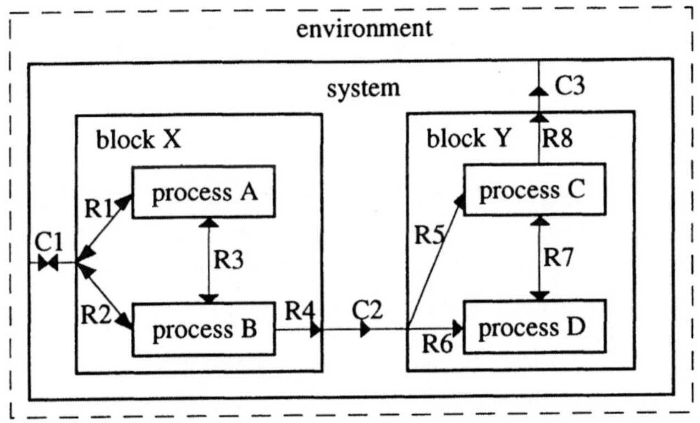

Figure 4.5: An SDL system architecture

All activities in the system are performed by processes. They can send and receive *signals* via *signalroutes* (only), which can be uni- or bi-directional. Blocks can be connected by *channels* (only), which are extended over block-boundaries by channels or signalroutes. An example of an SDL system architecture is shown in Figure 4.5. R1 to R8 are signalroutes, C1 to C3 are channels. The arrows indicate the direction of communication. C1 and C3 establish the link to the system's environment.

Signals in SDL have a signal type. Moreover, they may have a list of parameter values. Output and input of signals may be represented graphically. The sender of a signal is clear from the context. The receiver can - if not uniquely identified by the communication structure - be identified by a signalroute or its process identification.

With each process, *one* input port with a FIFO input queue is associated, where all incoming signals are temporarily stored. If in an arbitrary state of the process the input queue is not empty, the next signal is removed from the queue. It is checked whether a transition consuming that signal is defined. If this is the case, the transition is executed, otherwise the signal is discarded. Note that *all* signals intended for the process, no matter where they come from and independent of their route, are put into the same queue in the order of their arrival.

Of the above SDL concepts, the *input port* can be used to represent the interaction point. Interactions are called *signals* in SDL. The mode of interaction at the input port is asychronous, because signals are temporarily stored before consumption. The input port possesses the FIFO property, since all signals are stored in its associated FIFO input queue. Whenever a process proceeds, the next signal is accepted and processed. No inspection of signals takes place prior to acceptance. This is not necessary, because there is only one input port, and if a signal is not expected (unspecified reception, see [Zaf80]), it will be discarded.

We can ascribe the properties P2, P6, P9 and P13 to an SDL input port: $\mathcal{Seman}_{ip\_SDL} =_{Df} P2 \wedge P6 \wedge P9 \wedge P13$ (see Chapters 4.3 and 4.4; recall that this implies P1, P5, P7, P8, P11, and P12). This corresponds to the observations made so far. Other than in Estelle, no operation § is needed. As shown in Chapter 4.5.1, the conjunction of these properties is consistent.

The previous discussion does not cover the meaning of the input port completely. It is possible to keep unexpected signals for future consumption using the "save" construct. If such a signal is to be kept, it remains in the input queue. However, it is possible to consume signals after the sequence of kept signals. Therefore, the "save" mechanism violates the FIFO property.

Another problem for the semantics of input ports is the treatment of time in SDL. It is possible to define *timers*, that are objects owned by the declaring process. A timer can be set to a particular time and will generate a timer signal when this time has expired. The timer signal is appended to the input queue of the process where the timer has been defined, so the FIFO property is not violated here. However, conceptually the timer is now seen as an entity interacting with the process. It follows that there are two entities - the reliable medium and the timer - offering interactions to the process. Furthermore, by the statement RESET(T), every signal put into the input queue by timer T is removed from the queue *at once*, which violates the FIFO property.

4.5.4 Summary

The following is a table summarizing the investigation of the representation of interaction points in the FDTs Estelle, LOTOS, and SDL. It has already been explained why the conjunction of properties in each column is consistent. As mentioned in the previous sections, this does not fully cover the respective semantics. In particular, the full LOTOS semantics is not kept, because our treatment does not cover bi-directional

Features[31]	**Related properties**	**Properties of interaction points in**			
		Estelle (interaction point	**LOTOS** (gate[32])	**LOTOS** (process ip[33])	**SDL** (input port)
reliability	P1	P1	P1	P1	P1
mode of inter-action	P9, P10, P14	P9	P14	P9, P10	P9
progress	P5, P6	P5, P6	(P5)	P5, P6	P5, P6
strategies	P2, P7, P8	P2, P7, P8	P2	P2, P7, P8	P2, P7, P8
capacity	P3, P11, P12 P13, P14	P11, P12, P13	P14	P11, P12, P13	P11, P12, P13
context independence	given/ not given	given[34]	not given	not given	given[35]
selection of interactions	P4	-	-	-	-
inspection of interactions	P15, P16, P17, P18, P19, P20	P15, P16, P17, P18, P19, P20	-	-	-

Table 4.4: Comparison of interaction point representations

31 an informal explanation has been given in Chapter 4.2

32 with the reservations discussed in Chapter 4.5.2

33 the definition was given in Chapter 4.5.2

34 without common queues

35 for processes without timers, and without the use of the "save" mechanism

and multi-directional interactions as well as interaction points with a dynamically varying number of interacting entities. However, it is unclear whether these are essential features of the interaction point concept which must hold for interaction point representations. Our intention has been to investigate the basic architectural concept "interaction point" and possible representations, and not to fully cover the semantics of some FDT concepts.

4.6 Conformance between abstraction levels via the interaction point concept

In Chapter 4.1, we have given an intuitive informal definition of conformance for open systems. Since visible behaviour consisting of interactions between the system and its environment conceptually occurs at external interaction points, we can strengthen this intuitive notion of conformance as follows:

Definition 4.2: S1 is conforming to S2 (written "S1 *conf* S2") if and only if for all environments E, every behaviour of S1 in E, observed at external interaction points, is possible for S2 in E, observed at the corresponding interaction points.

Unfortunately, this informal definition is rather impractical, because the set of possible environments can be very large. Therefore, it is in general unfeasible to compare the behaviour of S1 in E against that of S2 in E for all possible environments. If the environment is already known, a weaker definition of conformance, taking only that environment into account, will be adequate. This can, for instance, be the case in protocol engineering: the environment of a protocol entity is often reduced to the underlying service provider and the peer entity such that reachability analysis can be performed. However, in the area of open systems this seems to be rather the exception; in general, the environment will not be predetermined. A way out of this difficulty would be a notion of conformance *conf** which relates S1 and S2 *independently* of the environment such that S1 *conf** S2 *implies* S1 *conf* S2. This condition ensures that it would suffice to compare S1 and S2 without taking the possible environments into consideration. It remains to be investigated whether environment-independent notions of conformance satisfying the condition actually exist. In the remainder of Chapter 4.6, we will address this issue and suggest a possible solution.

4.6.1 Problems with an environment-independent notion of conformance

A formal definition of conformance requires that the FDTs used to specify S1 and S2 are known. Existing proposals to formally capture conformance include:

- implication and equivalence between logical formulas;
- observational equivalence between CCS-processes ([Mil80]);
- the *conf*-relation and testing equivalence between LOTOS-processes ([BrScSt86]);
- the *satisfy*-relation between a CSP-process and a formula of trace-logic ([Hoa85]);
- correctness between a concurrent program and a formula of temporal logic ([Hai82]).

These notions of conformance indeed relate two descriptions independently of the environment. But they do not necessarily imply conformance as intuitively defined in Chapter 4.1, if we allow that interaction point representations on different levels of description may have different semantics. This, however, is typically the case when we start with an abstract specification (with an abstract semantics of interaction points) and move towards an implementation (where interaction points have to be realized using implementation language features). For instance, synchronous interaction found in many formalisms is usually implemented by a protocol using asynchronous communication. In order to see that this can sometimes lead to problems, consider the situation shown in Figure 4.6, where open systems S1 and S2 interact with the environment E via interaction points ip1 and ip2, respectively. Generally, S1 and S2 would be descriptions in different formalisms, for instance, in an implementation and a specification language. On account of simplicity, we assume that S1, S2, and E are specified in the same formalism. Also, we assume that the semantics of ip1 and ip2 is separated from S1, S2, and E. Furthermore, we decree that S1 and S2 are identical, so they will satisfy every meaningful, context-independent notion of conformance which may be defined between them. For expository purposes, we will use the formalism of communicating finite-state machines ([GoYu84]), however, similar examples can be found for other formalisms as well. An edge labeled "-n" stands for the offering of interaction n, i.e., ag.ip.!(n), "+n" corresponds to the acceptance of interaction n, i.e., ag.ip.?(n), where ag and ip are replaced appropriately by S1, S2, E, ip1, and ip2. An acceptance can only take place if there is a corresponding offer. An interaction n *occurs* when the acceptance takes place. The set of possible interaction sequences is determined by the specifications of S1, S2, and E, and the semantics of ip1 and ip2. In particular, interaction offers are constrained by the interaction point semantics (see Chapter 4.3).

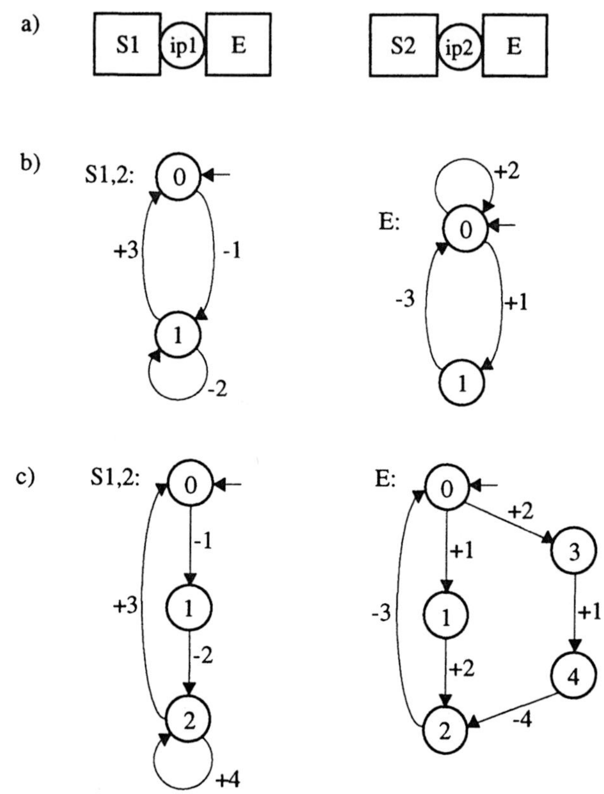

Figure 4.6: S1 and S2 embedded into environment E

Consider S1, S2, and E in Figure 4.6b, and assume that ip1 and ip2 have the FIFO property as defined by P2 in Chapter 4.3.3; additionally, let ip2 be synchronous. Formally, $\mathcal{S}eman_{ip1} =_{Df} P2$, $\mathcal{S}eman_{ip2} =_{Df} P2 \wedge P14$. Then interaction[36] sequences ⟨1,3⟩ and ⟨1,3,1,3⟩ are possible for (S1,ip1,E) and (S2,ip2,E); but sequences such as ⟨1,3,2⟩

36 Note that an interaction consists of offer *and* acceptance(s).

or ⟨1,3,2,2⟩, which may be observed in (S1,ip1,E), are not possible in (S2,ip2,E). So, despite the fact that S1 and S2 are identical, they do not satisfy the intuitive notion of conformance in Definition 4.2.

Another case is shown in Figure 4.6c, where it is assumed that ip1 is reliable as defined by P1 (Chapter 4.3.3), and ip2 has the FIFO property as defined by P2. Formally, $\mathcal{Seman}_{ip1} =_{Df} P1$, $\mathcal{Seman}_{ip2} =_{Df} P2$. Then some behaviours of (S1,ip1,E) are possible in (S2,ip2,E), but others such as ⟨2,1,4,3⟩ are not.

It is obvious that these difficulties with an environment-independent notion of conformance are due to the different interaction point semantics. Requiring that ip1 and ip2 have identical meaning would clearly solve the problem, but would also impose a strong restriction on interaction point representations on every level of abstraction. A weaker and still sufficient condition is that the semantics of ip1 is equivalent to or more specific than the semantics of ip2. This condition was violated in the previous examples. If it is satisfied, we say that ip1 is *compatible* with ip2 (written "ip1 *comp* ip2"). To show ip1 *comp* ip2, the following steps can be taken:

i) Identify interaction point representations on each level of description, including the requirement specification, the operational specification, the test system, and the implementation.
ii) Analyze the interaction point representations and capture their meaning in a mathematical formalism.
iii) Show that the semantics of the lower level representations is equivalent to or more specific than that of the corresponding higher level representations.

To capture the meaning of interaction point representations, the temporal logic proposed in Chapter 4.3.2 can be used. Showing compatibility between interaction point representations ip1 and ip2 amounts then to proving that the semantics of ip1 implies that of ip2. To show incompatibility, it suffices to prove that the implication does not always hold. We will make this precise in Chapter 4.6.2 and state some general results. In Chapter 4.6.3, we reconsider conformance as defined in Chapter 3.3.9. In Chapter 4.6.4, we outline how this methodology can be applied to OSI.

4.6.2 Compatibility between interaction points

Once the semantics of interaction points is captured in a mathematical formalism, it is possible to reason about their compatibility. Informally, ip1 is compatible with ip2 (written "ip1 *comp* ip2") if and only if the meaning of ip1 is equivalent to or more specific than the meaning of ip2. Based on the logical formalism in Chapter 4.3.2, we will now make this notion of interaction point compatibility precise and state some general results.

Consider a system S, some environment E, two interaction points ip1 and ip2, and the compositions (S,ip1,E) and (S,ip2,E). Let $\mathcal{Seman}_{ip1} =_{Df} P2 \wedge P5$ and $\mathcal{Seman}_{ip2} =_{Df} P2 \wedge P5 \wedge P14$ be formulas that capture their semantics completely (see Chapter 4.6.1 and Figure 4.6b). The only difference between ip1 and ip2 concerns the mode of interaction. At ip2, only synchronous interactions can occur, whereas the mode of interaction is undetermined for ip1. It follows that every sequence of interactions which can occur at ip2 can also occur at ip1 (safety). Moreover, if in a particular situation an interaction will occur at ip2, it must not be refused at ip1 in the same situation (liveness). So intuitively, ip2 *comp* ip1 holds. On the other hand, interaction sequences which can occur at ip1 can possibly not occur at ip2 (see Chapter 4.6.1), which means that ip1 is incompatible with ip2.

To make this intuition precise, we define relations *comp* and *incomp* between interaction points:

Definition 4.3: Let $\mathcal{Seman}_{ip1}$ and $\mathcal{Seman}_{ip2}$ be the precise meaning of the interaction points ip1 and ip2.

a) ip1 *comp* ip2 iff $\models \mathcal{Seman}_{ip1} \supset \mathcal{Seman}_{ip2}$
b) ip1 *incomp* ip2 iff $\not\models \mathcal{Seman}_{ip1} \supset \mathcal{Seman}_{ip2}$

It is important that $\mathcal{Seman}_{ip1}$ and $\mathcal{Seman}_{ip2}$ capture the semantics of ip1 and ip2 *precisely*. This means that all and only those interaction point properties constraining the set of possible interaction sequences at ip1 and ip2 are expressed by $\mathcal{Seman}_{ip1}$ and $\mathcal{Seman}_{ip2}$, respectively. If we are dealing with FDTs that have a formal semantics, it can be reasonably assumed that the meaning of interaction point representations is uniquely defined. What remains to be done is to capture it by a logical formula. If the above condition is violated, it could be possible to prove $\mathcal{Seman}_{ip1} \supset \mathcal{Seman}_{ip2}$ valid although ip1 is incompatible with ip2.

Proving $\mathcal{Seman}_{ip1} \supset \mathcal{Seman}_{ip2}$ valid is sufficient to guarantee that the problems discussed in Chapter 4.6.1 can not occur in any context. In case the context of ip1 and ip2 is determined, a weaker condition might do. However, in the area of open systems, the context is usually not known in advance. To prove ip1 *incomp* ip2, it is sufficient to give one counterexample for $\mathcal{S}eman_{ip1} \supset \mathcal{S}eman_{ip2}$, i.e., there exists a context in which problems as discussed in Chapter 4.6.1 can occur.

N1.	$P1 \supset P2$
N2.	$P7 \supset P8$
N3.	$P10 \supset P14$
N4.	$P14 \supset P10$

Table 4.5: Non-valid formulas

In the example above, the meaning of ip1 and ip2 has been captured by the conjunction of properties defined in Chapter 4.3. Further properties can be added when necessary. For the listed properties, the interdependencies shown in Table 4.3 (Chapter 4.4) and Table 4.5 have been proved valid and non-valid, respectively. For instance, it has been proved that the FIFO-property P2 implies reliability expressed by P1 (V2), but not vice versa (N1). V4 and V7 give a formal argument why P8 specifies a fair FIFO strategy: P8 together with the assumption that ag2 is ready to accept from time to time implies the FIFO property P2, and P2 together with the progress property P6 implies P8. Also, a fair FIFO strategy implies non-starvation as expressed by P7 (V8), but not vice versa (N2). These are general results, which can be applied when reasoning about the compatibility of particular interaction points. For instance, if we have $\mathcal{S}eman_{ip1} =_{Df} P2 \wedge P5$ and $\mathcal{S}eman_{ip2} =_{Df} P1 \wedge P5$, then from V2 we can conclude that $\mathcal{S}eman_{ip1} \supset \mathcal{S}eman_{ip2}$ is valid, therefore ip1 *comp* ip2. For $\mathcal{S}eman_{ip1} =_{Df} P1 \wedge P10$ and $\mathcal{S}eman_{ip2} =_{Df} P1 \wedge P14$, we conclude ip1 *incomp* ip2 and ip2 *incomp* ip1 from N3 and N4, respectively. This means that synchronous and asynchronous interaction points are incompatible, a fact which has already been known intuitively, but which can now be formally shown. Other facts may be less intuitive, but can be dealt with in the same way.

4.6.3 Environment-independent conformance based on interaction point compatibility

Having defined compatibility between interaction points, we can now reconsider conformance as informally defined in Chapter 4.6, and environment-independent notions of conformance:

Definition 4.4: Let *conf* be an environment-independent notion of conformance, S1 and S2 be formal descriptions of an open system. Then S1 *conf** S2 holds if and only if S1 *conf* S2, and additionally, all external interaction point representations of S1 are compatible with the corresponding interaction point representations of S2.

Clearly, *conf** is an environment-independent notion of conformance with the property S1 *conf** S2 *implies* S1 *conf* S2 (see Chapter 4.6).

The definition of *conf** can be applied to the conformance relation $conforms_{rep}$ from Chapter 3.3.9, which is environment-independent. Let $\mathcal{RS} = \langle \mathcal{Arch}, \mathcal{Behav} \rangle$ and $\mathcal{RS}' = \langle \mathcal{Arch}', \mathcal{Behav}' \rangle$ be requirement specifications such that $\mathcal{RS}'\ conforms_{rep}\ \mathcal{RS}$ under the refinement function ref, $\mathcal{Arch} = \langle \text{AG}, \text{IP}, \mathcal{Archf} \rangle$, and $\mathcal{Arch}' = \langle \text{AG}', \text{IP}', \mathcal{Archf}' \rangle$. Assume that all interaction points in IP are external, and that they are not refined, i.e., for all ip ∈ IP, ref(ip) = ip. This leads to the following relation *conf**:

(i) $\mathcal{RS}'\ conf^*\ \mathcal{RS} =_{Df} \mathcal{RS}'\ conforms_{rep}\ \mathcal{RS} \wedge \forall ip \in \text{IP}.\ \text{ref}(ip)\ comp\ ip$

Replacing *comp* by its definition and exploiting ref(ip) = ip yields:

(ii) $\mathcal{RS}'\ conf^*\ \mathcal{RS} \equiv \mathcal{RS}'\ conforms_{rep}\ \mathcal{RS} \wedge \forall ip \in \text{IP}.\ (\mathcal{Seman}'_{ip} \supset \text{rep}(\mathcal{Seman}_{ip}))$

Also, if the specifications of interaction points are semantically-local (see Chapter 3.3.8), then according to the definition of $conforms_{rep}$ in Chapter 3.3.9, we have

(iii) $\mathcal{RS}'\ conforms_{rep}\ \mathcal{RS} \supset (\bigwedge_{ip' \in \text{IP}'} \mathcal{Seman}'_{ip'} \supset \text{rep}(\bigwedge_{ip \in \text{IP}} \mathcal{Seman}_{ip}))$

Again exploiting the semantical locality and ref(ip) = ip,

(iv) $\mathcal{RS}'\ conforms_{rep}\ \mathcal{RS} \supset \forall ip \in \text{IP}.\ (\mathcal{Seman}'_{ip} \supset \text{rep}(\mathcal{Seman}_{ip}))$

is implied by (iii). From (ii) and (iv), it then follows that

(v) $\mathcal{RS}'\ conf^*\ \mathcal{RS} \equiv \mathcal{RS}'\ conforms_{rep}\ \mathcal{RS}$

In other words, under certain assumptions, $conforms_{rep}$ is an environment-independent notion that is already strong enough to avoid the problems outlined before. If we drop the assumptions that all interaction points in IP are external, and that they are not refined, we can formalize *conf** as follows:

(vi) $\mathcal{RS}'\ conf^*\ \mathcal{RS} =_{Df} \mathcal{RS}'\ conforms_{rep}\ \mathcal{RS}\ \wedge$
$$\forall ip \in IP.\ (\bigwedge_{ip' \in ref(ip)} \mathcal{S}eman'_{ip'} \wedge \bigwedge_{ag' \in ref(ip)} \mathcal{B}ehav'_{ag'} \supset rep(\mathcal{S}eman_{ip}))$$

Similar considerations as before show that even in this general case, (v) holds.

4.6.4 Application to OSI

In this chapter, we briefly discuss how the methodology outlined in Chapter 4.6.1 can be applied in the area of OSI. A detailed study of these issues is outside the scope of this book. Figure 4.7 shows a scenario, consisting of four levels of description. The conceptual view corresponds to the OSI Basic Reference Model (BRM), which introduces basic architectural concepts. These concepts can then be composed into conceptual system architectures. From the basic concepts of the BRM, the service access point corresponds to the interaction point.

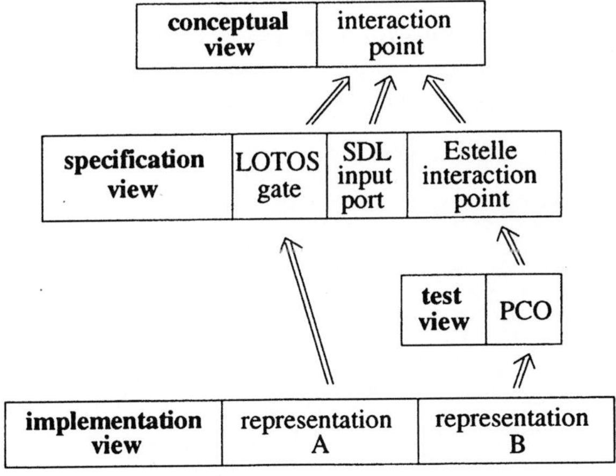

Figure 4.7: Compatibility between interaction point representations

On the specification level, the interaction point concept is represented in an operational specification. For the standardized FDTs Estelle, LOTOS, and SDL, the FDT concepts of Estelle interaction point, LOTOS gate, and SDL input port can be used to represent conceptual interaction points. On the test level, the point of control and observation (PCO) has been introduced as a corresponding concept. Finally, interaction point representations have to be identified on the implementation level.

After interaction point representations have been identified on each level of description, they are analysed in order to arrive at formulas capturing their semantics *precisely*. For the FDT concepts of Estelle interaction point, LOTOS gate, and SDL input port, an analysis has been presented in Chapter 4.5. For instance, the semantics of an Estelle interaction point has been captured by the conjunction of P2, P6, P9, and P13, which implies P1, P5, P7, P8, P11, and P12. Finally, compatibility has to be proved between corresponding interaction point representations, which is indicated by the arrows in Figure 4.7. It is sufficient to conduct this proof for neighbouring levels, because *comp* is transitive.

From the results of Chapters 4.5 and 4.6.2, it can be concluded that a given PCO cannot be compatible with both an Estelle interaction point and a LOTOS gate. As a consequence, PCOs with different semantics would have to be introduced on the test level. Alternatively, the representations of external interaction points on the specification level could be chosen such that they are compatible. For Estelle and SDL, for instance, this would require a restricted use of the corresponding FDT concepts. For Estelle and LOTOS, it seems sufficient to introduce LOTOS processes with the semantics of the corresponding Estelle interaction points.

5 Communication services

An important class of open systems are communication systems, which are, for instance, addressed in the framework of OSI (see Chapter 0.2). In the OSI Basic Reference Model (see Chapter 2.4), a number of architectural concepts such as service, protocol, entity, service access point, etc. are introduced. We will now investigate the service concept and demonstrate how temporal logic can be applied to specifying and reasoning about communication services. Based on the results of Chapter 4, the relationship between the service user view and the service provider view will be formally established. We argue that this is relevant both from a methodological and practical point of view.

5.1 The service concept

The service concept is one of the most important architectural concepts of Open Systems Interconnection (OSI) (see [Boc80], [ViLo85]). It has been introduced to consider a system from the user's point of view, which means that detail about the internal structure and operation of the system has to be omitted. What remains is the abstract behaviour of the system as it is visible at the system boundaries.

Usually, the service notion is explained in a conceptual context as given in Figure 5.1, which shows a number of service users and a service provider. Interactions between a user and the provider can take place through a service access point (SAP), which conceptually models a pervious system boundary between different components of the system. Depending on the kind of provided service, interactions at one SAP may be related to interactions at another SAP. Regarding a communication service, for instance, a request for transmission of data should cause the reception of these data.

Current standardization of OSI *services* is directed towards the formal description of *service providers*. The description of the service provider should define only *what* external behaviour the provider is supposed to exhibit, it should not explain *how* this behaviour can be realized. This will be done on a lower level of abstraction, where some internal structure is given to the service provider, and the behaviour of the internal components is defined such that their joint behaviour conforms to the external behaviour of the service provider. Therefore, the service provider forms a suitable abstraction and a basis for verification ([Boc83c], [ViLo85]).

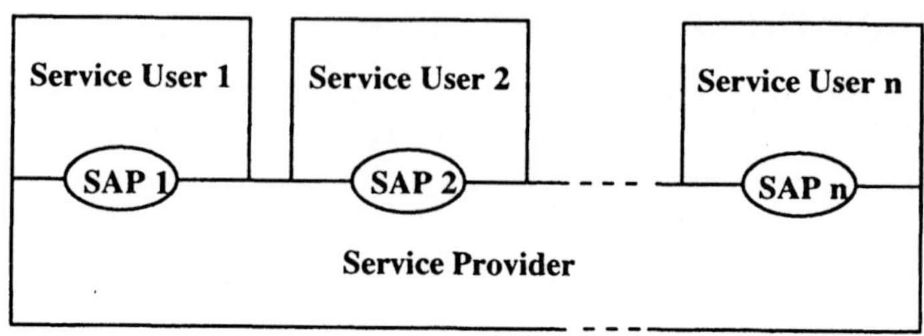

Figure 5.1: The service architecture

Different formal description techniques (FDTs), such as Estelle ([ISO89]), LOTOS ([ISO88c]), and SDL ([CCITT87]), have been applied to the specification of service providers (for instance, see [ISO86a], [ISO90a], [Hog88]). These specifications usually give some internal structure to the service provider, which is not mandatory for the implementation of the service provider. This serves two main purposes. Firstly, the service provider can be decomposed such that its behaviour is easier to understand. This is, for instance, achieved by having units defining phases of operation. Secondly, it might not be possible to give an adequate specification of the service provider without having some internal structure when using a particular FDT. While the first purpose is certainly justified, the second one reveals a lack of suitability of the FDT for the specification of services.

When specifying the external behaviour of the service provider, we not only intend to define a basis against which the joint behaviour of its internal components can be verified; we primarily want to supply a description being appropriate for the service user in the sense that it can understand which service is available and how to use it: "the service should be expressed simply in terms of user's needs" ([ViLo85]). This second second goal is not achieved, because the description of the service provider does not represent the user's point of view explicitly. Consequently, the user view has to be derived from the description of the service provider, which is in general very difficult, and to be defined in a separate description. It is this view of the service user that we call "*service*": the service is what the service user gets from the service provider. This draws a clear distinction between the notions of service and service provider.

5.2 Design methodology

From a methodological point of view, the specification of a communication system should start with the user view, i.e., the service (see Chapter 5.1), as shown in Figure 5.2. The service description defines explicitly what the requirements of the service users are, and indirectly restricts the behaviour of the service provider. To specify a service *explicitly*, a property-oriented description technique must be used. It is not possible to give an *explicit* service specification with an operational description technique. The reason is that in order to describe the view of the service users directly, a relationship between events of several users may have to be established. Also, to allow for a variety of different service users, restrictions on their behaviour should be kept small. We will apply the temporal logic designed in Chapter 3.3 to give a property-oriented formal description of a communication service.

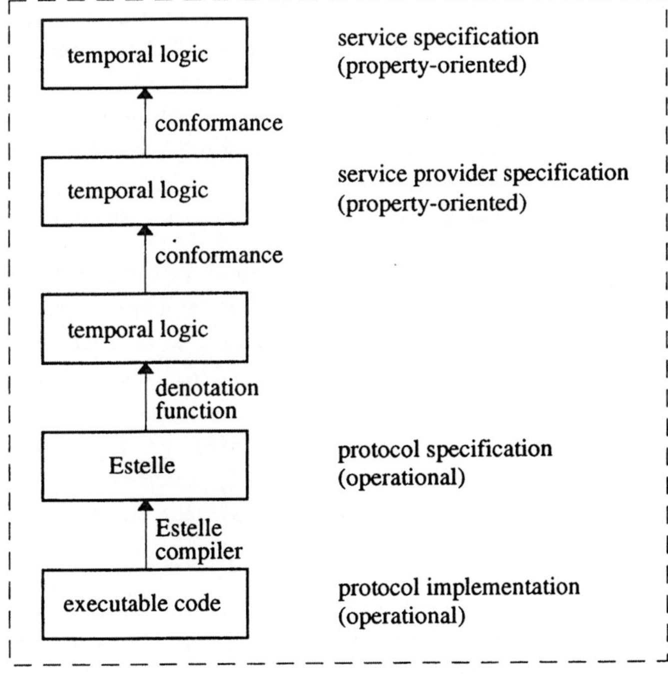

Figure 5.2: Design methodology

The next design step is then the specification of the service provider and of interaction points between the users and the provider according to the service architecture in Figure 5.1. At this point, we have a choice between a property-oriented and an operational description technique. Again, we will apply the temporal logic from Chapter 3.3 to formally specify the service provider and the interaction point semantics. In a subsequent analysis activity, it has to be shown that the service provider indeed provides the required service; in Figure 5.2, this is represented by the upper arrow and will be captured by the notion of conformance defined in Chapter 3.3.9. As it will be shown, the relationship between service and service provider crucially depends on the interaction point semantics.

Figure 5.2 shows further design steps down to the protocol implementation. Each design step introduces further design decisions and may also include a change of description technique. Whereas in the early design stages property-oriented techniques are preferable, operational techniques will typically be used when moving towards the implementation (see Chapter 1). For instance, Estelle ([ISO89]) could be used to specify the protocol entities, and an implementation language such as C could be used to generate executable code. Again, it has to be shown in subsequent analysis activities that the protocol entities correctly realize the service provider, and that the executable code correctly implements the protocol entities. These analyses are generally very difficult, partially because in both cases, a change of description language occurs.

To verify an Estelle specification against a logical specification, the proof technique of *model checking* ([ClEmSi86]) could be applied. This technique is feasible, if the semantics of the Estelle specification is given as an *explicit* transition system, and if this transition system has a finite number of states. The first condition is satisfied for the Estelle semantics in [ISO89]; the second condition does not hold, because the transition system associated with an Estelle specification may have an infinite number of states. Therefore, the model checking technique is in general not suited to perform an exhaustive analysis. However, it may serve to check certain aspects, if an appropriate abstraction step has resulted in a transition system with a finite number of states.

Instead of model checking, the proof technique of *theorem proving* could be applied. Therefor, the Estelle semantics has to be captured by a logical formula. In [BrGoVo92], a formal Estelle semantics supporting theorem proving is designed. This semantics is based on Lamport's *Temporal Logic of Actions* (*TLA*, [Lam91]) and Dijkstra's *predicate transformers* ([DiSc90]). For each Estelle specification, this semantics yields a temporal formula, which defines a transition system in an implicit manner (see Figure 5.2). This temporal formula can then be directly compared with the specification of the service provider.

Instead of formally proving that the executable code correctly implements the protocol entities specified in Estelle, a more pragmatic approach is usually applied. Since Estelle is an operational description technique, it is feasible to generate executable code automatically. Several compilers generating code for the sequential ([NBS87], [VuChCh88], [BUL89]) and parallel ([JaJe89], [SiSt91], [KrGo93]) execution of Estelle specifications have been developed recently.

A potential problem that results from a rigorous top-down design is the specification of a service for which it is impossible to find an appropriate service provider. To avoid this problem, both descriptions should be developed together. Similar concerns apply to the service provider and the protocol entities (see [ViLo85]).

In the following, we focus on the early design stages and show how temporal logic can be applied to the formal specification of a communication service and a suitable service provider. Furthermore, we establish a formal relationship between the two descriptions and prove that the service provider indeed provides the required service. Operational specifications of service providers and protocol entities can, for instance, be found in [ISO86a], [ISO86b], [ISO90a], [ISO90b], [Hog88], [Hog88a], [Hog92].

5.3 Example "modified InRes service"

To illustrate the methodological aspects of property-oriented service description, we have selected the InRes service (Initiator - Responder), which is taken from [Hog89] (see also [Hog89a] and [Hog92]). It is a simplified version of the Abracadabra service ([ISO88b]). To improve the InRes service, we have made several modifications. The modified InRes service is first described in the usual way, i.e., by prose and time sequence diagrams. We then give formal definitions from the point of view of the initiator, the responder, and the service provider, and show how these views are related. It turns out that this crucially depends on the semantics of the interaction points. A similar treatment of the original InRes service can be found in [Got90b].

5.3.1 Informal description

The modified InRes service provides the means for two entities to exchange data. It is asymmetrical, one entity assumes the role of the initiator, the other one is the responder. The initiator has the responsability to establish a connection, it can send data to the responder when the connection exists, and it can ask the responder for a receipt. The responder can accept or reject a connection request, receive data, send a receipt, and close a connection.

In Figure 5.3, several scenarios of the modified InRes service are described using time sequence diagrams. The horizontal dimension of these diagrams can be interpreted spatially or architecturally: initiator, service provider, and responder are located along this axis. Vertically, the lapse of time is represented. Thus, events in the diagram are associated with agents, and a global relative ordering in time is defined between them.

Figure 5.3a shows a time sequence diagram describing a successful connection establishment. The initiator requests a connection by issuing a CONreq to the service provider. This is followed by a CONind indicating the request to the responder, which then accepts the connection by issuing a CONresp. The connection is finally established by the confirmation CONconf, which is given to the initiator.

The connection establishment is a typical example for a double handshake, where the original message is followed by one acknowledgement. This is necessary because the responder may also refuse the connection by returning a CONref instead of a CONresp (see Figure 5.3b), in which case a rejection CONrej is issued to the initiator. Other reasons may exist why a connection can not be established, however, it is not always possible to explain them from the point of view of the service abstraction. It can be guessed from the time sequence diagrams that the initiator will get some response on a CONreq, either a CONconf or a CONrej.

When a connection has been established, data can be transferred from the initiator to the responder. Figure 5.3e shows a successful data transfer, however, it is possible that the data do not arrive (Figure 5.3f). From the time sequence diagrams we can guess that only data that have been sent by the initiator can be delivered to the responder. Furthermore, it is required that the service provider preserves the order of data requests.

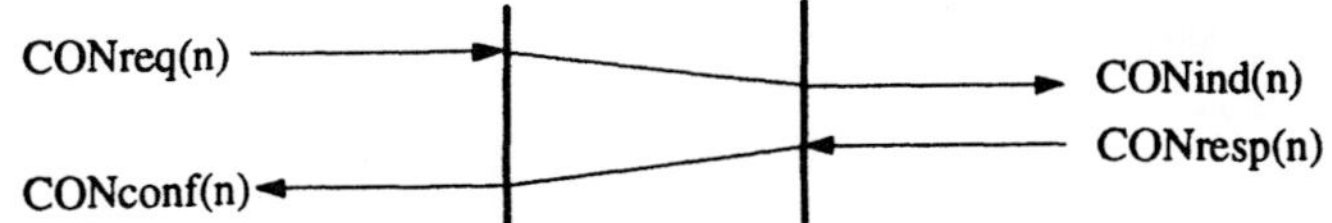

a) Successful connection establishment

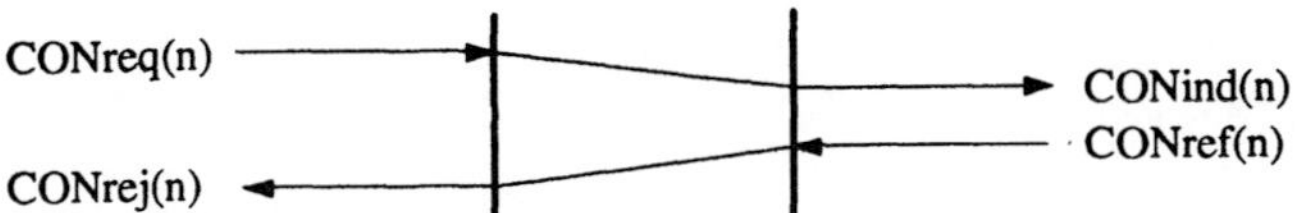

b) Unsuccessful connection establishment (rejection by the responder)

c) Unsuccessful connection establishment (unreliability of the service provider)

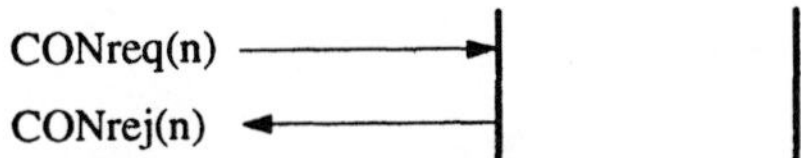

d) Unsuccessful connection establishment (unreliability of the service provider)

e) Successful data transfer

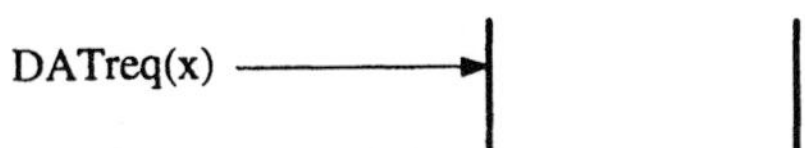

f) Unsuccessful data transfer

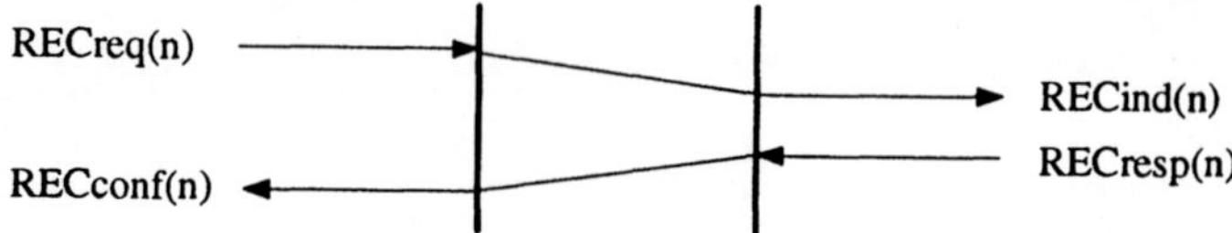

g) Successful receipt exchange

h) Unsuccessful receipt exchange
(unreliability of the service provider)

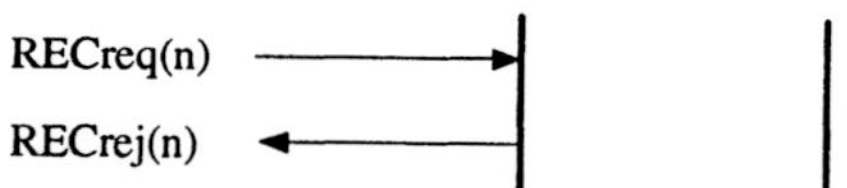

i) Unsuccessful receipt exchange
(unreliability of the service provider)

j) Successful disconnection

k) Unsuccessful disconnection

Figure 5.3: Time sequence diagrams for the modified InRes service

We modify the original InRes service by introducing a receipt phase. The initiator can ask the responder for a receipt by issuing a RECreq. This is followed by a RECind indicating the request to the responder which then issues a RECresp. The receipt is finally delivered to the initiator by a RECconf (Figure 5.3g). Like the connection establishment, the receipt exchange is a confirmed service. Note that it carries no message identification. Thus, it is only meaningful if the order of indications to the responder is the same as the order of corresponding requests. A RECreq is possibly not followed by a RECconf (Figures 5.3h-i). However, it can be guessed from the time sequence diagrams that the initiator will get some response, either a RECconf or a RECrej.

The responder has the right to close a connection by issuing a DISreq (Figure 5.3j). This shall cause a DISind to the initiator, but it is also legal that the DISreq has no effect.

In the original InRes service, the meaning of DISreq and DISind is overloaded. DISreq is used by the responder to close or refuse a connection; DISind indicates to the initiator that a connection is closed or refused, or that some data have not been delivered (see [Hog89]). Based on local information only, it is impossible to distinguish between these alternatives, which makes it difficult to specify a reasonable service from the user's point of view. For this reason, we have modified the original InRes service and have introduced additional service primitives CONref, CONrej, and RECrej (see Figure 5.3).

Another problem of the original InRes service is illustrated in Figure 5.4a. If the responder does not react "in time", the service provider may return a DISind to the initiator, which can then make another attempt to establish the connection. Meanwhile, the responder may have issued a CONresp leading to a CONconf. In the scenario in Figure 5.4a, this CONconf is related to the first CONreq, however, there are possible scenarios where it is related to the second CONreq. At first sight, this seems harmless, we could, for instance, define the connection as being established after the first CONconf. But a closer view reveals that this can lead to difficulties when we want to make statements about the reception of messages. The problem here is to find points of reference after which all messages sent by the initiator during a certain period of time have been received by the responder. The problem can be solved by associating parameter values with the service primitives of the connection phase as shown in Figure 5.4b: the initiator can recognize whether a CONconf is related to the previous

CONreq. For the same reasons, the service primitives of the receipt phase are associated with parameter values (see Figure 5.3).

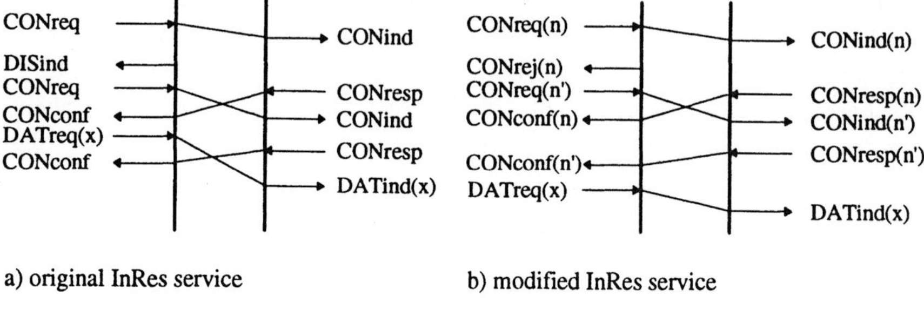

Figure 5.4: Cross-over between CONreq and CONresp

The informal description of the modified InRes service (including the time sequence diagrams) leaves many questions open[37]. E.g., how is successful behaviour distinguished from unsuccessful behaviour? Is the existence of successful behaviour a requirement, or is it sufficient to realize a service provider that always exhibits unsuccessful behaviour? Is unsuccessful behaviour a requirement, or does it suffice to implement successful behaviour? What is the precise definition of 'connection'? Must the initiator establish a connection before sending data? Has the initiator any possibility to find out whether the data it has sent within a certain period of time have been received by the responder up to a given moment in time? What other scenarios are allowed? A good service specification should provide explicit answers to these questions.

5.3.2 Customizing an appropriate temporal logic

The formal specification of service and service provider is based on the system architectures in Figures 5.5a and 5.5b, respectively. On a higher level of abstraction, the initiator A and the responder B have a common interaction point ip. On a lower level of abstraction, ip is refined into interaction points ip_A, ip_B, and the service provider M (see Chapter 2.2 and Figures 2.1a, 2.2a).

---

37 This applies to the original InRes service as well.

Formally, the system architecture in Figure 5.5a is defined by the tuple $\mathcal{Arch} = \langle AG, IP, \mathcal{Archf} \rangle$, where $AG = \{A,B\}$, $IP = \{ip\}$, and $\mathcal{Archf}(A) = \mathcal{Archf}(B) = \{ip\}$. The architecture in Figure 5.5b is defined by $\mathcal{Arch}' = \langle AG', IP', \mathcal{Archf}' \rangle$, where $AG' = \{A,B,M\}$, $IP' = \{ip_A, ip_B\}$, $\mathcal{Archf}'(A) = \{ip_A\}$, $\mathcal{Archf}'(B) = \{ip_B\}$, and $\mathcal{Archf}'(M) = \{ip_A, ip_B\}$. For the refinement function $ref(A) = \{A\}$, $ref(B) = \{B\}$, and $ref(ip) = \{M, ip_A, ip_B\}$, the relationship $\mathcal{Arch}'$ *refines* $\mathcal{Arch}$ holds, i.e., $\mathcal{Arch}'$ is an architectural refinement of $\mathcal{Arch}$ as defined in Chapter 2.3.

To specify properties characterizing the views of the initiator, the responder, and the service provider, we use the notation introduced in Chapter 4.3.2. As before, abstract operations ! and ? denote the offering and acceptance of an interaction, and situations where an agent is *at* the beginning and immediately *after* the operation are distinguished.

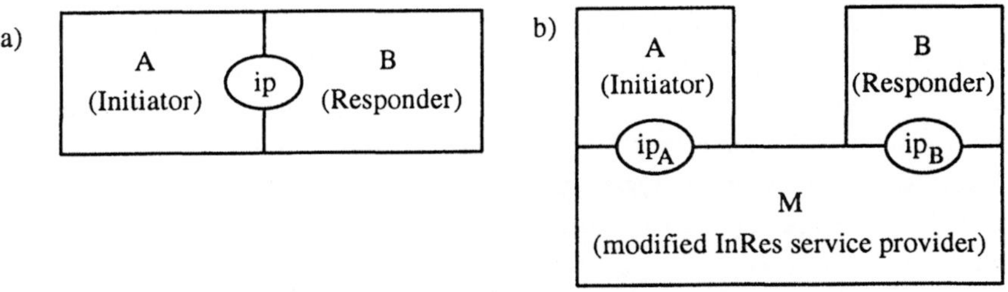

Figure 5.5: Conceptual system architecture

With these conventions, the atomic formulas of many-sorted first-order logic (Chapter 3.3.2) are determined as follows:

- A and B are constants of sort AG;
- ip is a constant of sort IP;
- ! and ? are constants of sort OP;
- p, p1, p2 and x, x1, x2 are individual variables of sorts P and X, respectively;
- CONreq, CONind, CONresp, CONconf, CONref, CONrej, DATreq, DATind, RECreq, RECind, RECresp, RECconf, RECrej, DISreq, and DISind are constants of sort P;
- n, n1, n2 are individual variables of sort $\mathbb{N}_0$;
- 1 is a constant of sort $\mathbb{N}_0$;

- at and after are relation symbols of arity 5, associated with sorts AG, IP, OP, P, X; we overload at and after to be also relation symbols of arity 3 and 4, associated with sorts AG, IP, OP and AG, IP, OP, P, respectively.

The temporal logic for specifying service properties can be customized by selecting building blocks At_F, Pr, Q, F_B, P, E_P, E_F, and I (see Section 3.3). At_F is selected because atomic formulas can then be decomposed, which makes it possible to associate architectural meaning with them. Q is selected because it allows quantification over infinite value domains. Since we allow the service and thus the service provider to be unreliable, F_B is chosen to refer to the future. I is selected to restrict the context in the past, for instance, in order to express properties restricted to the current connection.

5.3.3 Specification of the service

Following the design methodology outlined in Chapter 5.2, we start with the specification of the InRes *service*, i.e., the view of the service *users*. Because the InRes service is asymmetrical, we have different services for the initiator and the responder. Their formal specification is based on the system architecture in Figure 5.5a. Here, the initiator A and the responder B share a common interaction point ip. Later, ip will be refined into interaction points ip_A, ip_B, and a service provider M as shown in Figure 5.5b.

To specify the InRes service, it is appropriate and adequate to refer to local events of the service users occurring at the (conceptual) interaction point where the service is available. It is not desirable to explicitly introduce an agent "service provider" at this design stage, because this would reduce the degree of abstraction. The following properties reflect these conceptions. They are arranged in several tables related to the different phases of the service.

The properties listed in Table 5.1 define the connection phase from the initiator's point of view. S_A1 is a safety property specifying what the initiator may conclude from the occurrence of a local event [after A.ip.?(CONconf(n))]: it implies that several related events, namely [after A.ip.!(CONreq(n))], [after B.ip.?(CONind(n))], and [after B.ip.!(CONresp(n))] have previously occurred, *and* that they have occurred in this order. From S_A1, it is easy to show that if one of the related events does not occur, A will not accept an interaction CONconf(n). In particular, if A does not request a connection, no connection will be established.

Properties S_A2 and S_A3 state that if A accepts a CONconf or CONrej, it must have offered a corresponding CONreq. This allows the acceptance of both a CONconf and a CONrej following the same CONreq. Because this is only reasonable if the CONconf follows the CONrej, we rule out the other alternative: A can accept a CONrej only if it did not accept a CONconf since the corresponding CONreq, which is specified by S_A4.

S_A1.	AG ∀n. ([after A.ip.?(CONconf(n))] ⊃ ◆ ([after B.ip.!(CONresp(n))] ∧ ◆ ([after B.ip.?(CONind(n))] ∧ ◆ [after A.ip.!(CONreq(n))])))
S_A2.	AG ∀n.(#[after A.ip.?(CONconf(n))] ≤ #[after A.ip.!(CONreq(n))])
S_A3.	AG ∀n.(#[after A.ip.?(CONrej(n))] ≤ #[after A.ip.!(CONreq(n))])
S_A4.	AG ∀n. (⟨ [after A.ip.!(CONreq(n))] ⇐ [after A.ip.?(CONrej(n))] ⟩ ¬ ◆ [after A.ip.?(CONconf(n))])
S_A5.	AG ∀n. ([after A.ip.!(CONreq(n))] ⊃ EF ([after B.ip.?(CONind(n))] ∧ EF ([after B.ip.!(CONresp(n))] ∧ EF [after A.ip.?(CONconf(n))])))
S_A6.	AG ∀n. ([after A.ip.!(CONreq(n))] ⊃ AF ([after A.ip.?(CONconf(n))] ∨ [after A.ip.?(CONrej(n))]))

Table 5.1: Service from the initiator's point of view: connection phase

S_A5 is a liveness property stating that if A offers a CONreq(n), this will potentially be followed by corresponding event occurrences [after B.ip.?(CONind(n))], [after B.ip.!(CONresp(n))], and [after A.ip.?(CONconf(n))], in that order. Note that only potential behaviour is required by S_A5, which means that the service may be unreliable, but not completely unreliable. It may also be reliable, i.e., if A offers a CONreq(n), this will *inevitably* be followed by corresponding event occurrences. However, reliability is not requested by S_A5.

To cover further liveness aspects, S_A5 is supplemented by S_A6 stating that on a connection request, the initiator will inevitably get some response. This response will be a CONconf confirming the connection or a CONrej rejecting it.

The properties listed in Table 5.2 define the receipt phase from the initiator's point of view. They are similar to the properties in Table 5.1 defining the connection phase. Like a connection establishment, a receipt exchange between the initiator and the responder is a double handshake. If applied appropriately, it allows the initiator to draw conclusions on which messages have been received by the responder without using any message identification.

S_A7. AG ∀n. ([after A.ip.?(RECconf(n))]
⊃ ◆ ([after B.ip.!(RECresp(n))] ∧
◆ ([after B.ip.?(RECind(n))] ∧
◆ [after A.ip.!(RECreq(n))])))

S_A8. AG ∀n. (#[after A.ip.?(RECconf(n))] ≤ #[after A.ip.!(RECreq(n))])

S_A9. AG ∀n. (#[after A.ip.?(RECrej(n))] ≤ #[after A.ip.!(RECreq(n))])

S_A10. AG ∀n. (⟨ [after A.ip.!(RECreq(n))] ⇐ [after A.ip.?(RECrej(n))] ⟩
¬ ◆ [after A.ip.?(RECconf(n))])

S_A11. AG ∀n. ([after A.ip.!(RECreq(n))]
⊃ EF ([after B.ip.?(RECind(n))] ∧
EF ([after B.ip.!(RECresp(n))] ∧
EF [after A.ip.?(RECconf(n))])))

S_A12. AG ∀n. ([after A.ip.!(RECreq(n))]
⊃ AF ([after A.ip.?(RECconf(n))] ∨ [after A.ip.?(RECrej(n))]))

Table 5.2: Service from the initiator's point of view: receipt phase

The properties listed in Table 5.3 define the data and disconnection phase from the initiator's point of view. Property S_A13 states that B can not accept any data if A has never tried to establish a connection. S_A14 specifies that during the interval starting when A has accepted the last CONconf, only data which A has sent since then can have been accepted by B during this interval. S_A15 shows how the receipt exchange can be applied: if A accepts a RECconf, it can draw the conclusion that all data sent since the last CONconf have been accepted by B during that interval, and they have been accepted in the same order. This is one of the key properties of the service specification. Property S_A16 states that if A accepts a DISind, B must have previously offered a related DISreq.

$$S_A13.\ \ AG\,(\neg \blacklozenge\ [\text{after A.ip.!(CONreq)}] \supset \neg\ [\text{after B.ip.?(DATind)}])$$

$$S_A14.\ \ AG\,(\langle\ [\text{after A.ip.?(CONconf)}] \Rightarrow \rangle\ \ \forall x.\ (\#[\text{after A.ip.!(DATreq(x))}] \geq \#[\text{after B.ip.?(DATind(x))}]))$$

$$\begin{aligned} S_A15.\ \ AG\,(\langle\ &[\text{after A.ip.?(CONconf)}] \Leftarrow [\text{after A.ip.?(RECconf)}]\ \rangle \\ &\blacksquare\ ([\text{after A.ip.?(RECconf)}] \\ &\quad \supset \#[\text{after A.ip.!(DATreq)}] = \#[\text{after B.ip.?(DATind)}]) \wedge \\ &\forall x1,x2,n1,n2.\ \blacksquare\ (\#[\text{after B.ip.?(DATind(x1))}] = n1 \wedge \\ &\qquad \#[\text{after B.ip.?(DATind(x2))}] = n2 \\ &\qquad \supset \blacklozenge\ (\#[\text{after A.ip.!(DATreq(x1))}] = n1 \wedge \\ &\qquad\quad \#[\text{after A.ip.!(DATreq(x2))}] = n2))) \end{aligned}$$

$$S_A16.\ \ AG\,(\#[\text{after A.ip.?(DISind)}] \leq \#[\text{after B.ip.!(DISreq)}])$$

$$S_A17.\ \ AG\ \forall x.\ ([\text{after A.ip.!(DATreq(x))}] \wedge \text{connection}_{AB} \supset EF\ [\text{after B.ip.?(DATind(x))}])$$

Table 5.3: Service from the initiator's point of view: data and disconnection phase

Finally, S_A17 specifies the liveness requirement that if A offers data while there is a connection with B, these data will potentially be accepted by B. From the users' point of view, we can define the existence of a connection as follows:

$$
\begin{aligned}
\text{connection}_{AB} =_{Df}\ & \blacklozenge\ [\text{after A.ip.?(CONconf)}] \wedge \\
& \langle\ [\text{after B.ip.!(CONresp)}] \Rightarrow \rangle \\
& \qquad \neg \blacklozenge\ [\text{after B.ip.!(DISreq)}] \wedge \\
& \langle\ [\text{after A.ip.?(CONconf)}] \Rightarrow \rangle \\
& \qquad \neg \blacklozenge\ ([\text{after A.ip.?(DISind)}] \vee \\
& \qquad\qquad [\text{after A.ip.!(CONreq)}] \vee \\
& \qquad\qquad [\text{after A.ip.?(RECrej)}])
\end{aligned}
$$

This definition refers to local event occurrences of A and B. Because A can not directly observe event occurrences which are local to B, there will be some uncertainty about the actual existence of a connection.

The service for the responder is summarized in Table 5.4. Property S_B1 states that B can not accept any data if it has never issued a CONresp. S_B2 specifies that if in the interval starting with the last CONresp B accepts any data, they have been offered by A in the same ordering during this interval. Finally, S_B3 states that a DISreq will potentially lead to a DISind.

$$
\begin{aligned}
S_B1.\quad & AG\,(\neg \blacklozenge\ [\text{after B.ip.!(CONresp)}] \supset \neg\ [\text{after B.ip.?(DATind)}]) \\
S_B2.\quad & AG\,(\ \langle\ [\text{after B.ip.!(CONresp)}] \Rightarrow \rangle \\
& \qquad \forall x1,x2,n1,n2.\ \blacksquare\ (\#[\text{after B.ip.?(DATind(x1))}] = n1 \wedge \\
& \qquad\qquad \#[\text{after B.ip.?(DATind(x2))}] = n2 \\
& \qquad\qquad \supset \blacklozenge\ (\#[\text{after A.ip.!(DATreq(x1))}] = n1 \wedge \\
& \qquad\qquad\qquad \#[\text{after A.ip.!(DATreq(x2))}] = n2))) \\
S_B3.\quad & AG\,([\text{after B.ip.!(DISreq)}] \supset EF\ [\text{after A.ip.?(DISind)}])
\end{aligned}
$$

Table 5.4: Service from the responder's point of view

We have now formally characterized the modified InRes service by a number of properties. Each of these properties has established a relationship between local events from the point of view of the service users occurring at the interaction point ip. If we compare these properties with those of Chapter 4.3, we can see that there is no fundamental difference beside the fact that the service properties are more complex.

And indeed, to characterize the modified InRes service, we have listed properties that - taken together - define the semantics of the interaction point ip in Figure 5.5a:

$$\mathit{Seman}_{ip} =_{Df} \bigwedge_{1\leq i\leq 16} S_A i \wedge \bigwedge_{1\leq i\leq 3} S_B i$$

We conclude that a service can be understood as the semantics of a (complex) interaction point. Therefore, this architectural concept can be explained in terms of the basic concepts introduced in Chapter 2.1.

At this point, the question arises whether the modified InRes service can be provided. Is it possible to specify properties characterizing the service provider such that they imply the service properties? As it will turn out, the implication can indeed be formally proved, if some constraints on the behaviour of the service users and on the semantics of the interaction points ip_A and ip_B (see Figure 5.5b) are imposed. Stated otherwise, the service provider has to rely on properties of the environment in order to realize the specified service.

5.3.4 Specification of the service provider

In accordance with the design methodology outlined in Chapter 5.2, the interaction point ip between the initiator A and the responder B is now refined into interaction points ip_A, ip_B, and a service provider M as shown in Figure 5.5. This is formally defined by the system architecture Arch' in Chapter 5.3.2. The same logic as for the service is used, except that AG' = {A,B,M}, and IP' = {ip_A,ip_B}. It is our intention to specify the service provider such that it realizes the service defined in Chapter 5.3.3. Furthermore, it shall serve as a self-contained basis for implementation. Therefore, we will characterize the service provider by properties that refer to events local to M only. When the service provider is verified in Chapter 5.3.7, these events will be related to events of the service users by assigning a semantics to the interaction points ip_A and ip_B.

The properties listed in Table 5.5 define constraints for the connection phase from the service provider's point of view. C_M1 states that M may not offer more interactions CONind(n) at ip_B than it has accepted interactions CONreq(n) at ip_A. Similar constraints apply with respect to the other service primitives of the connection phase (C_M2, C_M3). C_M4 restricts the offer of a CONrej(n) to the case that no CONconf(n) has been offered since the acceptance of a CONreq(n). Note that only events which are local to the service provider are used. In particular, no assumptions about the environment are made. If this style can be sustained, the specification can serve as a self-contained basis for implementation.

C_M1. $\mathrm{AG}\ \forall n.\ (\#[\text{at } M.ip_B.!(\text{CONind}(n))] \le \#[\text{after } M.ip_A.?(\text{CONreq}(n))])$

C_M2. $\mathrm{AG}\ \forall n.\ (\#[\text{at } M.ip_A.!(\text{CONconf}(n))] \le \#[\text{after } M.ip_B.?(\text{CONresp}(n))])$

C_M3. $\mathrm{AG}\ \forall n.\ (\#[\text{at } M.ip_A.!(\text{CONrej}(n))] \le \#[\text{after } M.ip_A.?(\text{CONreq}(n))])$

C_M4. $\mathrm{AG}\ \forall n.\ (\langle[\text{after } M.ip_A.?(\text{CONreq}(n))] \Leftarrow [\text{after } M.ip_A.!(\text{CONrej}(n))]\rangle$
$\qquad \neg \blacklozenge\ [\text{after } M.ip_A.!(\text{CONconf}(n))])$

C_M5. $\mathrm{AG}\ \forall n.\ ([\text{after } M.ip_A.?(\text{CONreq}(n))] \supset \mathrm{EF}\ [\text{at } M.ip_B.!(\text{CONind}(n))])$

C_M6. $\mathrm{AG}\ \forall n.\ ([\text{after } M.ip_B.?(\text{CONresp}(n))] \supset \mathrm{EF}\ [\text{at } M.ip_A.!(\text{CONconf}(n))])$

C_M7. $\mathrm{AG}\ \forall n.\ ([\text{after } M.ip_A.?(\text{CONreq}(n))]$
$\qquad \supset \mathrm{AF}\ ([\text{at } M.ip_A.!(\text{CONconf}(n))] \vee [\text{at } M.ip_A.!(\text{CONrej}(n))]))$

Table 5.5: Constraints for the service provider: connection phase

The remaining properties in Table 5.5 are liveness properties. They state that the acceptance of a CONreq is potentially followed by the offer of a CONind (C_M5), and that a CONresp is potentially followed by a CONconf (C_M6). Finally, C_M7 requires that a CONreq is inevitably followed by a CONconf or a CONrej. Note that it is, for instance, not required that after the acceptance of a CONreq(n) at ip_A, an event [after $M.ip_A$.!(CONind(n))] will potentially occur. Instead, only [at $M.ip_A$.!(CONind(n))] is demanded. The reason is that it generally depends on the environment whether M can complete the abstract operation !. Therefore, the occurrence of the event [after $M.ip_A$.!(CONind(n))] can not be guaranteed by M alone. This reflects again a style without assumptions about the environment, leading to a self-contained basis for implementation.

The properties listed in Table 5.6 define the constraints for the receipt phase. They are similar to the properties in Table 5.5 defining the connection phase.

$C_M8.$ AG $\forall n.(\#[\text{at } M.ip_B.!(RECind(n))] \leq \#[\text{after } M.ip_A.?(RECreq(n))])$

$C_M9.$ AG $\forall n.\ (\#[\text{at } M.ip_A.!(RECconf(n))] \leq \#[\text{after } M.ip_B.?(RECresp(n))])$

$C_M10.$ AG $\forall n.\ (\#[\text{at } M.ip_A.!(RECrej(n))] \leq \#[\text{after } M.ip_A.?(RECreq(n))])$

$C_M11.$ AG $\forall n.\ (\langle[\text{after } M.ip_A.?(RECreq(n))] \Leftarrow [\text{after } M.ip_A.!(RECrej(n))]\rangle$
$\neg \blacklozenge [\text{after } M.ip_A.!(RECconf(n))])$

$C_M12.$ AG $\forall n.\ ([\text{after } M.ip_A.?(RECreq(n))] \supset EF\ [\text{at } M.ip_B.!(RECind(n))])$

$C_M13.$ AG $\forall n.\ ([\text{after } M.ip_B.?(RECresp(n))] \supset EF\ [\text{at } M.ip_A.!(RECconf(n))])$

$C_M14.$ AG $\forall n.\ ([\text{after } M.ip_A.?(RECreq(n))]$
$\supset AF\ ([\text{at } M.ip_A.!(RECconf(n))] \vee [\text{at } M.ip_A.!(RECrej(n))]))$

Table 5.6: Constraints for the service provider: receipt phase

$C_M15.$ AG $([\text{at } M.ip_B.!(DATind)] \supset connection_M)$

$C_M16.$ AG $(\langle [\text{after } M.ip_A.!(CONconf)] \Rightarrow \rangle$
$\forall x.(\#[\text{after } M.ip_A.?(DATreq(x))] \geq \#[\text{after } M.ip_B.?(DATind(x))]))$

$C_M17.$ AG $(\langle [\text{after } M.ip_A.!(CONconf)] \Leftarrow [\text{after } M.ip_A.!(RECconf)] \rangle$
$\blacksquare ([\text{after } M.ip_A.!(RECconf)]$
$\supset \#[\text{after } M.ip_A.!(DATreq)] = \#[\text{after } M.ip_B.?(DATind)]))$

$C_M18.$ AG $(\langle [\text{after } M.ip_A.!(CONconf)] \Rightarrow \rangle$
$\forall x1,x2,n1,n2.\ \blacksquare\ (\#[\text{after } M.ip_B.!(DATind(x1))] = n1 \wedge$
$\#[\text{after } M.ip_B.!(DATind(x2))] = n2$
$\supset \blacklozenge\ (\#[\text{after } M.ip_A.?(DATreq(x1))] = n1 \wedge$
$\#[\text{after } M.ip_A.?(DATreq(x2))] = n2)))$

$C_M19.$ AG $\forall x.\ ([\text{after } M.ip_A.?(DATreq(x))] \wedge connection_M$
$\supset EF\ [\text{at } M.ip_B.!(DATind(x))])$

$C_M20.$ AG $(\#[\text{at } M.ip_A.!(DISind)] \leq \#[\text{after } M.ip_B.?(DISreq)])$

$C_M21.$ AG $([\text{after } M.ip_B.?(DISreq)] \supset EF\ [\text{at } M.ip_A.!(DISind)])$

Table 5.7: Constraints for the service provider: data and disconnection phase

In Table 5.7, properties defining the data and disconnection phase are summarized. Property C_M15 specifies that M may only offer a DATind if a connection exists. From the point of view of M, we can define the existence of a connection as follows:

$$\begin{aligned} connection_M =_{Df} \; & \blacklozenge\, [\text{after } M.ip_A.!(CONconf)] \wedge \\ & \langle\, [\text{after } M.ip_B.?(CONresp)] \Rightarrow \rangle \\ & \qquad \neg \blacklozenge\, [\text{after } M.ip_B.?(DISreq)] \wedge \\ & \langle\, [\text{after } M.ip_A.!(CONconf)] \Rightarrow \rangle \\ & \qquad \neg \blacklozenge\, ([\text{after } M.ip_A.!(DISind)] \vee \\ & \qquad\quad [\text{after } M.ip_A.?(CONreq)] \vee \\ & \qquad\quad [\text{after } M.ip_A.!(RECrej)]) \end{aligned}$$

C_M16 states that in the interval beginning with the last offer of a CONconf, only data accepted at ip_A are offered at ip_B. C_M17 specifies that if a RECconf is offered at ip_A, all data accepted at ip_A since the last CONconf must have been offered at ip_B. C_M18 states that the FIFO property holds for every interval starting with a CONconf. This means that once data have been lost, no data may be offered at ip_B until the connection is reestablished. C_M19 specifies that if M accepts data at ip_A while there is a connection, these data will potentially be offered at ip_B.

In Table 5.8, some general liveness properties of the service provider are given. They state that M is prepared to accept interactions at ip_A and ip_B from time to time, provided it can always offer interactions.

C_M22. AG (AG (at $M.ip_A.!$ ⊃ AF [after $M.ip_A.!$]) ⊃ AG AF at $M.ip_A.?$)
C_M23. AG (AG (at $M.ip_B.!$ ⊃ AF [after $M.ip_B.!$]) ⊃ AG AF at $M.ip_B.?$)

Table 5.8: Constraints for the service provider: general liveness properties

The specification of the service provider ends with several ordering properties. They all follow the same pattern and ensure that certain contexts at ip_A have corresponding contexts at ip_B, and vice versa. We give two properties in Table 5.9 and list the remaining properties completing the specification of the service provider in Appendix

A.2. A significantly shorter list of ordering properties - two elements only - would result if related events at ip_A and ip_B had the same interaction type.

C_M24. AG $\forall$n1,n2.([after M.ip_A.!(CONconf(n1))] $\wedge$ $\blacklozenge$ [after M.ip_A.!(CONconf(n2))]
$\supset$ $\blacklozenge$ ([after M.ip_B.?(CONresp(n1))] $\wedge$ $\blacklozenge$ [after M.ip_B.?(CONresp(n2))]))

C_M25. AG $\forall$n. ([after M.ip_A.!(DISind)] $\wedge$ $\blacklozenge$ [after M.ip_A.!(CONconf(n))]
$\supset$ $\blacklozenge$ ([after M.ip_B.?(DISreq)] $\wedge$ $\blacklozenge$ [after M.ip_B.?(CONresp(n))]))

Table 5.9: Constraints for the service provider: ordering properties

5.3.5 Interaction point semantics

The joint behaviour of the system shown in Figure 5.5b is influenced by the semantics of each of its components, including the interaction points ip_A and ip_B. In particular, the question whether agent M indeed provides the required service can only be answered on the basis of a precise definition of the interaction point semantics. This will allow establishing a relationship between event occurrences of different agents at a common interaction point, which is a prerequisite for verifying the service provider with respect to the service (see Chapter 5.3.7).

For ip_A and ip_B, we require reliability, meaning that no loss, creation, duplication, or corruption of interactions may occur, and the FIFO property, meaning that interactions can only be accepted in the order in which they have been offered. Furthermore, two progress properties are demanded. If one agent is prepared to offer, and the other agent is ready to accept, then both will inevitably proceed. And if one agent is prepared to accept, and the other agent has offered more interactions than have been accepted, then it will progress.

With reference to Chapter 4.3, we characterize ip_A and ip_B by the properties P2, P5, and P6, which implies P1, P7, and P8, for each direction. It is necessary to select P2, because the service requires that the FIFO property holds for certain intervals. Otherwise, the FIFO property would be lost at the interaction points, even if it is satisfied by the service provider. Also note that we have not fixed the mode of interaction. This means that interaction point representations may be synchronous or asynchronous.

It should be pointed out that the interaction point properties have been specified in temporal logic with linear time operators to refer to the future (Chapter 4.3). Here, we use branching time operators. It turns out that we can keep the intended semantics by replacing every linear operator $\Box$ and $\Diamond$ by the branching operator AG and AF, respectively. A potential problem is that $\Box$ and $\Diamond$ are dual operators, but AG and AF are not. This can affect the results which we have obtained when reasoning about interaction points in Chapter 4.4. As it turns out, all proofs of linear time interdependencies also hold for the corresponding branching time interdependencies.

5.3.6 Constraints on the service users

The behaviour of the service provider as defined by the constraints in Chapter 5.3.4 and the constraints on interaction points from Chapter 5.3.5 are not sufficient to guarantee the service specified in Chapter 5.3.3[38]. It is, for instance, possible that the responder always ignores a CONind, or that it never accepts any interaction at ip_B. To exclude such uncooperative behaviour, we can require some minimal cooperation between the initiator and the responder by imposing a few local constraints.

$C_A1.$	AG ∀n. (⟨ [after A.ip.!(CONreq(n))] ⇐ [at A.ip.!] ⟩ ◆ ([after A.ip.?(CONconf(n))] ∨ [after A.ip.?(CONrej(n))])))
$C_A2.$	AG ∀n. (#[after A.ip.!(CONreq(n))] ≤ 1)
$C_A3.$	AG ∀n. (⟨ [after A.ip.!(RECreq(n))] ⇐ [at A.ip.!] ⟩ ◆ ([after A.ip.?(RECconf(n))] ∨ [after A.ip.?(RECrej(n))])))
$C_A4.$	AG ∀n. (#[after A.ip.!(RECreq(n))] ≤ 1)
$C_A5.$	AG AF at A.ip.?

Table 5.10: Constraints for the initiator

38 This is an example where a syntactically-local specification, namely $\mathcal{Seman}_{ip}$, is not semantically-local (see Chapter 3.3.8).

Restrictions sufficient to prove that the service provider is correct with respect to the service (see Chapter 5.3.7) are listed in Tables 5.10 and 5.11. These constraints are neither a consequence of the service specification nor are they uniquely determined by the specification of the service provider. Other constraints permitting the correctness proof, and other service providers needing different constraints on the service users may exist.

The constraints imposed on the initiator are listed in Table 5.10. C_A1 states that once A has offered a CONreq(n), it must wait for a related acceptance, i.e. a CONconf(n) or a CONrej(n), before it may be prepared to offer another interaction. A similar constraint applies to the receipt phase (C_A3). C_A2 and C_A4 require that a parameter value n may only be used once for a CONreq and a RECreq, respectively. This is necessary to distinguish between possible overlappings of connection establishments (see Figure 5.4) or receipt exchanges. Finally, C_A5 states that A must be ready to accept from time to time.

C_B1.	AG ∀n. (#[at B.ip.!(CONresp(n))] + #[at B.ip.!(CONref(n))] ≤ #[after B.ip.?(CONind(n))])
C_B2.	AG ∀n. ([after B.ip.?(CONind(n))] ⊃ EF [at B.ip.!(CONresp(n))])
C_B3.	AG ∀n. (#[at B.ip.!(RECresp(n))] ≤ #[after B.ip.?(RECind(n))])
C_B4.	AG ∀n. ([after B.ip.?(RECind(n))] ⊃ AF [at B.ip.!(RECresp(n))])
C_B5.	AG AF at B.ip.?

Table 5.11: Constraints for the responder

Constraints imposed on the responder are given in Table 5.11. C_B1 and C_B3 specify that interactions CONresp(n), CONref(n), and RECresp(n) may only be offered if there are related interactions CONind(n) and RECind(n), respectively. C_B2 states that B may not always refuse a connection request, C_B4 requires that B will inevitably offer a RECresp(n), when it accepts a RECind(n). Finally, C_B5 states that B must be ready to accept from time to time.

5.3.7 Verification of the service provider

The objective of verifying the service provider is to formally prove that it indeed provides the specified service. More precisely, the verification has to show that the requirement specification $\mathcal{RS}' = \langle \mathcal{Arch}', \mathcal{Behav}' \rangle$ with $\mathcal{Arch}' = \langle \text{AG}', \text{IP}', \mathcal{Archf}' \rangle$ as defined in Chapter 5.3.2, and $\mathcal{Behav}' = \bigwedge_{ag \in AG'} \mathcal{Behav}'_{ag} \wedge \bigwedge_{ip \in IP'} \mathcal{Seman}'_{ip}$, conforms to the requirement specification $\mathcal{RS} = \langle \mathcal{Arch}, \mathcal{Behav} \rangle$ with $\mathcal{Arch} = \langle \text{AG}, \text{IP}, \mathcal{Archf} \rangle$ as defined in Chapter 5.3.2, and $\mathcal{Behav} = \bigwedge_{ag \in AG} \mathcal{Behav}_{ag} \wedge \bigwedge_{ip \in IP} \mathcal{Seman}_{ip}$, under a representation function rep. With $\mathcal{Seman}_{ip} = \bigwedge_{1 \le i \le 16} S_A i \wedge \bigwedge_{1 \le i \le 3} S_B i$, $\mathcal{Behav}_A = \mathcal{Behav}_B$ = true, $\mathcal{Behav}'_A = \mathcal{Behav}'_B$ = true, $\mathcal{Behav}'_M = \bigwedge_{1 \le i \le 39} S_M i$, $\mathcal{Seman}'_{ipA}$ = (P2 $\wedge$ P5 $\wedge$ P6) [ag1\A, ag2\M, ip\ip$_A$] $\wedge$ (P2 $\wedge$ P5 $\wedge$ P6) [ag1\M, ag2\A, ip\ip$_A$], and $\mathcal{Seman}'_{ipB}$ = (P2 $\wedge$ P5 $\wedge$ P6) [ag1\B, ag2\M, ip\ip$_B$] $\wedge$ (P2 $\wedge$ P5 $\wedge$ P6) [ag1\M, ag2\B, ip\ip$_B$], it must be shown that $\mathcal{RS}'$ *conforms*$_{\text{rep}}$ $\mathcal{RS}$.

We define a representation function rep by mapping interactions of A and B at ip to interactions at ip$_A$ and ip$_B$, respectively:

rep (at A.ip.!(p(x)))	= at A.ip$_A$.!(p(x))
rep (after A.ip.!(p(x)))	= after A.ip$_A$.!(p(x))
rep (at A.ip.?)	= at A.ip$_A$.?
rep (after A.ip.?(p(x)))	= after A.ip$_A$.?(p(x))
rep (at B.ip.!(p(x)))	= at B.ip$_B$.!(p(x))
rep (after B.ip.!(p(x)))	= after B.ip$_B$.!(p(x))
rep (at B.ip.?)	= at B.ip$_B$.?
rep (after B.ip.?(p(x)))	= after B.ip$_B$.?(p(x))
rep ($\neg\varphi$)	= $\neg$ rep (φ)
rep ($\varphi_1 \wedge \varphi_2$)	= rep (φ_1) $\wedge$ rep (φ_2)
rep ($\forall$x.φ)	= $\forall$x. rep (φ)
rep (AG φ)	= AG rep (φ)
rep (AF φ)	= AF rep (φ)
rep ($\blacksquare$ φ)	= $\blacksquare$ rep (φ)
rep ([φ])	= [rep (φ)]
rep (#[φ])	= #[rep (φ)]
rep ($\langle \beta \rangle$ φ)	= $\langle$ rep (β) $\rangle$ rep (φ)

Table 5.12: The representation function rep

To prove $\mathcal{RS}'$ *conforms*$_{rep}$ $\mathcal{RS}$, it must be shown that $\mathcal{Arch}'$ *refines* $\mathcal{Arch}$, and that $\mathcal{Behav}' \supset$ rep($\mathcal{Behav}$) is initially-valid. $\mathcal{Arch}'$ *refines* $\mathcal{Arch}$ holds for the refinement function given in Chapter 5.3.2. The proof of $\mathcal{Behav}' \supset$ rep($\mathcal{Behav}$) is more difficult. As it turns out, some assumptions concerning the behaviour of the service users and the relations at and after have to be made before a formal proof can be conducted. The first aspect has been addressed in Chapter 5.3.6, where properties constraining the behaviour of the initiator and the responder are listed. These constraints concern both requirement specifications: $\mathcal{Behav}_A = \bigwedge_{1 \le i \le 5} C_A i$, $\mathcal{Behav}_B = \bigwedge_{1 \le i \le 5} C_B i$, $\mathcal{Behav}'_A$ = rep ($\mathcal{Behav}_A$), $\mathcal{Behav}'_B$ = rep ($\mathcal{Behav}_B$). To cover the second aspect, we assume that the relations at and after satisfy the properties listed in Table 4.1 (Chapter 4.3.2). With these preparations, we consider the service provider to be correct with respect to the service, if the following can be proved:

Theorem 5.1: $\mathcal{Arch}'$ *refines* $\mathcal{Arch}$
$\models_{iB}$ $\mathcal{Behav}' \supset$ rep ($\mathcal{Behav}$)

A rigorous proof of Theorem 5.1 has been conducted. It depends partially on the properties constraining the environment of the service provider. These constraints concern both the behaviour of the service users A and B and the semantics of the interaction points ip_A and ip_B. If we drop constraints which are necessary to conduct the correctness proof, the service is not guaranteed anymore. This clearly shows that a correct implementation of the service is in general *not* independent of the environment of the service provider. Consequently, the correct implementation of the service provider is not sufficient to guarantee the required service.

The service property S_A17 can be proved if it is additionally assumed that the interaction points ip_A and ip_B are synchronous, i.e., P14 (Chapter 4.3.4) holds for both directions. It can then be shown that $connection_{AB}$ holds if and only if $connection_M$ is satisfied. With C_M19, the proposition follows.

Experience gained during the verification activity shows that proving non-local interval properties of distributed systems requires "suitable" local constraints. Examples are the service properties S_A14 and S_A15 which become non-local when the interaction point ip is refined into ip_A, M, and ip_B. The problem here is to identify and characterize related intervals at different locations of the distributed system. In the previous case study, this problem has been solved by enforcing sufficient synchronization between the initiator and the responder during a connection establishment and a receipt exchange.

5.4 Conclusion

In the previous chapter, it has been demonstrated how the formalism of temporal logic can be successfully applied to specifying and reasoning about communication services in a methodologically clean fashion. We have specified properties defining the service as perceived by the service users, and properties defininig the service provider. We have then proved that if some restrictions on the behaviour of the service users and interaction points are respected, the service provider is correct with respect to the service.

In the course of the service specification, it has been discovered that a service can be understood as the semantics of a (complex) interaction point. Therefore, the service concept can be explained in terms of the basic architectural concepts introduced in Chapter 2.1.

The specification of the communication service has been based on a conceptual system architecture consisting of the service users and a common interaction point only. Since the service description reflects the users' point of view, this degree of structural abstraction is appropriate and adequate at this early design stage. Later, the interaction point of the service users has been refined into a service provider and two interaction points. This proceeding demonstrates that abstraction from internal structure is well-supported.

Three kinds of modularity have been used. Firstly, modularity results from the distributed nature of the system. Each architectural constituent can be replaced or refined without affecting the remaining parts of the system, if its properties are preserved. Secondly, the specification of an architectural constituent is given as the conjunction of a list of properties. Each of these properties is a segregatable part that can be easily understood, modified, removed, or replaced. Thirdly, properties with a semantical relationship are grouped in order to define phases of operation. Again, this kind of modularity serves a better understanding, but has no architectural significance.

If the conceptual system architecture of a system is to be carried into lower levels of description, it is important to describe each architectural constituent by referring to its local aspects only. Each part can then be considered separately, which supports modularity of realization and verification. In the previous case study where an event-oriented specification style has been used, local aspects are related to the occurrence of local events. Architectural constituents, i.e., agents and interaction points, should therefore be characterized by referring to their local event occurrences. References to non-local events can be made when non-local properties are stated. Because non-local properties are proved from local constraints, it is sufficient to implement the local constraints to ensure the non-local properties.

Experience gained during the specification activity shows that the future operators for branching time are sufficiently expressive to distinguish between successful and unsuccessful behaviour in the context of unreliable systems[39]. Behaviour which is specified as "inevitable" or "potential" is considered as successful. Unsuccessful behaviour is not required; however, it may be implemented, if if does not contradict the specification. In the service case study, unsuccessful behaviour is implicitly permitted when successful behaviour occurs potentially. This disallows implementations where only unsuccessful behaviour can occur. However, an implementation that exhibits only successful behaviour is correct with respect to this specification. It is interesting to observe that the important distinction between successful and unsuccessful behaviour can not be drawn in the standardized FDTs Estelle, LOTOS, and SDL, which have been developed by ISO and CCITT especially for the specification of communication services and protocols (see Chapter 4.5).

The important step towards the verification of the service provider with respect to the service has been to establish a formal relationship between the service user view and the service provider view. This has made a formal proof feasible. Further verification activities are required when the service users and the service provider are implemented. However, it will not be necessary to reconsider the entire system, which is a consequence of modularity. It is rather sufficient to verify the implementation of the service provider against its local specification, and to verify the implementation of the service users against their local constraints. Furthermore, the interaction point representations have to be checked for compatibility (see Chapter 4.6). This leads to a decomposition of verification activities and to a reduction of verification efforts, when the implementation of a service user or the service provider has to be replaced.

We emphasize that the term "protocol" has been avoided throughout the service case study in Chapter 5.3. This underlines our systematic approach and view that the

[39] In the context of reliable systems, future operators for linear time suffice.

service is independent of any protocol and therefore has to be described without reference to a protocol. Consequently, we must not explain why a connection request, for instance, can lead to "unsuccessful" behaviour, by referring to the internal structure of the service provider or the protocol of its entities.

It should be stressed again that current standardization of OSI *services* is directed towards the formal description of *service providers*. The previous case study has provided evidence that the definition of service providers falls short of the objective to define services. To perform the task of specifying and reasoning about services *and* service providers, the temporal logic designed in Chapter 3.3 has proved to be an appropriate, adequate, and versatile formal technique.

6 An epistemic logic for open distributed systems

With the temporal logic introduced in Chapter 3, the system designer can specify the architecture and the behaviour of open distributed systems. In Chapter 4, this logic has been applied to capture the meaning of interaction points. In Chapter 5, a communication service and a service provider have been specified, and the relationship between the views of the service users and the service provider have been formally established. To allow for an even more natural and adequate treatment of open distributed systems, the expressiveness of the logic from Chapter 3 will now be extended by epistemic concepts.

6.1 The role of knowledge

In Chapter 0.4, it has already been pointed out that there is a close relationship between the areas of open distributed systems and distributed artificial intelligence (DAI). In DAI, "the central problem is the *cooperation* among multiple agents to achieve a common goal" ([Wer88]), such as the operation of a factory or the provision of a communication service. Cooperation, in turn, requires communication to resolve uncertainty about intentions of other agents, or to find out which alternatives they have chosen, i.e., to acquire knowledge. Therefore, the purpose of communication can be understood as the increase of the agents' knowledge about the world.

The concept of knowledge is often used in the informal description of communication services and protocols (for instance, see [ISO88], [Hal87]), where statements such as "once the sender receives the acknowledgement, it *knows* that the current packet has been delivered; it can then safely discard the current packet and send the next packet" ([Hal87]) can be found. In this statement, two important aspects are expressed. Firstly, reception of an acknowledgement changes the sender's state of knowledge: it knows that the current packet has been delivered, which explains the purpose of the acknowledgement. On the other hand, this part of the statement expresses *how* the increase of knowledge is achieved, namely by the exchange of an acknowledgement. Secondly, when the sender has acquired sufficient knowledge, it can safely process the next packet. This part of the statement expresses *what* to do in a certain state of knowledge. A more abstract specification can be obtained by omitting the first part of the statement, leaving it open how the sender acquires sufficient knowledge to safely process the next packet. Protocols written in such a style have been termed "*knowledge-based protocols*" in [HaFa85]. Note that without reference to the concept of knowledge, the above protocol would read "Once the sender receives an acknowledgement, it sends the next packet", which provides no insight into the purpose of the acknowledgement, and is on a lower level of abstraction.

This small example shows that the concept of knowledge can help to treat open distributed systems in a more natural and abstract way. "Reasoning about knowledge seems to play a fundamental role in distributed systems" ([HaMo87]). In order to use knowledge in formal specification and reasoning, it is necessary to define its meaning precisely. The formal study of knowledge is a branch of philosophy, known as *epistemic logic* ([Hin62]). Currently, epistemic logic is investigated and studied in a variety of fields, ranging from artificial intelligence ([Ros85]), DAI ([Wer88]), distributed systems ([Hal87]) and robotics ([Ros87]) to game theory ([Aum76]), psychology ([ClMa81]), linguistics and economics. In Chapter 6.2, we will look at several notions of knowledge in these areas. In Chapter 6.3, we will define a modular epistemic logic suitable for specifying and reasoning about open distributed systems.

6.2 Notions of knowledge

The notions of knowledge found in the literature can be classified into individual knowledge and group knowledge. Individual knowledge refers to the knowledge of a single agent, group knowledge applies to sets of agents. The following survey focuses on several notions of knowledge, which seem to be of particular interest in the context of open distributed systems.

6.2.1 Possible-worlds semantics

In order to use the notion of knowledge for specifying and reasoning about open distributed systems, its semantics has to be formally defined. However, there is no general agreement on what the properties of knowledge are or should be ([Len78]). For instance, does an agent know what it knows? Or does it know what it doesn't know? Does it know only true facts? Therefore, different notions of knowledge have been proposed in the literature.

To formally model knowledge, Hintikka has introduced the *model of possible worlds* ([Hin62]). The idea is that at each moment in time, an agent is in one of a set of *situations* (or *worlds*). However, if only part of a situation is visible to the agent, there may be other situations which - from its local point of view - it could possibly be in. It is with respect to these situations that knowledge is ascribed to the agent: the agent is said to *know* a fact φ (written "$K\varphi$") exactly if φ is true in all situations which it considers possible. In other words, "knowledge corresponds to the extent to which [the agent] can determine what world he is in" ([HaMo85]).

This model of possible worlds is directly related to Kripke structures (see Chapter 3.3.1) introduced in [Kri63]. A *Kripke structure* is a tuple $\mathcal{M} = \langle W,R,V \rangle$ ([HuCr68]), where W is a set of *worlds* (also called "*states of affairs*"), $R \subseteq W \times W$ is a *seeing-relation* (also called "*epistemic accessibility relation*" when used to model knowledge), and $V: \Phi \times W \rightarrow \{0,1\}$ is a *value assignment* determining the truth value of every atomic proposition in every world. If R is chosen such that for all worlds $w, w' \in W$, $(w,w') \in R$ exactly if the agent being in situation w considers w' possible, then knowledge of a fact φ can be formalized as follows:

$$\mathcal{M},w \models K\varphi \text{ iff for all } w' \in W, (w,w') \in R \text{ implies } \mathcal{M},w' \models \varphi$$

"That is, the agent in a situation w is viewed as knowing a fact φ if φ is true, no matter which of the alternative states of affairs compatible with his knowledge (in w) turns out to actually be the case" ([Ros85]).

Using Kripke structures, it is possible to model different notions of knowledge. First of all, it can be shown that every notion of knowledge modeled in a Kripke structure as described above has the following properties:

K1. $K(\varphi_1 \supset \varphi_2) \supset (K\varphi_1 \supset K\varphi_2)$ (consequence closure)

K2. $\vdash \varphi$ implies $\vdash K\varphi$ (epistemic necessitation)

K1 and K2 make an agent *logically omniscient* ([Hin75]): it knows all logical consequences of its knowledge, and it knows all tautologies. Further properties which are more commonly considered to characterize knowledge are the following:

K3. $K\varphi \supset \varphi$ (knowledge axiom)

K4. $K\varphi \supset K\,K\varphi$ (positive introspection)

K5. $\neg K\varphi \supset K \neg K\varphi$ (negative introspection)

The knowledge axiom expresses that only true facts can be known, it is usually taken as the property distinguishing knowledge from belief ([HaMo85]). Properties K4 and

K5 express that the agent knows what it knows and what it does not know, respectively.

In the context of modal logic, the system consisting of the axioms and inference rules of propositional logic (see Chapter 3.3.2), and K1, K2, K3 is known as T, T + K4 is known as S4, and S4 + K5 is known as S5. To model the properties K3, K4, K5 in a Kripke structure, constraints on the seeing-relation R can be imposed. K3 corresponds to reflexivity, K4 to transitivity, and K5 holds if R is Euclidean.

6.2.2 Situated-Automata Knowledge

In [Ros85], two views of what it means for a machine to know a fact are contrasted. "In the current view, the machine is regarded as knowing a fact if its state either explicitly encodes the fact as a sentence of an interpreted formal language or if such a sentence can be derived from other encoded sentences according to the rules of an appropriate logical system" ([Ros85]). This conception is termed "*interpreted-symbolic-structure (ISS) approach*", and can be seen as the classical AI approach to ascribe knowledge to agents. Under the ISS approach, much research has been dedicated to the representation of knowledge in data objects. However, it depends on the interpretation of the designer what knowledge is represented by a given data object. Stated otherwise, the same data object can represent different pieces of knowledge. This means that the properties of knowledge can vary with the interpretation of data objects the designer has in mind.

To put the notion of knowledge on objective grounds, another view termed "*Situated-Automata Approach*" is suggested in [Ros85]. Here, a deterministic automaton T interacting with an environment E as shown in Figure 6.1 is considered. The automaton is determined by a structure $T = \langle S,I,O,\delta,\lambda,s_0 \rangle$, where S is a (finite or infinite) set of states, I is a set of inputs (also called "*stimuli*"), O is a set of outputs ("*actions*"), δ: $S \times I \rightarrow S$ is a next-state function, l: $S \rightarrow O$ is an output function, and $s_0 \in S$ is the initial state. Furthermore, the environment is in some state. By composing the states of T and E, a so-called "world-state" w is obtained.

A metalanguage is used to express logical assertions about the world termed "*world conditions*". Let Ψ be the set of all world conditions. With each world state w, the subset $\Psi' \subseteq \Psi$ of world conditions holding in w can be associated.

The automaton T can distinguish different states of the world only on the basis of the inputs it observes. These inputs can be related to world conditions in the following way. Let $\psi_0 \in \Psi$ be the strongest world condition that is guaranteed to hold when T is in its initial state. With each input $x \in I$, a function from Ψ into itself mapping a world condition $\psi \in \Psi$ to the most specific world condition guaranteed to hold after the input x (written "ψ/x") can be associated. This function can be extended to input sequences $x^* \in I^*$. With these definitions, ψ_0/x^* denotes the strongest world condition to hold after T has accepted the input sequence x^*. Thus, the conditions which T can *in principle* discriminate are determined by $\{ \psi_0/x^* \mid x^* \in I^* \}$.

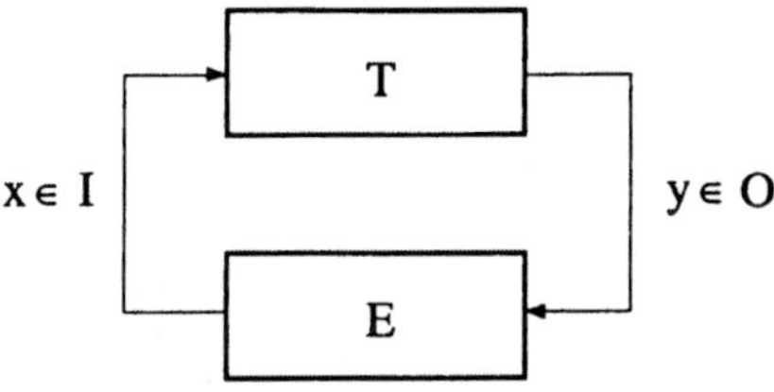

Figure 6.1: An automaton coupled to its environment ([Ros85])

Whether T can *in fact* discriminate between these conditions additionally depends on how much input history is encoded in its internal states. In other words, with each internal state s the set of input histories leading to that state (i.e., $\{ x^* \in I^* \mid \delta^*(s_0,x^*) = s \}$, where δ^* extends δ to input sequences) can be associated, yielding an equivalence relation on the set of input sequences (recall that T is deterministic). Since T is in the same internal state for all input histories of the corresponding equivalence class, it can not distinguish between them. The strongest condition guaranteed to hold after any of a set $\{ x_1^*,...,x_n^* \}$ of input sequences has occurred can be expressed as $\psi_0/x_1^* \vee ... \vee \psi_0/x_n^*$. If $L_s = \{ x^* \in I^* \mid \delta^*(s_0,x^*) = s \}$ denotes the set of input sequences leading to state s, then the information content info(s) of state s is given by $\bigvee_{x^* \in L_s} (\psi_0/x^*)$.

This model of information can be directly related to the possible-worlds model (see Chapter 6.2.1). If suffices to define the epistemic accessibility relation R, which can be done as follows:

$$(w,w') \in R \text{ iff } state(w) = state(w')$$

where state(w) denotes the state of the automaton T in world state w. Since under this definition R is an equivalence relation, the notion of knowledge termed "*Situated-Automata Knowledge (SAK)*" satisfies the axioms of the system S5[40].

The important difference to the ISS approach is that the knowledge of the automaton T is not explicitly encoded in T's state nor is it explicitly manipulated by T. Instead, the designer of the automaton uses a metalanguage to state world conditions, which he "uses ... only to express (to himself!) various background assumptions he is making and to characterize (again for himself) the information content of the states of the machine he is designing. His purpose is to comprehend the emerging design and verify that the machine will behave as desired" ([Ros85]).

Situated-Automata Knowledge is a notion related to the architecture of Figure 6.1 under the additional assumption that the automaton T is deterministic. From the definition of SAK it follows that placing T into a different environment in general changes the knowledge ascribed to T. This appears to be too restrictive in the context of open distributed systems. Here, it should be possible to ascribe some knowledge to a system independently of its environment, or with the environment being only partially determined. The reason is that the environment is in general not known during the design of an open system. Furthermore, distribution aspects should be treated.

6.2.3 View-based knowledge interpretation

In [HaMo87], the notion of knowledge is considered in the context of distributed systems. A distributed system is viewed as a finite set $\{ ag_1,...,ag_m \}$ of agents (or *processors*) interacting by the exchange of messages over a communication network. A *run* σ of a distributed system is an infinite execution sequence. A *point* is a tuple (σ,n), where σ is a run and $n \in \mathbb{N}_0$ is a time. A distributed system is identified with the set Σ of possible runs.

With each agent ag_i and each point (σ,n), the *history* $h(ag_i,\sigma,n)$ given by the sequence of events which are local to ag_i is associated. In particular, ag_i wakes up at time $n_0(i,\sigma)$; until then, $h(ag_i,\sigma,n)$ is empty. The internal state of ag_i at time $n_0(i,\sigma)$ is the initial state of ag_i. For $n \geq n_0(i,\sigma)$, $h(ag_i,\sigma,n)$ is given by the initial state of ag_i and the

40 Note that a relation is reflexive, transitive, and symmetrical if and only if it is reflexive and Euclidean.

sequence of messages ag_i has sent and received up to (σ,n). It is required that the history contains only local events.

In order to express *ground facts* about the system, the existence of an underlying logical language is assumed (a ground fact is a fact not involving knowledge). A ground fact is interpreted on the points of the set Σ of possible runs: for a ground fact φ, $\pi(\varphi) \subseteq \Sigma \times \mathbb{N}_0$ is the set of points where φ holds. The logical language is extended to a language which is closed under operators for individual knowledge of agents, and under propositional operators. The semantics of these operators is then defined with respect to the views of the agents. The *view* $v(ag_i,\sigma,n)$ of the agent ag_i at point (σ,n) is an abstraction of ag_i's history. This takes into account that although ag_i has observed all local events, it records only an aggregation of the complete history. It follows that the agent's view at any point is a function of its history. Formally: $h(ag_i,\sigma,n) = h(ag_i,\sigma',n')$ implies $v(ag_i,\sigma,n) = v(ag_i,\sigma',n')$. The inversion holds only if the agent records the entire history. Two points (σ,n) and (σ',n') are *indistinguishable* for agent ag_i, if ag_i has the same view at both points, i.e., $v(ag_i,\sigma,n) = v(ag_i,\sigma',n')$. Agent ag_i is then said to know a fact φ at point (σ,n), if and only if φ holds at all points which it can not distinguish from (σ,n).

The previous interpretation of knowledge is called "*view-based interpretation*" ([HaMo87]). Under this interpretation, the knowledge of a single agent ag_i at a point (σ,n) is a function of its history $h(ag_i,\sigma,n)$, which is a property any reasonable notion of knowledge in the context of distributed systems must satisfy. Another property is that at any point, an agent can know only facts which hold at that point, which distinguishes knowledge from belief ([HaMo85]).

The model of distributed systems together with the interpretation of ground facts and the view function can be directly related to the possible-worlds model and Kripke structures (see Chapter 6.2.1). If W is the set of points and V is determined by the interpretation of ground facts, the epistemic accessibility relation R_i for agent ag_i can be defined as follows:

$$((\sigma,n),(\sigma',n')) \in R_i \text{ iff } v(ag_i,\sigma,n) = v(ag_i,\sigma',n')$$

In fact, for each agent, an accessibility relation R_i has to be defined, which leads to an extended Kripke structure $\mathcal{M} = \langle W,R_1,\ldots,R_m,V \rangle$ to model a system of m agents. Because under this definition R_i is an equivalence relation, the view-based interpretation of knowledge satisfies the axioms of the system S5. It immediately follows that apart from the properties mentioned above, the properties of positive and negative introspection hold.

Previous work (see [Hal87]) for a survey) has shown that the view-based interpretation provides a notion of knowledge which is useful for designing and analyzing distributed systems. It is closely related to Situated Automata Knowledge (ground facts correspond to world conditions) and can be understood as a generalization of SAK to distributed systems. Again, knowledge is ascribed "to a processor without the processor necessarily being 'aware' of this knowledge, and without the processor needing to perform any particular computation in order to obtain such knowledge" ([HaMo87]). As for SAK, placing an agent ag_i into a different environment in general changes the knowledge ascribed to ag_i.

The view-based interpretation probably captures the strongest reasonable and intuitive notion of individual knowledge in the context of distributed systems. For certain applications, different notions seem to be more appropriate. It can, for instance, be required that the knowledge ascribed to an agent is explicitly represented in its state, or that it can be computed with a limited amount of resources. With respect to open systems, it should be possible to ascribe knowledge to a system independently of its environment, or with the environment being only partially determined. Provided such a notion of knowledge, epistemic properties of the open system will continue to hold when it is placed into a different environment.

6.2.4 Group knowledge

When specifying and reasoning about distributed systems, i.e., systems consisting of two or more agents, it is often useful to refer to the knowledge of these agents collectively and concisely. This idea has lead to the introduction of several notions of *group knowledge* ([HaMo84], [Hal87], [HaMo87], [Bar88]). In the framework of the model of distributed systems used in [HaMo87] (see Chapter 6.2.3), it is, for instance, possible to state that some agent knows a fact φ (written "$S\varphi$", "*S-knowledge*" for short), or that every agent knows φ (written "$E\varphi$", "*E-knowledge*" for short). Another notion particularly interesting in the context of distributed systems captures the *combined knowledge*[41] of a fact φ (written "$I\varphi$", "*I-knowledge*" for short): $I\varphi$ holds if by pooling the individual knowledge of all agents together, φ can be deduced.

[41] In [HaMo87], this notion of knowledge has been termed "implicit knowledge". In the following, implicit knowledge will be used in a different sense.

Furthermore, *common knowledge* of a fact φ (written "$C\varphi$", "*C-knowledge*" for short), i.e., every agent knows φ, and every agent knows that every agent knows φ, and so on, is often used. Intuitively, all these notions of group knowledge should collapse into individual knowledge in case of a single-agent system.

The intuitive meaning of group knowledge can be made precise in a Kripke structure $\mathcal{M} = \langle W, R_1, ..., R_m, V \rangle$, which is related to the model of distributed systems as explained in Chapter 6.2.3. In particular, each epistemic accessibility relation R_i captures the view of agent ag_i. A world $w' \in W$ is called "*reachable*" from a world w if there is some sequence $w_1, ..., w_n$ of worlds such that $w = w_1$, $w' = w_n$, and for all $j = 1, ..., n-1$, there is some R_i such that $(w_j, w_{j+1}) \in R_i$. For a world w of a Kripke structure $\mathcal{M}$, the meaning of the previous notions of group knowledge can be defined as follows:

$\mathcal{M}, w \models S\varphi$ iff for some $i \in \{1, ..., m\}$, for all $w' \in W$, $(w,w') \in R_i$ implies $\mathcal{M}, w' \models \varphi$

$\mathcal{M}, w \models E\varphi$ iff for all $i \in \{1, ..., m\}$, for all $w' \in W$, $(w,w') \in R_i$ implies $\mathcal{M}, w' \models \varphi$
iff for all $w' \in W$, $(w,w') \in R_1 \cup ... \cup R_m$ implies $\mathcal{M}, w' \models \varphi$

$\mathcal{M}, w \models I\varphi$ iff for all $w' \in W$, $(w,w') \in R_1 \cap ... \cap R_m$ implies $\mathcal{M}, w' \models \varphi$

$\mathcal{M}, w \models C\varphi$ iff for all $w' \in W$ reachable from w, $\mathcal{M}, w' \models \varphi$

From these definitions, it follows that the notions of group knowledge form the following hierarchy: $C\varphi \supset E\varphi \supset S\varphi \supset I\varphi$. In general, this hierarchy is strict. Moreover, it can be observed that in a single-agent system, S-knowledge, E-knowledge, and I-knowledge collapse into individual knowledge as defined in Chapter 6.2.1. Under view-based knowledge interpretations (see Chapter 6.2.3), this is also the case for common knowledge.

Some notions of group knowledge can be defined syntactically in terms of individual knowledge. Let $K_i\varphi$ denote that ag_i knows φ:

$$S\varphi =_{Df} \bigvee_{i \in \{1,...,m\}} K_i\varphi$$

$$E\varphi =_{Df} \bigwedge_{i \in \{1,...,m\}} K_i\varphi$$

$$E^1\varphi =_{Df} E\varphi$$

$$E^{k+1}\varphi =_{Df} E\, E^k\varphi, \text{ for } k \geq 1$$

$$C\varphi =_{Df} \bigwedge_{k \in \mathbb{N}} E^k\varphi$$

It has been shown that under view-based knowledge interpretations, combined knowledge and common knowledge both have the properties of the modal system S5 ([HaMo85]). For S-knowledge, the axioms of consequence closure and negative introspection do not hold. E-knowledge does not satisfy the axioms of positive and negative introspection.

According to [ClMa81], there are two basic ways in which a group can acquire common knowledge. One is by *membership in a community*. If we design, for instance, a communication system, we define such a community, and all invariant properties are common knowledge of the system's agents. The other is *copresence with the occurrence of a fact*. This is, for instance, the case for synchronous communication, as it is usually assumed in process algebra (for instance, see [Mil80], [Hoa85], [ISO88c]). However, common knowledge can not be attained if synchronous communication is implemented by asynchronous exchange of messages, even if message delivery is guaranteed, but there is an uncertainty about message delivery times ([HaMo84]). This follows from the fact that when common knowledge is attained, it is attained by all agents simultaneously. To capture the group knowledge which can be acquired in case of asynchronous reliable message exchange, another notion termed "*eventual common knowledge*" (denoted by $C^{\Diamond}$) has been introduced in [HaMo84]. Informally, $C^{\Diamond}\varphi$ expresses that every agent eventually knows φ, and every agent eventually knows that every agent eventually knows φ, and so on. Since this is strictly less than common knowledge, systems with asynchronous interaction between agents can not be equivalent[42] to systems with synchronous interaction.

It is not clear from the first what kind of group knowledge is most suitable to capture the knowledge ascribed to a distributed system as a whole. Reasonable choices range from combined knowledge (upper bound) to E-knowledge (lower bound). As pointed out earlier, all of these notions collapse into individual knowledge in case of a one-agent system. We will readdress this important issue in Chapter 6.3.9.

The notions of group knowledge considered in [HaMo84] and [HaMo85] quantify over all agents of a distributed system. It can also be useful to refer to arbitrary subsets of agents, which can be formally expressed by indexing the operators with the corresponding set of agents (see [Hal87], [HaMo87]). For instance, if G is an arbitrary set of agents, φ a fact, then $I_G\varphi$ expresses that the agents in G have combined

42 A strong equivalence in terms of the acquired knowledge.

knowledge of φ. The adaptation of the model-theoretic semantics to this generalization is obvious.

It has already been pointed out that in the context of open systems, it should be possible to specify and reason about such systems independently of the environments into which they are embedded later. This can be achieved by ascribing knowledge which is stable with respect to modifications of the environment. Clearly, the notions of group knowledge considered in this chapter do not have this property.

6.2.5 Awareness

As pointed out in the literature (for instance, see [Hin75], [FaHa88]), possible-worlds semantics (see Chapter 6.2.1) does not seem appropriate for modeling human knowledge. The reason is that under this semantics, every notion of knowledge has the properties of consequence closure and epistemic necessitation. In particular, this means that an agent knows all logical consequences of its knowledge, and it knows all tautologies, which has been called "*logical omniscience*" in [Hin75]. However, in real life people are certainly not omniscient. In [FaHa88], several sources for the lack of logical omniscience are identified:

- people are only aware of a subset of facts,
- people are resource-bounded,
- people don't always know the relevant rules to deduce knowledge,
- people don't focus on all issues simultaneously.

An approach to model these different aspects termed "*logic of general awareness*" has been published in [FaHa88]. In that work, several notions of belief are investigated. However, since these notions have obvious counterparts with respect to knowledge[43], we will outline that approach in terms of knowledge rather than belief.

In the logic of general awareness, a distinction is drawn between implicit and explicit knowledge. An agent ag_i *implicitly knows* a fact φ (written "$K_i φ$") if φ is true in all situations it considers possible. In other words, implicit knowledge exactly corresponds to individual knowledge under possible-worlds semantics. An agent ag_i *explicitly knows* a fact φ (written "$K'_i φ$") if it implicitly knows φ and additionally is

[43] Recall that usually, the knowledge axiom (see Chapter 6.2.1) is taken as the property distinguishing knowledge from belief.

aware of φ. If $A_i\varphi$ denotes the latter, the relationship between implicit and explicit knowledge is the following:

$$K_i'\varphi \equiv K_i\varphi \wedge A_i\varphi$$

The idea is that an agent can only have explicit knowledge of facts it is aware of. However, it is not discussed in [FaHa88] what "*awareness*" really is: "the precise interpretation we give to the notion of awareness will depend on the intended application of the logic". Assuming, for instance, that agents are aware of all facts implies that explicit knowledge is reduced to implicit knowledge.

The intuitive meaning of implicit and explicit knowledge can be made precise in an extended Kripke structure $\mathcal{M} = \langle W, R_1, \ldots, R_m, B_1, \ldots, B_m, V \rangle$, where for each agent ag_i, B_i is a function associating with each world the set of formulas ag_i is aware of in that world (*awareness function*). The meaning of knowledge and awareness can then be defined as follows:

$$\mathcal{M},w \models K_i\varphi \quad \text{iff} \quad \text{for all } w' \in W, (w,w') \in R_i \text{ implies } \mathcal{M},w' \models \varphi$$

$$\mathcal{M},w \models K_i'\varphi \quad \text{iff} \quad \text{for all } w' \in W, (w,w') \in R_i \text{ implies } \mathcal{M},w' \models \varphi, \text{ and } \varphi \in B_i(w)$$

$$\mathcal{M},w \models A_i\varphi \quad \text{iff} \quad \varphi \in B_i(w)$$

The generality of this approach is due to the awareness function, which can be customized with respect to the particular application. By placing different restrictions on this function, several interesting notions of explicit knowledge can be captured. According to [FaHa88], "typical" restrictions include:

- If the order of conjuncts has no influence on awareness, the restriction "$\varphi_1 \wedge \varphi_2 \in B_i(w)$ implies $\varphi_2 \wedge \varphi_1 \in B_i(w)$" can be imposed on the awareness function. "$\varphi \in B_i(w)$ iff $\neg\varphi \in B_i(w)$" states that ag_i is aware of a fact if and only if it is aware of its negation.
- Awareness can be closed under subformulas, i.e., if $\varphi \in B_i(w)$ and φ' is a subformula of φ, then $\varphi' \in B_i(w)$.
- Awareness of ag_i can be restricted to a subset of atomic formulas, and additionally be closed under certain formation rules for formulas. The subset could, for instance, consist of all "local" atomic formulas. The formation rules could exclude rules mentioning other agents, for

instance, the rule stating that if φ is a formula, then $K_j\varphi$ is a formula, for $j \neq i$.

- A self-reflective agent is aware of what it is aware of, i.e., $\varphi \in B_i(w)$ implies $A_i\varphi \in B_i(w)$. Syntactically, this corresponds to the axiom $A_i\varphi \supset A_iA_i\varphi$.
- The formulas an agent is aware of can be exactly those explicitly represented in its state, or computable with a limited amount of resources.

Some restrictions on the awareness function can be captured axiomatically. For instance, for a propositional logic with operators for implicit and explicit knowledge, and awareness, closure under subformulas has been expressed in [FaHa88] as follows:

$$A_i(\neg\varphi) \supset A_i\varphi$$
$$A_i(\varphi_1 \wedge \varphi_2) \supset A_i\varphi_1 \wedge A_i\varphi_2$$
$$A_i(K_j\varphi) \supset A_i\varphi$$
$$A_i(K_j'\varphi) \supset A_i\varphi$$
$$A_i(A_j\varphi) \supset A_i\varphi$$

Note that from these restrictions, it follows that if an agent is aware of $\varphi_1 \vee \varphi_2$, $\varphi_1 \supset \varphi_2$, or $\varphi_1 \equiv \varphi_2$, then it is aware of both φ_1 *and* φ_2:

$$A_i(\varphi_1 \vee \varphi_2) \supset A_i\varphi_1 \wedge A_i\varphi_2$$
$$A_i(\varphi_1 \supset \varphi_2) \supset A_i\varphi_1 \wedge A_i\varphi_2$$
$$A_i(\varphi_1 \equiv \varphi_2) \supset A_i\varphi_1 \wedge A_i\varphi_2$$

Since the meaning of implicit knowledge is identical to the possible-worlds semantics (see Chapter 6.2.1), it is clear that it satisfies the axioms of the modal system S5 under a view-based interpretation. The properties of explicit knowledge clearly depend on restrictions on the awareness function. In general, the consequence closure axiom does not hold for explicit knowledge. However, if awareness is closed under subformulas, it does, which means that this assumption is certainly inappropriate for resource-bounded reasoning. Furthermore, if an agent is aware of what it explicitly knows and what it does not explicitly know, the axioms of positive and negative introspection are valid, respectively. Clearly, the knowledge axiom holds for arbitrary awareness assumptions.

With respect to open systems, it seems that by using an appropriate notion of explicit knowledge, i.e., by placing suitable restrictions on the awareness function, it will be possible to ascribe knowledge to a system independently of its environment, or with the environment being partially determined. This would have the consequence that epistemic properties of the open system can be guaranteed to be invariant with respect to modifications of the environment.

6.3 A modular epistemic logic for open distributed systems

In the previous survey, several notions of individual knowledge and group knowledge from the literature have been considered. We take them as the starting point for the design of an epistemic logic for open distributed systems. This epistemic logic extends the modular temporal logic from Chapter 3.3 by adding a number of building blocks, each consisting of a group of epistemic operators. It will then be possible to customize temporal epistemic logics according to the needed expressiveness.

6.3.1 Semantical models

The epistemic logics introduced in the following can be based on propositional logic as well as first-order logic. In the propositional framework, a state is defined by a set of true atomic propositions; in the first-order framework, it is given by a set of functions and relations. To interpret epistemic formulas in these different settings, the following types of semantical models will be used:

- $\mathcal{M}_{PLE}$ model of propositional linear time temporal epistemic logic
- $\mathcal{M}_{PBE}$ model of propositional branching time temporal epistemic logic
- $\mathcal{M}_{FLE}$ model of many-sorted first-order linear time temporal epistemic logic
- $\mathcal{M}_{FBE}$ model of many-sorted first-order branching time temporal epistemic logic

When only a distinction between linear and branching time is to be drawn, we write $\mathcal{M}_{LE}$ and $\mathcal{M}_{BE}$, respectively. To define the structure of these model types, the notational conventions from Chapter 3.3.1 are used.

Definition 6.1: A model $\mathcal{M}_{PLE}$ of propositional linear time temporal epistemic logic is a structure $\langle AG, S, S_0, \Sigma, \Phi, lp, h, v, af \rangle$, where

- AG, S, S_0, Σ, Φ, and lp are defined as for $\mathcal{M}_{PL}$ (see Definition 3.1);

- h is a function defining the *local history* of an agent ag $\in$ AG in *global situations* (σ,n), where $\sigma \in \Sigma$ and $n \in \mathbb{N}_0$;
- v is a function defining the *view* of an agent ag $\in$ AG in global situations (σ,n). It is required that the view is a function of the history, i.e., $h(ag,\sigma,n) = h(ag,\sigma',n')$ implies $v(ag,\sigma,n) = v(ag,\sigma',n')$;
- *af* is a function associating with each agent the set of formulas it is *aware* of; *af* is closed under subformulas and formation rules.

Definition 6.2: A model $\mathcal{M}_{PBE}$ of propositional branching time temporal epistemic logic is a structure $\langle$ AG,S,S_0,Π,Φ,lp,h,v,*af* $\rangle$, where

- AG, S, S_0, Π, Φ, and lp are defined as for $\mathcal{M}_{PB}$ (see Definition 3.2);
- h, v, and *af* are defined as for $\mathcal{M}_{PLE}$ (see Definition 6.1).

Definition 6.3: A model $\mathcal{M}_{FLE}$ of many-sorted first-order linear time temporal epistemic logic is a structure $\langle$ AG,IP,E,$\mathcal{A}rch$,S,S_0,Σ,h,v,*af* $\rangle$, where

- AG, IP, E, $\mathcal{A}rch$, S, S_0, Σ are defined as for $\mathcal{M}_{FL}$ (see Definition 3.3);
- h, v, and *af* are defined as for $\mathcal{M}_{PLE}$ (see Definition 6.1).

Definition 6.4: A model $\mathcal{M}_{FBE}$ of many-sorted first-order branching time temporal epistemic logic is a structure $\langle$ AG,IP,E,$\mathcal{A}rch$,S,S_0,Π,h,v,*af* $\rangle$, where

- AG, IP, E, $\mathcal{A}rch$, S, S_0, Π are defined as for $\mathcal{M}_{FB}$ (see Definition 3.4);
- h, v, and *af* are defined as for $\mathcal{M}_{PLE}$ (see Definition 6.1).

For the models $\mathcal{M}_{PLE}$, $\mathcal{M}_{PBE}$, $\mathcal{M}_{FLE}$, and $\mathcal{M}_{FBE}$, the notions of satisfaction and validity as defined in Chapter 3.3.1, Definitions 3.5 and 3.6, apply.

A global situation is completely characterized by a tuple (σ,n) not only in linear time models, but also in branching time models. The reason is that a state sequence σ uniquely determines a state tree $\pi \in \Pi$ such that $\sigma \in \pi$, because there exists only one state tree with $r(\pi) = \sigma_0$ (see Definition 3.2). Also, it suffices to define the history function h on state sequences rather than on state trees, because the history concerns the past, which is linear. Furthermore, since the view of an agent is a function of its local history, the same observation applies to the view function v.

Note that we assume the function *af* to be static, i.e., the awareness of an agent is the same in all global situations. This conception seems justified by our intention to specify and reason about systems from the designer's point of view, and not to model human knowledge.

The previous definitions determine the structure of semantical models and some general restrictions. For a given application, further constraints can be added, in particular, the functions *h*, *v*, and *af* may have to be defined in detail. In the propositional framework, one option is to define the local history in terms of the global situation and lp. Recall that lp is a function associating with each agent the set of its local atomic propositions. For each global situation (σ,n), the *local situation* of agent ag can be defined as (σ',n), where $\sigma_i' =_{Df} \sigma_i \cap lp(ag)$ for all $i \in \mathbb{N}_0$. The local history is then given as the sequence of local states up to the current moment in time, i.e., $h(ag,\sigma,n) =_{Df} \langle \sigma_0' ... \sigma_n' \rangle$.

Two global situations (σ,n) and (σ',n') are called "*indistinguishable*" for agent ag if and only if ag has the same view in both situations, i.e., *v*(ag,σ,n) = *v*(ag,σ',n'). Since the view of an agent is a function of its local history, it follows from *h*(ag,σ,n) = *h*(ag,σ',n') that the global situations (σ,n) and (σ',n') are indistinguishable for ag. The converse only holds if ag has a complete-history view. For each agent, indistinguishability is an equivalence relation on the set of global situations.

In each of the semantical models, it is possible to define the meaning of various notions of individual knowledge, group knowledge, and awareness. In the following, a number of building blocks covering epistemic aspects will be introduced. They extend the modular temporal logic of Chapter 3.3 to yield a modular temporal epistemic logic.

6.3.2 Operators for implicit individual knowledge

In this and the following chapters, the modular temporal logic from Chapter 3.3 is extended by several building blocks of epistemic operators. For each of these building blocks, formation rules defining syntactically correct formulas are presented. Then, the semantics of these formulas when interpreted in the models $\mathfrak{M}_{PLE}$, $\mathfrak{M}_{PBE}$, $\mathfrak{M}_{FLE}$, and $\mathfrak{M}_{FBE}$ (see Chapter 6.3.1) is recursively defined. If available, an axiomatic basis is provided for each group of operators. In the appendix, selections of theorems and valid formulas are listed.

With operators for implicit individual knowledge, the knowledge of a single agent about itself and its environment can be formally expressed. In a distributed system, an agent can also know something about the knowledge of other agents. The knowledge is called "*implicit*", because it will be ascribed to an agent regardless of what facts the agent is actually aware of. Thus, this notion of knowledge will be useful for the designer of the system, but it is inappropriate if the agent will have to answer queries based on its knowledge.

To refer to implicit individual knowledge, the building block *K* is introduced. For each agent ag $\in$ AG, an operator K_{ag} is defined and interpreted as follows:

<u>Syntax *K*</u>

i) Let φ be a formula, ag $\in$ AG be an agent, then $K_{ag}\varphi$ is a formula.

<u>Semantics *K*</u>

Let φ be a formula, ag $\in$ AG be an agent, then

i) $\mathcal{M}_{LE'}(\sigma,i,j) \models K_{ag}\varphi$ iff $\forall \sigma' \in \Sigma, k \geq 0. (\nu(ag,\sigma,j) = \nu(ag,\sigma',k)$ implies $\mathcal{M}_{LE'}(\sigma',0,k) \models \varphi)$

ii) $\mathcal{M}_{BE'}(\pi,\sigma,i,j) \models K_{ag}\varphi$ iff $\forall \pi' \in \Pi, \sigma' \in \pi', k \geq 0. (\nu(ag,\sigma,j) = \nu(ag,\sigma',k)$ implies $\mathcal{M}_{BE'}(\pi',\sigma',0,k) \models \varphi)$

An agent ag implicitly knows a fact φ in a global situation (σ,j) exactly if φ is true in all global situations (σ',k) which it can not distinguish from (σ,j), i.e., where $\nu(ag,\sigma,j) = \nu(ag,\sigma',k)$. This semantics has been called "*view-based interpretation*" in [HaMo87] (see Chapter 6.2.3). Note that if the formula $K_{ag}\varphi$ is interpreted in a restricted context, i.e., $i > 0$, φ is evaluated on the entire context. This choice is in accordance with the intended meaning.

<u>Axiomatic basis *K*</u>

Let φ, φ_1, φ_2 be formulas, ag $\in$ AG be an agent:

A27: $K_{ag}\varphi \supset \varphi$ (knowledge axiom)

A28: $K_{ag}(\varphi_1 \supset \varphi_2) \supset (K_{ag}\varphi_1 \supset K_{ag}\varphi_2)$ (consequence closure)

A29: $K_{ag}\varphi \supset K_{ag}K_{ag}\varphi$ (positive introspection)

A30: $\neg K_{ag}\varphi \supset K_{ag}\neg K_{ag}\varphi$ (negative introspection)

Tr6: $\vdash \varphi$ implies $\vdash K_{ag}\varphi$ (epistemic necessitation)

As explained in Chapter 6.2.3, the view function determines, for each agent, an epistemic accessibility relation on the set of global situations. Thus, a relationship between the semantical models in Chapter 6.3.1 and Kripke structures (see Chapter 6.2.3) can be established. Since the accessibility relations obtained from the view function are equivalence relations, implicit individual knowledge satisfies the axioms of the modal system S5. In particular, agents know only true facts (A27), they are logically omniscient (A28 and Tr6), and they know what they know (A29) and what they don't know (A30).

6.3.3 Operators for explicit individual knowledge

The notion of implicit knowledge is too strong if agents have to answer queries based on their knowledge. Moreover, in the context of open systems, implicit knowledge has the counterintuitive property that the knowledge of an agent is partially determined by the environment into which it is embedded. If the environment is changed, the implicit knowledge ascribed to the agent is in general also changed. However, during the design of an open system, it should be possible to ascribe to the system and its agents epistemic properties which are invariant with respect to modifications of the environment. Therefore, the notion of *explicit individual knowledge* (see Chapter 6.2.5) is incorporated into the modular temporal logic.

To refer to explicit individual knowledge, the building block *K'* is introduced. For each agent ag ∈ AG, an operator K'_{ag} is defined and interpreted as follows:

Syntax *K'*

i) Let φ be a formula, ag ∈ AG be an agent, then $K'_{ag}\varphi$ is a formula.

Semantics *K'*

Let φ be a formula, ag ∈ AG be an agent, then

i) $\mathcal{M}_{LE'}(\sigma,i,j) \models K'_{ag}\varphi$ iff $\varphi \in af(ag)$ and $\forall \sigma' \in \Sigma, k \geq 0.$
$(v(ag,\sigma,j) = v(ag,\sigma',k)$ implies $\mathcal{M}_{LE'}(\sigma',0,k) \models \varphi)$

ii) $\mathcal{M}_{BE'}(\pi,\sigma,i,j) \models K'_{ag}\varphi$ iff $\varphi \in af(ag)$ and $\forall \pi' \in \Pi, \sigma' \in \pi', k \geq 0.$
$(v(ag,\sigma,j) = v(ag,\sigma',k)$ implies $\mathcal{M}_{BE'}(\pi',\sigma',0,k) \models \varphi)$

An agent ag explicitly knows a fact φ in a global situation (σ,j) exactly if it implicitly knows φ, i.e., if φ is true in all global situations (σ',k) which it can not distinguish from (σ,j), *and* if it is aware of φ, i.e., φ ∈ *af*(ag).

Axiomatic basis *K'*

Let φ, φ_1, φ_2 be formulas, ag ∈ AG be an agent:

A31: $K'_{ag}\varphi \supset \varphi$ (knowledge axiom)

A32: $K'_{ag}(\varphi_1 \supset \varphi_2) \supset (K'_{ag}\varphi_1 \supset K'_{ag}\varphi_2)$ (consequence closure)

A33: $K'_{ag}\varphi \supset K'_{ag}K'_{ag}\varphi$ (positive introspection)

The properties of explicit knowledge depend on the view function v and the awareness function *af*. The knowledge axiom A31 holds for arbitrary awareness functions. Recall that *af* is static, i.e., the awareness of an agent is the same in all global situations, and that *af* is closed under subformulas and formation rules. Clearly, the latter restriction is sufficient to ensure the consequence closure axiom A32 and the positive introspection axiom A33. Additional constraints on *af* may exist within a given application, which could lead to stronger properties of explicit knowledge. Note that in general agents have no explicit individual knowledge of all tautologies, so they are not logically omniscient under this notion of knowledge.

6.3.4 Operators for individual awareness

The notion of explicit individual knowledge is based on the facts an agent is aware of. To model awareness, the awareness function *af* associating with each agent a set of formulas has been introduced (see Chapter 6.3.1). So far, we have assumed that *af* is static, and closed under subformulas and formation rules. However, in a given application, additional more specific constraints will be imposed on *af*. In a distributed system, for instance, the primitive propositions an agent is aware of could be defined to be those local to the agent, i.e., for all $p \in \Phi$, $p \in lp(ag)$ iff $p \in af(ag)$. Furthermore, the precise modeling of awareness will depend on the intentions of the system designer.

To formally specify individual awareness, the building block A is introduced. For each agent ag $\in$ AG, an operator A_{ag} is defined and interpreted as follows:

<u>Syntax A</u>

i) Let φ be a formula, ag $\in$ AG be an agent, then $A_{ag}\varphi$ is a formula.

<u>Semantics A</u>

Let φ be a formula, ag $\in$ AG be an agent, then

i) $\mathcal{M}_{LE'}(\sigma,i,j) \models A_{ag}\varphi$ iff $\varphi \in af(ag)$

ii) $\mathcal{M}_{BE'}(\pi,\sigma,i,j) \models A_{ag}\varphi$ iff $\varphi \in af(ag)$

With these operators for individual awareness, it is possible to state the relationship between implicit and explicit individual knowledge axiomatically. Let φ be a formula, $ag \in AG$ be an agent, then the following formula is valid:

$$K'_{ag}\varphi \equiv K_{ag}\varphi \wedge A_{ag}\varphi$$

It is obvious that under the above semantics, individual awareness is static. The assumption that it is closed under subformulas and formation rules can be captured (for awareness and propositional operators) as follows:

<u>Axiomatic basis *A*</u>

Let φ, φ_1, φ_2 be formulas, ag, ag' $\in$ AG be agents:

A34: $A_{ag}\neg\varphi \equiv A_{ag}\varphi$

A35: $A_{ag}(\varphi_1 \wedge \varphi_2) \equiv A_{ag}\varphi_1 \wedge A_{ag}\varphi_2$

A36: $A_{ag}A_{ag'}\varphi \equiv A_{ag}\varphi$

Further constraints on awareness in a given application can be specified analogously.

6.3.5 Operators for implicit group knowledge

When specifying and reasoning about distributed systems, it is often useful to refer to the knowledge of subsets of agents collectively and concisely. As discussed in Chapter 6.2.4, this idea has lead to the introduction of several notions of group knowledge. We take these notions in a more general form where it is possible to refer to arbitrary sets of agents, and redefine them in the semantical models of Chapter 6.3.1.

Let $G \subseteq AG$ be a non-empty set of agents. A global situation (σ',j') is called "*G-reachable*" from a global situation (σ,j) if there is some sequence $(\sigma_1,j_1),\ldots,(\sigma_n,j_n)$ of global situations such that $(\sigma,j) = (\sigma_1,j_1)$, $(\sigma',j') = (\sigma_n,j_n)$, and for all $k = 1,\ldots,n-1$, there is some $ag \in G$ such that $\nu(ag,\sigma_k,j_k) = \nu(ag,\sigma_{k+1},j_{k+1})$. The semantics of operators for group knowledge is given for models $\mathcal{M}_{LE}$. For models $\mathcal{M}_{BE}$, it can be defined analogously by replacing $\mathcal{M}_{LE}$ and (σ,i,j) by $\mathcal{M}_{BE}$ and (π,σ,i,j), respectively.

To refer to implicit group knowledge, the building block *G* is introduced. For each non-empty set $G \subseteq AG$ of agents, operators S_G, E_G, I_G, and C_G are defined and interpreted as follows:

Syntax G

i) Let φ be a formula, $G \subseteq AG$ be a non-empty set of agents, then $S_G\varphi$, $E_G\varphi$, $I_G\varphi$, and $C_G\varphi$ are formulas.

Semantics G

Let φ be a formula, $G \subseteq AG$ be a non-empty set of agents, then

i) $\mathcal{M}_{LE'}(\sigma,i,j) \models S_G\varphi$ iff $\exists ag \in G.\ \forall\sigma' \in \Sigma, k \geq 0.\ (\nu(ag,\sigma,j) = \nu(ag,\sigma',k)$ implies $\mathcal{M}_{LE'}(\sigma',0,k) \models \varphi)$

ii) $\mathcal{M}_{LE'}(\sigma,i,j) \models E_G\varphi$ iff $\forall ag \in G, \sigma' \in \Sigma, k \geq 0.\ (\nu(ag,\sigma,j) = \nu(ag,\sigma',k)$ implies $\mathcal{M}_{LE'}(\sigma',0,k) \models \varphi)$

iii) $\mathcal{M}_{LE'}(\sigma,i,j) \models I_G\varphi$ iff $\forall\sigma' \in \Sigma, k \geq 0.\ (\forall ag \in G.\ \nu(ag,\sigma,j) = \nu(ag,\sigma',k)$ implies $\mathcal{M}_{LE'}(\sigma',0,k) \models \varphi)$

iv) $\mathcal{M}_{LE'}(\sigma,i,j) \models C_G\varphi$ iff $\forall\sigma' \in \Sigma, k \geq 0.\ ((\sigma',k)$ is G-reachable from (σ,j) implies $\mathcal{M}_{LE'}(\sigma',0,k) \models \varphi)$

This means that $S_G\varphi$ holds in a global situation (σ,j) exactly if some agent $ag \in G$ has implicit individual knowledge of the fact φ in that situation ("*S_G-knowledge*" for short). $E_G\varphi$ is true exactly if every agent $ag \in G$ implicitly knows φ ("*E_G-knowledge*" for short). $I_G\varphi$ holds if by pooling the implicit knowledge of all agents $ag \in G$ together, φ can be deduced (referred to as "*combined knowledge in G*" or "*I_G-knowledge*"). Finally, $C_G\varphi$ means that every agent in G knows φ, and every agent in G knows that every agent in G knows φ, and so on (referred to as "*common knowledge in G*" or "*C_G-knowledge*").

For an arbitrary set G of agents, these notions of group knowledge form the hierarchy $C_G\varphi \supset E_G\varphi \supset S_G\varphi \supset I_G\varphi$, which in general is strict. For a singleton set G, all notions collapse into implicit individual knowledge. Extending the group of agents leads to an increase of S-knowledge and I-knowledge, i.e., for $G \subseteq G'$, $S_G\varphi$ and $I_G\varphi$ imply $S_{G'}\varphi$ and $I_{G'}\varphi$, respectively. However, it has a reciprocal effect on E-knowledge and C-knowledge, namely $E_{G'}\varphi$ and $C_{G'}\varphi$ imply $E_G\varphi$ and $C_G\varphi$, respectively. These and other properties of implicit group knowledge are captured by the following axioms and inference rules:

Axiomatic basis G

Let φ, φ_1, φ_2 be formulas, $G, G' \subseteq AG$ be non-empty sets of agents, where $G \subseteq G'$:

A37: $S_G\varphi \supset \varphi$ (knowledge axiom)

A38: $S_G\varphi \supset S_GS_G\varphi$ (positive introspection)
Tr7: $\vdash \varphi$ implies $\vdash S_G\varphi$ (epistemic necessitation)

A39: $E_G\varphi \supset \varphi$ (knowledge axiom)
A40: $E_G(\varphi_1 \supset \varphi_2) \supset (E_G\varphi_1 \supset E_G\varphi_2)$ (consequence closure)
Tr8: $\vdash \varphi$ implies $\vdash E_G\varphi$ (epistemic necessitation)

A41: $I_G\varphi \supset \varphi$ (knowledge axiom)
A42: $I_G(\varphi_1 \supset \varphi_2) \supset (I_G\varphi_1 \supset I_G\varphi_2)$ (consequence closure)
A43: $I_G\varphi \supset I_GI_G\varphi$ (positive introspection)
A44: $\neg I_G\varphi \supset I_G\neg I_G\varphi$ (negative introspection)
Tr9: $\vdash \varphi$ implies $\vdash I_G\varphi$ (epistemic necessitation)

A45: $C_G\varphi \supset \varphi$ (knowledge axiom)
A46: $C_G(\varphi_1 \supset \varphi_2) \supset (C_G\varphi_1 \supset C_G\varphi_2)$ (consequence closure)
A47: $C_G\varphi \supset C_GC_G\varphi$ (positive introspection)
A48: $\neg C_G\varphi \supset C_G\neg C_G\varphi$ (negative introspection)
Tr10: $\vdash \varphi$ implies $\vdash C_G\varphi$ (epistemic necessitation)

A49: $C_G\varphi \supset E_G\varphi$
A50: $E_G\varphi \supset S_G\varphi$
A51: $S_G\varphi \supset I_G\varphi$

A52: $S_G\varphi \supset S_{G'}\varphi$
A53: $E_{G'}\varphi \supset E_G\varphi$
A54: $I_G\varphi \supset I_{G'}\varphi$
A55: $C_{G'}\varphi \supset C_G\varphi$

Note that groups of agents are logically omniscient under E_G-knowledge, I_G-knowledge, and C_G-knowledge, but not under S_G-knowledge, because the consequence closure axiom does not hold in that case.

6.3.6 Operators for group awareness

A consequent and systematical extension of the epistemic operators so far is the inclusion of operators for group awareness. Following the notions of implicit group knowledge, corresponding notions of group awareness can be defined. In particular, we can state that somebody (everybody) in a group is aware of a fact, and that a group has combined awareness of a fact. To model individual awareness, the awareness function *af*, which is static and closed under subformulas and formation rules, has been introduced (see Chapter 6.3.1). *af* associates with each agent the set of formulas it is aware of. Based on *af*, it is also possible to formally define group awareness.

To refer to group awareness, the building block A_G is introduced. For each non-empty set $G \subseteq AG$ of agents, operators R_G, D_G, and H_G are defined and interpreted as follows:

Syntax A_G

i) Let φ be a formula, $G \subseteq AG$ be a non-empty set of agents, then $R_G\varphi$, $D_G\varphi$, and $H_G\varphi$ are formulas.

Semantics A_G

Let φ be a formula, $G \subseteq AG$ be a non-empty set of agents, and let *Cl* denote closure under formation rules, then

i) $\mathcal{M}_{LE}, (\sigma,i,j) \models R_G\varphi$ iff $\varphi \in \bigcup_{ag \in G} af(ag)$

ii) $\mathcal{M}_{LE}, (\sigma,i,j) \models D_G\varphi$ iff $\varphi \in \bigcap_{ag \in G} af(ag)$

iii) $\mathcal{M}_{LE}, (\sigma,i,j) \models H_G\varphi$ iff $\varphi \in Cl\,(\bigcup_{ag \in G} af(ag))$

This means that $R_G\varphi$ holds if some agent $ag \in AG$ is aware of the fact φ ("*R_G-awareness*" for short). $D_G\varphi$ is true if every agent $ag \in AG$ is aware of φ ("*D_G-awareness*" for short). Finally, $H_G\varphi$ holds if φ consists of subformulas φ' such that for each φ', some agent $ag \in AG$ is aware of φ' (referred to as "*combined awareness in G*" or "*H_G-awareness*").

Since the semantics of group awareness is defined in terms of individual awareness, its properties are determined by the awareness function *af*. If *af* is static and closed under subformulas for all agents $ag \in AG$, then $\bigcup_{ag \in G} af(ag)$, $\bigcap_{ag \in G} af(ag)$, and $Cl\,(\bigcup_{ag \in G} af(ag))$ also have these properties for all sets $G \subseteq AG$. If *af* is static and closed under formation rules for all agents $ag \in AG$, then so is $\bigcap_{ag \in G} af(ag)$. $Cl\,(\bigcup_{ag \in G} af(ag))$ has this property by definition.

For an arbitrary set G of agents, the notions of group awareness form the hierarchy $D_G\varphi \supset R_G\varphi \supset H_G\varphi$, which in general is strict. For a singleton set G, all notions collapse into individual awareness. Extending the group of agents leads to an increase of R-awareness and H-awareness, i.e. for $G \subseteq G'$, $R_G\varphi$ and $H_G\varphi$ imply $R_{G'}\varphi$ and $H_{G'}\varphi$, respectively. However, it leads to a decrease of D-awareness, i.e., $D_{G'}\varphi$ implies $D_G\varphi$. The properties of group awareness are captured by the following axioms:

Axiomatic basis A_G

Let φ, φ_1, φ_2 be formulas, G, G' $\subseteq$ AG be non-empty sets of agents, where $G \subseteq G'$:

A56: $R_G\neg\varphi \equiv R_G\varphi$

A57: $R_G(\varphi_1 \wedge \varphi_2) \supset R_G\varphi_1 \wedge R_G\varphi_2$

A58: $R_GR_{G'}\varphi \equiv R_G\varphi$

A59: $D_G\neg\varphi \equiv D_G\varphi$

A60: $D_G(\varphi_1 \wedge \varphi_2) \equiv D_G\varphi_1 \wedge D_G\varphi_2$

A61: $D_GD_{G'}\varphi \equiv D_G\varphi$

A62: $H_G\neg\varphi \equiv H_G\varphi$

A63: $H_G(\varphi_1 \wedge \varphi_2) \equiv H_G\varphi_1 \wedge H_G\varphi_2$

A64: $H_GH_{G'}\varphi \equiv H_G\varphi$

A65: $D_G\varphi \supset R_G\varphi$

A66: $R_G\varphi \supset H_G\varphi$

A67: $R_G\varphi \supset R_{G'}\varphi$

A68: $D_{G'}\varphi \supset D_G\varphi$

A69: $H_G\varphi \supset H_{G'}\varphi$

Further constraints on group awareness can be defined in the same way.

6.3.7 Operators for explicit group knowledge

Another systematical extension of the epistemic operators is the inclusion of operators for explicit group knowledge. As in the case of explicit individual knowledge, it should be possible to ascribe knowledge to the agents of a system that is invariant with respect to modifications of the environment. We have deliberately decided to introduce the explicit versions of S_G-knowledge, E_G-knowledge, and I_G-knowledge (see Chapter 6.3.5), since those are candidates to capture the knowledge ascribed to a distributed system as a whole. Explicit common knowledge is excluded here, however, it can be defined analogously.

To refer to explicit group knowledge, the building block *G'* is introduced. For each non-empty set $G \subseteq AG$ of agents, operators S'_G, E'_G, and I'_G are defined and interpreted as follows:

Syntax *G'*

i) Let φ be a formula, $G \subseteq AG$ be a non-empty set of agents, then $S'_G\varphi$, $E'_G\varphi$, and $I'_G\varphi$ are formulas.

Semantics *G'*

Let φ be a formula, $G \subseteq AG$ be a non-empty set of agents, and let *Cl* denote closure under formation rules, then

i) $\mathcal{M}_{LE'},(\sigma,i,j) \models S'_G\varphi$ iff $\exists ag \in G.\ (\varphi \in af(ag)$ and $\forall \sigma' \in \Sigma, k \geq 0.$
$(\nu(ag,\sigma,j) = \nu(ag,\sigma',k)$ implies $\mathcal{M}_{LE'},(\sigma',0,k) \models \varphi))$

ii) $\mathcal{M}_{LE'},(\sigma,i,j) \models E'_G\varphi$ iff $\forall ag \in G.\ (\varphi \in af(ag)$ and $\forall \sigma' \in \Sigma, k \geq 0.$
$(\nu(ag,\sigma,j) = \nu(ag,\sigma',k)$ implies $\mathcal{M}_{LE'},(\sigma',0,k) \models \varphi))$

iii) $\mathcal{M}_{LE'},(\sigma,i,j) \models I'_G\varphi$ iff $\varphi \in Cl(\bigcup_{ag \in G} af(ag))$ and $\forall \sigma' \in \Sigma, k \geq 0.$ $(\forall ag \in G.$
$\nu(ag,\sigma,j) = \nu(ag,\sigma',k)$ implies $\mathcal{M}_{LE'},(\sigma',0,k) \models \varphi)$

This means that $S'_G\varphi$ holds in a global situation (σ,j) exactly if some agent $ag \in AG$ has explicit individual knowledge of the fact φ in that situation ("S'_G-*knowledge*" for short). $E'_G\varphi$ is true exactly if every agent $ag \in AG$ explicitly knows φ ("E'_G-*knowledge*" for short). $I'_G\varphi$ holds if the agents in G have implicit combined knowledge *and* combined awareness of φ ("I'_G-*knowledge*" for short).

From these definitions, it follows immediately that there is the following relationship between implicit and explicit group knowledge and group awareness:

$$S'_G\varphi \supset S_G\varphi \wedge R_G\varphi$$
$$E'_G\varphi \equiv E_G\varphi \wedge D_G\varphi$$
$$I'_G\varphi \equiv I_G\varphi \wedge H_G\varphi$$

For an arbitrary set G of agents, the notions of explicit group knowledge form the hierarchy $E'_G\varphi \supset S'_G\varphi \supset I'_G\varphi$. For a singleton set G, they collapse into explicit individual knowledge. Extending the group of agents leads to an increase of S'_G-

knowledge and I'_G-knowledge, and to a decrease of E'_G-knowledge. These and other properties are captured by the following axioms:

<u>Axiomatic basis G'</u>

Let φ, φ_1, φ_2 be formulas, G, G' $\subseteq$ AG be non-empty sets of agents, where G $\subseteq$ G':

A70: $S'_G\varphi \supset \varphi$ (knowledge axiom)

A71: $S'_G\varphi \supset S'_GS'_G\varphi$ (positive introspection)

A72: $E'_G\varphi \supset \varphi$ (knowledge axiom)

A73: $E'_G(\varphi_1 \supset \varphi_2) \supset (E'_G\varphi_1 \supset E'_G\varphi_2)$ (consequence closure)

A74: $I'_G\varphi \supset \varphi$ (knowledge axiom)

A75: $I'_G(\varphi_1 \supset \varphi_2) \supset (I'_G\varphi_1 \supset I'_G\varphi_2)$ (consequence closure)

A76: $I'_G\varphi \supset I'_GI'_G\varphi$ (positive introspection)

A77: $E'_G\varphi \supset S'_G\varphi$

A78: $S'_G\varphi \supset I'_G\varphi$

A79: $S'_G\varphi \supset S'_{G'}\varphi$

A80: $E'_{G'}\varphi \supset E'_G\varphi$

A81: $I'_G\varphi \supset I'_{G'}\varphi$

Note that in general, groups of agents have no explicit knowledge of all tautologies, since the rules of epistemic necessitation do not hold. Therefore, they are not logically omniscient, whatever notion of explicit group knowledge is used.

6.3.8 Customizing temporal epistemic logics

In the previous chapters, several building blocks, each consisting of a group of epistemic operators, have been introduced. Together with the modular temporal logic from Chapter 3.3, they form a modular temporal epistemic logic. For a given problem, a subset of these building blocks can be selected and combined, i.e., the formation rules, semantics, and axiomatic bases are joined together, in order to customize the appropriate temporal epistemic logic. Apart from the restrictions listed in Chapter 3.3.7, no further constraints apply to the combination of building blocks.

The heuristics for the selection of building blocks given in Chapter 3.3.7 can be extended as follows:

- select K to specify constraints on the view function;
- select A to specify constraints on the awareness function;
- select K' to specify individual knowledge that is independent of the environment;
- select G to specify group knowledge, and to reason about distributed systems;
- select A_G to specify group awareness, and to reason about distributed systems;
- select G' to specify group knowledge that is independent of the environment, and to reason about distributed systems.

To specify and reason about the mutual exclusion problem, a logic consisting of At_P, Pr, F_L, K, K', and A will be used in Chapter 7. Furthermore, logics consisting of At_P, Pr, F_L, K, K', A, G, G', A_G and At_F, Pr, F_L, E_P, E_F, K, K', A, G, G', A_G will be applied to a drink server.

6.3.9 Some remarks on conformance

In Chapter 3.3.9, we have introduced a notion of conformance based on the representation of formulas via the function rep. For the verification of the communication service, where purely temporal concepts have been used, the definition of rep has been obvious (see Chapter 5.3.7). However, it is not clear how epistemic concepts such as knowledge and awareness should be represented[44]. In particular, how should $rep(K_{ag}\varphi)$, $rep(K'_{ag}\varphi)$, and $rep(A_{ag}\varphi)$ be defined?

Recall that when moving to a lower level of abstraction, a single agent is refined into a set of agents and interaction points. This includes as a special case that an agent may be refined into a single agent, i.e., part of the higher level system architecture may be kept on the lower level. If an agent ag is refined into ag', then intuitively, there must be a direct correspondance between the knowledge and the awareness of ag and ag'. More specifically, whenever ag knows a fact φ, then ag' must know $rep(\varphi)$, and if ag is aware of φ, the ag' must be aware of $rep(\varphi)$. We can capture this correspondance by defining $rep(K_{ag}\varphi) =_{Df} K_{ag'}\, rep(\varphi)$, $rep(K'_{ag}\varphi) =_{Df} K'_{ag'}\, rep(\varphi)$, and $rep(A_{ag}\varphi) =_{Df} A_{ag'}\, rep(\varphi)$.

44 Note that we address here the representation of higher level epistemic formulas by epistemic formulas on a lower level of abstraction. We do not refer to knowledge representation in the sense of encoding knowledge in data objects.

In the general case where an agent is refined into a set of agents and interaction points, the knowledge and awareness of that agent can be represented by some form of group knowledge and group awareness. Possible candidates have been introduced in Chapters 6.3.5, 6.3.6, and 6.3.7. Since for a singleton set, all the group notions collapse into the corresponding individual notion, each choice is in accordance with the previous definition of rep in the special case. However, a closer look reveals at least two other important criteria resulting in fewer options.

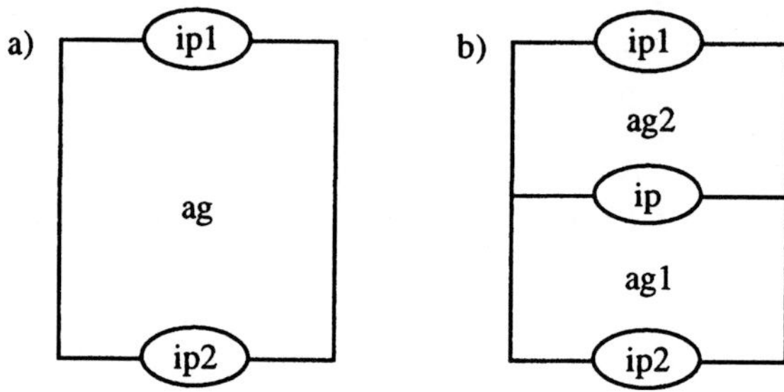

Figure 6.2: System architectures

Consider, for instance, a system with the system architecture shown in Figure 6.2a. Agent ag accepts and offers interactions at ip1 and ip2, respectively, such that the number of offers never exceeds the number of acceptances. From ag's point of view, these are local facts, therefore, we assume that ag knows them explicitly. Now consider the system architecture in Figure 6.2b, where ag is refined into ag1, ag2, and ip. Here, the acceptance of an interaction at ip1 is local to ag1, but not to ag2. Also, offers at ip2 are local to ag2, but not to ag1. And the fact that the number of offers never exceeds the number of acceptances is neither local to ag1 nor to ag2. If we assume that ag1 and ag2 have explicit knowledge of local facts, what notions of group knowledge (awareness) are appropriate to make sure that whenever ag knows (is aware of) some fact φ, then ag1 and ag2 together know (are aware of) rep(φ)?

To begin with, consider implicit individual knowledge of ag as related to implicit group knowledge of G = {ag1,ag2}. Under the previous assumptions, E_G-knowledge and C_G-knowledge are ruled out, since offers and acceptances of interactions are known by ag, but not by ag1 *and* ag2. Furthermore, there are facts that are local to ag, but not to ag1 or ag2, which rules out S_G-knowledge. The remaining candidate is implicit combined knowledge under which the facts in the previous example are implicitly known in G whenever they are known by ag. Similar arguments lead to the selection of combined awareness and explicit combined knowledge in order to represent individual awareness and explicit individual knowledge. This can be captured by defining $rep(K_{ag}\varphi) =_{Df} I_G\, rep(\varphi)$, $rep(K'_{ag}\varphi) =_{Df} I'_G\, rep(\varphi)$, and $rep(A_{ag}\varphi) =_{Df} H_G\, rep(\varphi)$.

Another important criterion for the representation of knowledge and awareness is that if a formula is provable on the higher level of abstraction, its representation has to be provable on the lower level of abstraction, i.e., $\vdash \varphi$ implies $\vdash rep(\varphi)$. Only then are properties of the higher level respected on the lower level of abstraction. With respect to epistemic concepts, this means that the notions of group knowledge and group awareness must have the same or stronger properties than the notions of individual knowledge and individual awareness they represent. This rules out, for instance, E_G-knowledge, which does not satisfy the introspection axioms, and S_G-knowledge, because the axiom of consequence closure does not hold. Under this criterion, we obtain the same representations as before.

The previous ideas can be generalized to arbitrary architectures. Let $\mathcal{RS} = \langle \mathcal{Arch}, \mathcal{Behav} \rangle$ and $\mathcal{RS}' = \langle \mathcal{Arch}', \mathcal{Behav}' \rangle$ be requirement specifications such that $\mathcal{Arch}'$ *refines* $\mathcal{Arch}$. Then there exists a refinement function ref: $AG \cup IP \rightarrow 2^{AG' \cup IP'}$ as defined in Chapter 2.3. By ref, the agents of $\mathcal{RS}$ are refined into disjoint sets of agents and interactions points of $\mathcal{RS}'$, which leads to the following representations:

$$rep(K_{ag}\,\varphi) =_{Df} I_G\, rep(\varphi) \text{ for all } ag \in AG, \text{ where } G = ref(ag) \setminus IP$$
$$rep(K'_{ag}\,\varphi) =_{Df} I'_G\, rep(\varphi) \text{ for all } ag \in AG, \text{ where } G = ref(ag) \setminus IP$$
$$rep(A_{ag}\,\varphi) =_{Df} H_G\, rep(\varphi) \text{ for all } ag \in AG, \text{ where } G = ref(ag) \setminus IP$$

7 Applying temporal epistemic logics to open distributed systems

To illustrate how temporal epistemic logics can be applied to specifying and reasoning about open distributed systems, a number of small examples will be presented and discussed. The purpose here is to outline some of the principles and ideas, which can then be applied to problems of practical interest.

7.1 Example "mutual exclusion"

To begin with, we reconsider the well-known mutual exclusion problem for a finite set of agents (for instance, see [ClEmSi86]). To specify this problem, a logic consisting of the building blocks At_P, Pr, F_L, K, K', and A is used, formulas are interpreted in a model $\mathcal{M}_{PLE}$ (see Definition 6.1). We partially constrain the set of correct solutions by considering only models where $AG = \{ag_1,...,ag_m\}$, $\Phi = \bigcup_{i\in\{1,...,m\}} \{N_i,T_i,C_i\}$, and $lp(ag_i) = \{N_i,T_i,C_i\}$ for $1 \leq i \leq m$. As explained in Chapter 3.3.1, these aspects can be modeled in $\mathcal{M}_{PLE}$, but they can not be expressed by propositional formulas. The following informal interpretation is associated with the primitive propositions in Φ:

N_i :	agent ag_i is in the non-critical region
T_i :	agent ag_i is in the trying region
C_i :	agent ag_i is in the critical region

For a system of two agents ($m = 2$), any correct solution of the mutual exclusion problem must satisfy the following properties:

ME1.	$\neg \Diamond (C_1 \wedge C_2)$	mutual exclusion
ME2a.	$\Box (T_1 \supset \Diamond C_1)$	absence of starvation for ag_1
ME2b.	$\Box (T_2 \supset \Diamond C_2)$	absence of starvation for ag_2

7.1.1 Implicit knowledge

Based on this specification, we can reason about the system and analyze what the agents know implicitly and explicitly. First of all, we observe that no reference to knowledge is made in the specification, in particular, there is no property stating what agents are supposed to know. Consequently, any model $\mathcal{M}_{PLE}$ whose state sequences initially-satisfy ME1, ME2a, and ME2b, is acceptable, no matter how the view function and the awareness function are defined. This means that if ag_1, for instance, is in some state where the primitive proposition C_1 is true, it is well possible that ag_1 neither implicitly knows C_1 nor is it aware of C_1, although C_1 is a local proposition of ag_1 according to lp.

Although no properties describing the agents' knowledge are contained in the specification, there is still quite a bit of knowledge ascribed to each agent. From the semantics of implicit individual knowledge, it follows that if a formula φ is valid in a model $\mathcal{M}_{PLE}$, then so is $K_{ag}\varphi$:

K-GEN. $\mathcal{M}_{PLE} \models \varphi$ implies $\mathcal{M}_{PLE} \models K_{ag}\varphi$
K-GEN$_i$. $\mathcal{M}_{PLE} \models_i \Box\, \varphi$ implies $\mathcal{M}_{PLE} \models_i \Box\, K_{ag}\varphi$

This means that not only are all tautologies implicitly known by each agent under any given view function, as expressed by the rule of generalization (Tr6, Chapter 6.3.2); also, all invariant properties of the model are implicit individual knowledge. Since ME1, ME2a, and ME2b are invariant[45] and must hold for all correct solutions of the mutual exclusion problem, they are implicitly known by ag_1 and ag_2. Moreover, other invariant properties that can be derived, such as $\Box\,(C_1 \supset \neg\, C_2)$ and $\Box\,(T_1 \wedge T_2 \supset \Diamond\, C_1 \wedge \Diamond\, C_2)$, are known by both agents. As reported in [HaMo87], all invariant properties of the model are even implicit *common* knowledge of all agents, i.e. $\mathcal{M}_{PLE} \models \varphi$ implies $\mathcal{M}_{PLE} \models C_{AG}\varphi$, regardless of the view function. The basic way how common knowledge is acquired here is by membership in a community (see [ClMa81]), which consists of the set AG of agents.

Another consequence of the semantics of implicit individual knowledge is that if a formula $\varphi_1 \supset \varphi_2$ is valid in a model $\mathcal{M}_{PLE}$, then so is $K_{ag}\varphi_1 \supset K_{ag}\varphi_2$:

K-GEN'. $\mathcal{M}_{PLE} \models \varphi_1 \supset \varphi_2$ implies $\mathcal{M}_{PLE} \models K_{ag}\varphi_1 \supset K_{ag}\varphi_2$
K-GEN'$_i$. $\mathcal{M}_{PLE} \models_i \Box\,(\varphi_1 \supset \varphi_2)$ implies $\mathcal{M}_{PLE} \models_i \Box\,(K_{ag}\varphi_1 \supset K_{ag}\varphi_2)$

Note that this is different from $(\varphi_1 \supset \varphi_2) \supset (K_{ag}\varphi_1 \supset K_{ag}\varphi_2)$, which is not valid in $\mathcal{M}_{PLE}$. From K-GEN'$_i$ and the specification of the mutual exclusion problem, the following properties can be derived no matter how the view function is defined:

45 Invariance can be expressed by the prefixed "henceforth" operator. Note that ME1 is equivalent to $\Box\,\neg\,(C_1 \wedge C_2)$.

$$\Box (K_1 C_1 \supset K_1 \neg C_2)$$
$$\Box (K_1 T_1 \supset K_1 \Diamond C_1)$$
$$\Box (K_1 (T_1 \wedge T_2) \supset K_1 (\Diamond C_1 \wedge \Diamond C_2))$$

However, the following properties can not be derived from ME1, ME2a, and ME2b:

$$\Box (C_1 \supset K_1 C_1)$$
$$\Box (C_1 \supset K_1 \neg C_2)$$

This means that even if ag_1 is in some state where C_1 is true, it is possible that it does not know C_1 or $\neg C_2$. Intuitively, an agent should have knowledge about its local state. In the mutual exclusion example, for instance, each agent should know whether or not it is in the non-critical region, the trying region, or the critical region. We can formally specify that by adding the following properties to our specification:

ME3a. $\Box ((p \supset K_1 p) \wedge (\neg p \supset K_1 \neg p))$ for all $p \in lp(ag_1)$
ME3b. $\Box ((p \supset K_2 p) \wedge (\neg p \supset K_2 \neg p))$ for all $p \in lp(ag_2)$

ME3a and ME3b state what ag_1 and ag_2 are supposed to know, which constrains the set of models to those with a suitable view function. In particular, models where $p \wedge \neg K_i p$ or $\neg p \wedge \neg K_i \neg p$ can be satisfied although p is local to ag_i are excluded from the set of correct solutions. With ME3a and ME3b, it is possible to show

$$\Box (C_1 \supset K_1 \neg C_2)$$
$$\Box (T_1 \supset K_1 \Diamond C_1)$$
$$\Box (T_1 \supset K_1 \Diamond \neg C_2)$$

However, it is not possible to derive $\Box (C_2 \supset K_1 C_2)$ and $\Box (T_1 \wedge T_2 \supset K_1 \Diamond C_2)$, since this would require that ag_1 has knowledge about the local state of ag_2.

7.1.2 Knowledge-oriented specification

Starting point for the discussion of the agents' knowledge were the properties ME1, ME2a, and ME2b. It has been pointed out that they make no reference to knowledge. An alternative and, as we believe, more natural approach is to specify the mutual exclusion problem from a knowledge-oriented point of view. We can then directly define that each agent implicitly knows about the mutual exclusion, i.e., if it is in the critical region, it *knows* that the other agent is not. Also, we can state that if an agent is in the trying region, it *knows* that it will eventually enter the critical region, which tells the agent how to get there. Formally, these properties can be expressed as follows:

ME1a'. $\Box (C_1 \supset K_1 \neg C_2)$
ME1b'. $\Box (C_2 \supset K_2 \neg C_1)$
ME2a'. $\Box (T_1 \supset K_1 \Diamond C_1)$
ME2b'. $\Box (T_2 \supset K_2 \Diamond C_2)$

Note that the first specification of the mutual exclusion problem is logically implied by these properties; the converse, however, is not true, so this specification is strictly stronger. If we add the properties ME3a and ME3b to both versions, they become equivalent.

We believe that the knowledge-oriented specification of the mutual exclusion problem is preferable, because it serves a better understanding and provides more insight. In particular, we can conclude from the formal description that some cooperation between ag_1 and ag_2, possibly with the support of a mediating agent, is necessary to achieve the specified knowledge goals. But it is not determined how that knowledge will be acquired, which, of course, is a matter of implementation.

7.1.3 Explicit knowledge

Implicit knowledge is a useful notion for the designer to reason about distributed systems. It helps to express distribution aspects in the specification and to argue what knowledge agents can *in principle* acquire about the local states and the knowledge of the other agents. While this is useful and necessary during the design verification, it will in general not be required to represent implicit knowledge in the implementation. In fact, both agents in our example will behave well without explicitly knowing about the existence of the other agent. More generally, if we add further agents to the system, this should not change the knowledge of the already existing agents. This idea can be modeled by imposing constraints on the awareness function, and by using explicit instead of implicit individual knowledge.

Constraints on the awareness function can be specified syntactically. We can express that each agent is aware precisely of its local propositions by adding the following properties:

ME4a. A_1p for all $p \in lp(ag_1)$
ME4b. A_2p for all $p \in lp(ag_2)$
ME5a. $\neg A_1p$ for all $p \in \Phi \setminus lp(ag_1)$
ME5b. $\neg A_2p$ for all $p \in \Phi \setminus lp(ag_2)$

Recall that awareness is static, i.e., $A_ip \supset \Box A_ip$. Moreover, awareness is closed under formation rules and subformulas, which can be captured axiomatically:

ME6a. $A_i\varphi \equiv A_i\neg\varphi$
ME6b. $A_i\varphi_1 \wedge A_i\varphi_2 \equiv A_i(\varphi_1 \wedge \varphi_2)$
ME6c. $A_i\varphi \equiv A_i\Box\varphi$
ME6d. $A_i\varphi \equiv A_i\Diamond\varphi$
ME6e. $A_i\varphi \equiv A_iA_j\varphi$
ME6f. $A_i\varphi \equiv A_iK_j\varphi$
ME6g. $A_i\varphi \equiv A_iK'_j\varphi$

Stated otherwise, awareness of an agent is generated by the set of its local primitive propositions, i.e., $A_i\varphi$ if and only if φ contains only primitive propositions local to ag_i. It follows that ag_1 is aware of ME2a', but not of ME1a', ME1b', and ME2b'. Since ME2a' is implicit knowledge of ag_1, it is therefore also explicit knowledge: $K'_1 \Box (T_1 \supset K_1 \Diamond C_1)$. Since ag_1 is aware of $\Diamond C_1$, it can be concluded that $\Box(T_1 \supset K'_1 \Diamond C_1)$ holds; $\Box (C_1 \supset K'_1 \neg C_2)$ is not true, because ag_1 is not aware of C_2.

It is possible to tune the notion of awareness in order to capture a variety of conceptions (see [FaHa88]). For instance, we could add the properties A_1C_2 and A_2C_1, meaning that an agent is aware of the fact that the other agent could also be in the critical region. This does *not* imply that ag_1 knows when ag_2 is in the critical region, or vice versa, because knowledge depends on the view function. But as a consequence, ME1a' and ME1b' become explicit knowledge to both agents, and $\Box (C_1 \supset K'_1 \neg C_2)$ and $\Box (C_2 \supset K'_2 \neg C_1)$ hold. So whenever ag_1 is in the critical region, it explicitly knows that ag_2 is not, and vice versa. This means that from its local state, each agent can draw some conclusions about the state of the other agent.

7.2 Example "drink server"

A drink server[46] DS takes orders for tea and coffee from customers at interaction point ip1. For each tea order, one cup of tea is served at ip2. For each coffee order, one cup of coffee is served at ip3. The system architecture of DS is shown in Figure 7.1. Its internal structure is not revealed. Note that DS is an open system, therefore, it has external interaction points. DS can later be embedded into an environment, for instance, a self-service restaurant or a faculty club.

Drink servers often work in rounds, i.e., when a drink is ordered, it is served before the next drink can be ordered. More sophisticated drink servers might be able to take new orders while still serving drinks. Such concurrent behaviour should not be excluded.

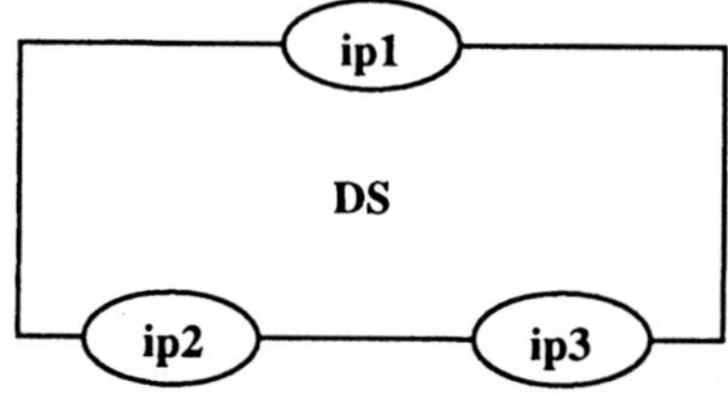

Figure 7.1: Conceptual system architecture of a drink server

When the behaviour of DS is specified, no assumptions about the environment are to be made. This means that only the *readiness* of DS to take orders and to serve drinks can be described. Whether orders will be taken when DS is placed into some environment depends on whether they are actually given, and whether drinks will actually be served depends on the readiness of the environment to accept them. We abstract from limitations of resources, i.e., tea and coffee are always available, and from failures.

7.2.1 Specification based on propositional logic

To specify the drink server, a logic consisting of the building blocks At_P, Pr, F_L, K, K', and A is used, formulas are interpreted in a model $\mathcal{M}_{PLE}$ (see Definition 6.1). The drink

[46] A preliminary version of the drink server has been presented in Chapters 3.3.7 through 3.3.9.

server is described as a single agent, i.e., AG = {DS}. The set $\Phi = \Phi_{DS}$ consists of the following primitive propositions:

tea_order:	one or more unsatisfied orders for tea
coffee_order:	one or more unsatisfied orders for coffee
ready_to_take_order:	DS is ready to take an order at ip1
ready_to_serve_tea:	DS is ready to serve tea at ip2
ready_to_serve_coffee:	DS is ready to serve coffee at ip3

All primitive propositions are local to DS, i.e., lp(DS) = Φ. The desired behaviour of DS can be captured by the following properties:

DS1. $\Box \Diamond$ ready_to_take_order

DS2. $\Box$ (K'_{DS} tea_order $\supset \Diamond$ ready_to_serve_tea)

DS3. $\Box$ ($\neg K'_{DS}$ tea_order $\supset \neg$ ready_to_serve_tea)

DS4. $\Box$ (K'_{DS} coffee_order $\supset \Diamond$ ready_to_serve_coffee)

DS5. $\Box$ ($\neg K'_{DS}$ coffee_order $\supset \neg$ ready_to_serve_coffee)

Table 7.1: Specification of DS

Property DS1 expresses that DS is ready to take an order at ip1 from time to time. DS2 states that if DS explicitly knows that there is an unsatisfied tea order, it will eventually be ready to serve tea at ip2. DS3 covers the complementary situations where DS does not explicitly know about unsatisfied tea orders: in these situations, it is required that DS is not ready to serve tea. DS4 and DS5 state analogous behaviour in case of coffee orders.

It is worthwhile having a closer look at the specification of DS, because it illustrates some principles of knowledge-oriented specification. First of all, we consider the liveness properties DS2 and DS4. They follow the pattern that if the agent DS explicitly knows that a certain condition holds, it guarantees that a certain *local* behaviour occurs or will eventually occur. Stated otherwise, *explicit knowledge can trigger local activities.*

The fact that the primitive propositions in DS2 and DS4 are local to DS can not be expressed in the specification itself. The reason is that atomic formulas can not be decomposed in the framework of propositional logic, and therefore, locality can not be *specified.* However, it has been *modeled* by the function lp.

The properties DS2 and DS4 can be understood as a commitment for DS. If DS acquires the specified knowledge, it is committed to perform certain activities. It is important in our example that these activities are entirely under the control of DS, because no assumptions have been made about the environment. In the general case, an agent could be committed to non-local activities, which also requires that it can control them to some degree.

The liveness property DS1 can be reformulated as $\Box (K'_{DS}$ true $\supset \Diamond$ ready_to_take_order$)$, which follows the same pattern as DS2 and DS4. The difference here is that DS is committed to exhibit a certain local behaviour under any condition, i.e., no particular explicit knowledge is required to trigger this kind of local activity.

The safety properties DS3 and DS5 follow the pattern that if DS does *not* explicitly know that a certain condition holds, it guarantees that a certain *local* behaviour is currently *not* displayed. In other words, *lack of explicit knowledge can inhibit local activities.*

DS6. $\Box ((p \supset K_{DS}p) \wedge (\neg p \supset K_{DS}\neg p))$ for all $p \in lp(DS)$

DS7. $A_{DS}p$ for all $p \in lp(DS)$

Table 7.2: Specification of DS (continued)

The specification in Table 7.1 can be satisfied for arbitrary view functions and awareness functions. In particular, in a model where DS never knows whether tea or coffee have been ordered, it will not serve any drinks. To exclude such undesired solutions, the specification of the drink server can be supplemented as shown in Table 7.2. Property DS6 expresses that DS has implicit knowledge of its local situation. To correctly implement this requirement, an appropriate aggregation of DS's local history will have to be recorded. From this aggregation, which could, for instance, be encoded in a local state component, a view function satisfying DS6 has to be derived. Property DS7 determines the awareness of DS.

7.2.2 Refinement

In the following design step, the internal architecture of the agent DS is revealed. According to the rules of architectural refinement (see Chapter 2), DS is decomposed into a waiter W, a tea girl TG, a coffee boy CB, and internal interaction points ip4 and ip5 (see Figure 7.2). The behaviour of these agents shall be defined such that it conforms to the already specified behaviour of DS.

Informally, the waiter takes orders for tea and coffee from customers at interaction point ip1. If tea is ordered, the waiter asks the tea girl at ip4 to serve tea. If coffee is ordered, the waiter asks the coffee boy to serve coffee. When asked to serve tea, the tea girl serves tea at ip2. When asked to serve coffee, the coffee boy serves coffee at ip3.

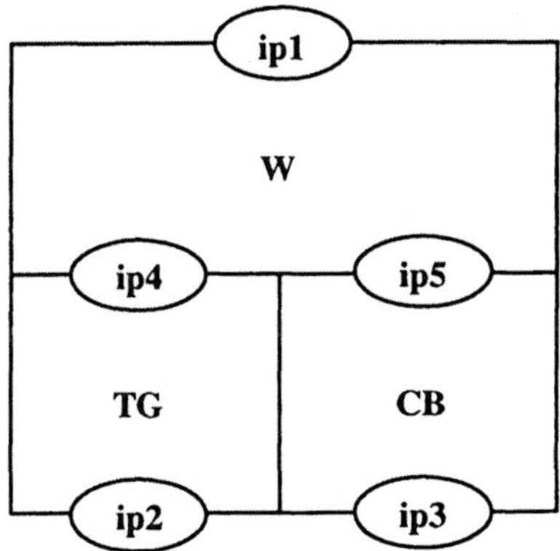

Figure 7.2: Refined system architecture of the drink server

To specify the waiter, the tea girl, and the coffee boy, a logic consisting of the building blocks At_P, Pr, F_L, K, K', and A is used. Additionally, we select G, G', and A_G, which will be needed for verification purposes (see Chapter 7.2.3). Formulas are interpreted in a model $\mathcal{M}_{PLE}$ with AG = {W,TG,CB}, $\Phi = \Phi_W \cup \Phi_{TG} \cup \Phi_{CB}$, and $\mathrm{lp}(W) = \Phi_W$,

$lp(TG) = \Phi_{TG}$, $lp(CB) = \Phi_{CB}$. The set Φ_W consists of the following primitive propositions, the desired behaviour of W is captured by the properties in Table 7.3:

tea_to_request:	one or more orders for tea to be passed on
coffee_to_request:	one or more orders for coffee to be passed on
ready_to_take_order:	W is ready to take an order at ip1
ready_to_request_tea:	W is ready to ask for tea at ip4
ready_to_request_coffee:	W is ready to ask for coffee at ip5

W1. $\Box \Diamond$ ready_to_take_order

W2. $\Box (K'_W$ tea_to_request $\supset \Diamond$ ready_to_request_tea$)$

W3. $\Box (\neg K'_W$ tea_to_request $\supset \neg$ ready_to_request_tea$)$

W4. $\Box (K'_W$ coffee_to_request $\supset \Diamond$ ready_to_request_coffee$)$

W5. $\Box (\neg K'_W$ coffee_to_request $\supset \neg$ ready_to_request_coffee$)$

W6. $\Box ((p \supset K_W p) \wedge (\neg p \supset K_W \neg p))$ for all $p \in lp(W)$

W7. $A_W p$ for all $p \in lp(W)$

W8. $\neg A_W p$ for all $p \in \Phi \setminus lp(W)$

Table 7.3: Specification of W

The set Φ_{TG} consists of the following primitive propositions, the specification of TG is listed in Table 7.4:

tea_to_serve:	one or more unsatisfied requests for tea
ready_to_take_tea_request:	TG is ready to take a tea request at ip4
ready_to_serve_tea:	TG is ready to serve tea at ip2

TG1. $\Box \Diamond$ ready_to_take_tea_request

TG2. $\Box (K'_{TG}$ tea_to_serve $\supset \Diamond$ ready_to_serve_tea)

TG3. $\Box (\neg K'_{TG}$ tea_to_serve $\supset \neg$ ready_to_serve_tea)

TG4. $\Box ((p \supset K_{TG}p) \wedge (\neg p \supset K_{TG}\neg p))$ for all $p \in lp(TG)$

TG5. $A_{TG}p$ for all $p \in lp(TG)$

TG6. $\neg A_{TG}p$ for all $p \in \Phi \setminus lp(TG)$

Table 7.4: Specification of TG

The set Φ_{CB} consists of the following primitive propositions, the specification of CB is listed in Table 7.5:

coffee_to_serve:	one or more unsatisfied requests for coffee
ready_to_take_coffee_request:	CB is ready to take a coffee request at ip5
ready_to_serve_coffee:	CB is ready to serve coffee at ip3

CB1. $\Box \Diamond$ ready_to_take_coffee_request

CB2. $\Box (K'_{CB}$ coffee_to_serve $\supset \Diamond$ ready_to_serve_coffee)

CB3. $\Box (\neg K'_{CB}$ coffee_to_serve $\supset \neg$ ready_to_serve_coffee)

CB4. $\Box ((p \supset K_{CB}p) \wedge (\neg p \supset K_{CB}\neg p))$ for all $p \in lp(CB)$

CB5. $A_{CB}p$ for all $p \in lp(CB)$

CB6. $\neg A_{CB}p$ for all $p \in \Phi \setminus lp(CB)$

Table 7.5: Specification of CB

The specifications of W, TG, and CB are very similar to the specification of DS which has been explained in detail in Chapter 7.2.1.

7.2.3 Verification of the drink server refinement

To formally verify that the refinement of the drink server conforms to the specification of DS, we have to establish a formal relationship between both descriptions and to prove that the description of the refinement logically implies the specification of DS. More precisely, the verification has to show that the requirement specification $\mathcal{RS}' = \langle \mathcal{Arch}', \mathcal{Behav}' \rangle$ with $\mathcal{Arch}' = \langle AG' \rangle$, where $AG' = \{W, TG, CB\}$, and $\mathcal{Behav}' = \bigwedge_{ag \in AG'} \mathcal{Behav}'_{ag}$ conforms to the requirement specification $\mathcal{RS} = \langle \mathcal{Arch}, \mathcal{Behav} \rangle$ with $\mathcal{Arch} = \langle AG \rangle$, where $AG = \{DS\}$, and $\mathcal{Behav} = \bigwedge_{ag \in AG} \mathcal{Behav}_{ag}$, under a representation function rep. With $\mathcal{Behav}_{DS} = \bigwedge_{1 \le i \le 7} DSi$, $\mathcal{Behav}'_{W} = \bigwedge_{1 \le i \le 8} Wi$, $\mathcal{Behav}'_{TG} = \bigwedge_{1 \le i \le 6} TGi$, and $\mathcal{Behav}'_{CB} = \bigwedge_{1 \le i \le 6} CBi$, it must be shown that $\mathcal{RS}'$ $conforms_{rep}$ $\mathcal{RS}$.

As explained in Chapter 3.3.9, conformance addresses both architectural and behavioural aspects. In particular, if $\mathcal{RS}'$ $conforms_{rep}$ $\mathcal{RS}$ is to be shown, then $\mathcal{Arch}'$ *refines* $\mathcal{Arch}$ (see Definition 2.3) must hold, which is the case for the refinement function ref: $AG \rightarrow 2^{AG'}$ with ref(DS) = {W,TG,CB}. To prove $\models_i \mathcal{Behav}' \supset rep(\mathcal{Behav})$, we define a representation function rep by mapping formulas of the more abstract description level to corresponding formulas of the lower level:

rep (tea_order)	=	tea_to_request ∨ tea_to_serve
rep (coffee_order)	=	coffee_to_request ∨ coffee_to_serve
rep (ready_to_take_order)	=	ready_to_take_order
rep (ready_to_serve_tea)	=	ready_to_serve_tea
rep (ready_to_serve_coffee)	=	ready_to_serve_coffee
rep ($\neg\varphi$)	=	$\neg$ rep (φ)
rep ($\varphi_1 \wedge \varphi_2$)	=	rep (φ_1) $\wedge$ rep (φ_2)
rep ($\Box\, \varphi$)	=	$\Box$ rep (φ)
rep ($K_{DS}\varphi$)	=	$I_{\{W,TG,CB\}}$ rep(φ)
rep ($K'_{DS}\varphi$)	=	$I'_{\{W,TG,CB\}}$ rep(φ)
rep ($A_{DS}\varphi$)	=	$H_{\{W,TG,CB\}}$ rep(φ)

Table 7.6: The representation function rep

Each primitive proposition of Φ_{DS} is mapped to a formula of the lower level description. The representations of individual knowledge and individual awareness are defined in accordance with the restrictions explained in Chapter 6.3.9.

I1.	$\Box$ (ready_to_request_tea $\wedge$ $\Diamond$ ready_to_take_tea_request $\supset$ $\Diamond$ tea_to_serve)
I2.	$\Box$ (ready_to_request_coffee $\wedge$ $\Diamond$ ready_to_take_coffee_request $\supset$ $\Diamond$ coffee_to_serve)

Table 7.7: Interaction properties

It turns out that to conduct a formal proof of $\models_i \mathcal{Behav}' \supset \text{rep}(\mathcal{Behav})$, further assumptions are necessary. The reason is that in order to exhibit the behaviour of the drink server, the agents W, TG, and CB have to interact. The properties of these interactions are listed in Table 7.7 and are in fact rather obvious. Together with I1 and I2, conformance between $\mathcal{RS}'$ and $\mathcal{RS}$ is straightforward to prove.

7.2.4 Specification based on first-order logic

In Chapter 7.2.1, the drink server has been specified in a temporal epistemic logic which was based on propositional logic. To model the system architecture, the set of agents has been defined to consist of the drink server. To specify the system behaviour, a number of primitive propositions have been introduced, and several properties characterizing the legal behaviour have been stated. We believe that the outcome is easily understood, and that it can serve as a first formalization of the problem. Nevertheless, several aspects deserving improvement can be identified.

First of all, there is a discrepancy between the system architecture shown in Figure 7.1 and the architecture being actually formalized. While the former introduces agents and interaction points, the latter is restricted to agents only. Consequently, the fact that the drink server is an open system is not expressed, and it is not clear from the formalization how the drink server can be embedded into an environment. Taking interaction points into consideration would require a change of the underlying semantical model (see Chapter 3.3.1).

Further inaccuracies come along with the introduction of primitive propositions. Since these are formulas which can not be decomposed within the framework of propositional logic, their intended meaning had to be given informally. But how should truth and falsity of these propositions be related to the visible behaviour of implementations? Under what circumstances are orders taken, and how do they affect the truth values of the propositions tea_order and coffee_order? When should the readiness to serve a drink result in visible behaviour, and how are tea_order and coffee_order affected?

DS1'. $\Box \Diamond$ at DS.ip1.?

DS2'. $\Box$ (K'_{DS} (#[after DS.ip1.?(order(tea))] > #[after DS.ip2.!(serve(tea))])
$\supset \Diamond$ at DS.ip2.!(serve(tea)))

DS3'. $\Box$ ($\neg$ K'_{DS} (#[after DS.ip1.?(order(tea))] > #[after DS.ip2.!(serve(tea))])
$\supset \neg$ at DS.ip2.!(serve(tea)))

DS4'. $\Box$ (K'_{DS} (#[after DS.ip1.?(order(coffee))] > #[after DS.ip3.!(serve(coffee))])
$\supset \Diamond$ at DS.ip3.!(serve(coffee)))

DS5'. $\Box$ ($\neg$ K'_{DS} (#[after DS.ip1.?(order(coffee))] >#[after DS.ip3.!(serve(coffee))])
$\supset \neg$ at DS.ip3.!(serve(coffee)))

DS6a'. $\Box$ ((q $\supset K_{DS}$q) $\wedge$ ($\neg$q $\supset K_{DS}\neg$q) $\wedge$ ([q] $\supset K_{DS}$[q]))
for all q $\in$ {at ag.ip.!(p(x)), after ag.ip.!(p(x)), at ag.ip.?, after ag.ip.?(p(x))},
where ag = DS, ip $\in$ Archif(DS), p $\in$ P, and x $\in$ X

DS6b'. $\Box$ ((q $\supset K_{DS}$q) $\wedge$ ($\neg$q $\supset K_{DS}\neg$q))
for all q $\in$ {#[after DS.ip1.?(order(tea))] > #[after DS.ip2.!(serve(tea))],
#[after DS.ip1.?(order(coffee))] > #[after DS.ip3.!(serve(coffee))]}

DS7'. A_{DS}q for all q $\in$ {at ag.ip.!(p(x)),after ag.ip.!(p(x)),at ag.ip.?,
after ag.ip.?(p(x))}, where ag = DS, ip $\in$ Archif(DS), p $\in$ P, and x $\in$ X

Table 7.8: Specification of DS

To overcome the problems outlined before, we give a more detailed specification of the drink server in a temporal epistemic logic which is based on many-sorted first-order logic instead of propositional logic. The logic consists of the building blocks At_F, Pr, Q, E_P, E_F, F_L, K, K', and A, formulas are interpreted in a model $\mathcal{M}_{FLE}$ (see Definition 6.3). The system architecture in Figure 7.1 (Chapter 7.2.1) is completely captured by the tuple $\mathcal{Arch} = \langle$ AG,IP,$\mathcal{Archf}\rangle$, where AG = {DS}, IP = {ip1,ip2,ip3}, and $\mathcal{Archf}$(DS) = {ip1,ip2,ip3}. To specify the behaviour of the drink server, we use the notation that has been introduced in Chapter 4.3.2. Abstract operations ! and ? denote the offering and acceptance of an interaction, and situations where an agent is *at* the beginning and immediately *after* the operation are distinguished. With these conventions, the atomic formulas of many-sorted first-order logic (Chapter 3.3.2) are determined as follows:

- DS is a constant of sort AG;
- ip1, ip2, ip3 are constants of sort IP;
- ! and ? are constants of sort OP;
- order and serve are constants of sort P;
- tea and coffee are constants of sort X;
- at and after are relation symbols of arity 5, associated with sorts AG, IP, OP, P, X; we overload at and after to be also relation symbols of arity 3, associated with sorts AG, IP, OP.

The specification of the drink server is listed in Table 7.8. The behaviour of DS at its interaction points is now precisely specified. In particular, it is now clear that orders are taken by an interaction with the environment at ip1, and that each order eventually leads to the serving of the requested drink. Moreover, it can be proved from the specification that drinks are only served if they have been ordered. Differently from the specification based on propositional logic, locality is expressed in the *specification*. All atomic formulas are related to events that are local to DS according to the system architecture $\mathcal{Arch}$. Properties DS6a' and DS6b' restrict the view function such that DS always knows about its present local situation. In particular, DS implicitly knows about local events occurring at its interaction points. DS7' ensures that DS is aware of all local aspects.

Clearly, the specification in Table 7.8 is more precise and more detailed than the specification in Tables 7.1 and 7.2. It is even possible to relate both specifications, as shown in Table 7.9. If we replace the primitive propositions in DSi, $1 \leq i \leq 5$, accordingly, then we obtain the properties DSi', $1 \leq i \leq 5$. The replacement in DS6 yields a property that is logically implied by DS6a' $\wedge$ DS6b'. Finally, replacing the propositions in DS7 results in a property implied by DS7' together with closure under formation rules. From these observations, it follows that the first formalization of the drink server is in accordance with the specification in Table 7.8.

ready_to_take_tea_order $=_{Df}$ at DS.ip1.?
ready_to_serve_tea $=_{Df}$ at DS.ip2.!(serve(tea))
ready_to_serve_coffee $=_{Df}$ at DS.ip3.!(serve(coffee))
tea_order $=_{Df}$ #[after DS.ip1.?(order(tea))] > #[after DS.ip2.!(serve(tea))]
coffee_order $=_{Df}$ #[after DS.ip1.?(order(coffee))] > #[after DS.ip3.!(serve(coffee))]

Table 7.9: Relationship to the propositional version of the drink server specification

7.2.5 Refinement

In Chapter 7.2.2, the refinement of the drink server has been specified in a temporal epistemic logic that was based on propositional logic. Again we believe that the outcome is easily understood, and that it can serve as a first formalization of the problem. Nevertheless, several aspects similar to those identified in the previous chapter deserve improvement. Therefore, we provide a more detailed specification of the refinement in a temporal epistemic logic, which is based on many-sorted first-order logic. As before, the logic is formed from the building blocks At_F, Pr, Q, E_P, E_F, F_L, K, K', and A. Additionally, we select G, G', and A_G, which will be needed for verification purposes (see Chapter 7.2.6).

According to the rules of architectural refinement (see Chapter 2), DS is decomposed as shown in Figure 7.2 (Chapter 7.2.2). The system architecture is captured by the tuple $\mathcal{Arch}' = \langle$ AG',IP',$\mathcal{Archf}' \rangle$, where AG' = {W,TG,CB}, IP' = {ip1,ip2,ip3,ip4,ip5}, $\mathcal{Archf}'$(W) = {ip1,ip4,ip5}, $\mathcal{Archf}'$(TG) = {ip2,ip4}, and $\mathcal{Archf}'$(CB) = {ip3,ip5}. The atomic formulas of the logic are determined as follows:

- W, TG, and CB are constants of sort AG;
- ip1, ip2, ip3, ip4, ip5 are constants of sort IP;
- ! and ? are constants of sort OP;
- order, serve, and request are constants of sort P;

- tea and coffee are constants of sort X;
- at and after are relation symbols of arity 5, associated with sorts AG, IP, OP, P, X; we overload them to be also relation symbols of arity 3 and 4, associated with sorts AG, IP, OP, and AG, IP, OP, P, respectively.

W1'. $\Box \Diamond$ at W.ip1.?

W2'. $\Box$ (K'_W (#[after W.ip1.?(order(tea))] > #[after W.ip4.!(request)])
$\supset \Diamond$ at W.ip4.!(request))

W3'. $\Box$ ($\neg K'_W$ (#[after W.ip1.?(order(tea))] > #[after W.ip4.!(request)])
$\supset \neg$ at W.ip4.!(request))

W4'. $\Box$ (K'_W (#[after W.ip1.?(order(coffee))] > #[after W.ip5.!(request)])
$\supset \Diamond$ at W.ip5.!(request))

W5'. $\Box$ ($\neg K'_W$ #[after W.ip1.?(order(coffee))] > #[after W.ip5.!(request)]
$\supset \neg$ at W.ip5.!(request))

W6a'. $\Box ((q \supset K_W q) \wedge (\neg q \supset K_W \neg q) \wedge ([q] \supset K_W[q]))$
for all $q \in$ {at ag.ip.!(p(x)), after ag.ip.!(p(x)), at ag.ip.?, after ag.ip.?(p(x))},
where ag = W, ip $\in \mathcal{Arch}'$(W), p $\in$ P, and x $\in$ X

W6b'. $\Box ((q \supset K_W q) \wedge (\neg q \supset K_W \neg q))$
for all $q \in$ {#[after W.ip1.?(order(tea))] > #[after W.ip4.!(request)],
#[after W.ip1.?(order(coffee))] > #[after W.ip5.!(request)]}

W6c'. $\Box \forall n$. (#[after W.ip4.!(request) = n $\supset K_W$ #[after W.ip4.!(request) = n)

W6d'. $\Box \forall n$. (#[after W.ip5.!(request) = n $\supset K_W$ #[after W.ip5.!(request) = n)

W7'. $A_W q$ for all $q \in$ { at ag.ip.!(p(x)), after ag.ip.!(p(x)), at ag.ip.?,
after ag.ip.?(p(x)) }, where ag = W, ip $\in \mathcal{Arch}'$(W), p $\in$ P, and x $\in$ X

W8'. $\neg A_W q$ for all $q \in$ { at ag.ip.!(p(x)), after ag.ip.!(p(x)), at ag.ip.?,
after ag.ip.?(p(x)) }, where ag $\in$ AG \ {W}, ip $\in$ IP, p $\in$ P, and x $\in$ X

Table 7.10: Specification of W

The specifications of W and TG are listed in Tables 7.10 and 7.11. The specification of CB is very similar to that of TG. Note that interactions by which the waiter requests tea and coffee from the tea girl and the coffee boy, respectively, are now explicitly specified. It can be proved from the specification that the waiter only asks TG and CB to serve drinks if there is a corresponding request. The specifications of W, TG, and CB follow the specification of DS with the exception of properties W6c', W6d', TG4c', and CB4c'. They require that W, TG, and CB know about the number of requests at interaction points ip4 and ip5, which will be necessary to prove conformance (next chapter).

To complete the refinement, we define the semantics of the interaction points ip4 and ip5. Since requests are only passed in one direction, it suffices to define $\mathcal{S}eman'_{ip4} = (P1 \wedge P5 \wedge P6)$ [ag1/W,ag2/TG,ip/ip4] and $\mathcal{S}eman'_{ip5} = (P1 \wedge P5 \wedge P6)$ [ag1/W,ag2/CB,ip/ip5] (compare Chapter 4.3.3).

TG1'. $\Box \Diamond$ at TG.ip4.?
TG2'. $\Box$ (K'_{TG} (#[after TG.ip4.?(request)] > #[after TG.ip2.!(serve(tea))]) $\supset \Diamond$ at TG.ip2.!(serve(tea)))
TG3'. $\Box$ ($\neg K'_{TG}$(#[after TG.ip4.?(request)] > #[after TG.ip2.!(serve(tea))]) $\supset \neg$ at TG.ip2.!(serve(tea)))
TG4a'. $\Box$ $((q \supset K_{TG}q) \wedge (\neg q \supset K_{TG}\neg q) \wedge ([q] \supset K_{TG}[q]))$ for all $q \in$ {at ag.ip.!(p(x)), after ag.ip.!(p(x)), at ag.ip.?, after ag.ip.?(p(x))},   where ag = TG, ip $\in \mathcal{A}rch'$(TG), $p \in P$, and $x \in X$
TG4b'. $\Box$ $((q \supset K_{TG}q) \wedge (\neg q \supset K_{TG}\neg q))$ where q = #[after TG.ip4.?(request)] > #[after TG.ip2.!(order(tea))]
TG4c'. $\Box$ $\forall$n. (#[after TG.ip4.?(request) = n $\supset K_{TG}$ #[after TG.ip4.?(request) = n)
TG5'. $A_{TG}q$ for all $q \in$ { at ag.ip.!(p(x)), after ag.ip.!(p(x)), at ag.ip.?,   after ag.ip.?(p(x)) }, where ag = TG, ip $\in \mathcal{A}rch'$(TG), $p \in P$, and $x \in X$
TG6'. $\neg A_{TG}q$ for all $q \in$ {at ag.ip.!(p(x)), after ag.ip.!(p(x)), at ag.ip.?,   after ag.ip.?(p(x)) }, where ag $\in$ AG \ TG, ip $\in$ IP, $p \in P$, and $x \in X$

Table 7.11: Specification of TG

As before, it is straightforward to relate the propositional specifications in Chapter 7.2.2 to the first-order descriptions of W, TG, and CB. If we replace the primitive propositions in Chapter 7.2.2 by appropriate first-order formulas, it follows that the first formalization of the refinement is in accordance with the specification in this chapter.

7.2.6 Verification of the drink server refinement

The verification has to show that the requirement specification $\mathcal{RS}' = \langle \mathcal{Arch}', \mathcal{Behav}' \rangle$ with $\mathcal{Arch}' = \langle AG', IP', \mathcal{Archf}' \rangle$, where $AG' = \{W, TG, CB\}$, $IP' = \{ip1, ip2, ip3, ip4, ip5\}$, $\mathcal{Archf}'(W) = \{ip1, ip4, ip5\}$, $\mathcal{Archf}'(TG) = \{ip2, ip4\}$, and $\mathcal{Archf}'(CB) = \{ip3, ip5\}$, and $\mathcal{Behav}' = \bigwedge_{ag \in AG'} \mathcal{Behav}'_{ag} \wedge \bigwedge_{ip \in IP'} \mathcal{Seman}'_{ip}$ conforms to the requirement specification $\mathcal{RS} = \langle \mathcal{Arch}, \mathcal{Behav} \rangle$ with $\mathcal{Arch} = \langle AG, IP, \mathcal{Archf} \rangle$, where $AG = \{DS\}$, $IP = \{ip1, ip2, ip3\}$, $\mathcal{Archf}(DS) = \{ip1, ip2, ip3\}$ and $\mathcal{Behav} = \bigwedge_{ag \in AG} \mathcal{Behav}_{ag}$, under a representation function rep. With $\mathcal{Behav}_{DS} = \bigwedge_{1 \le i \le 7} DSi'$, $\mathcal{Behav}'_{W} = \bigwedge_{1 \le i \le 8} Wi'$, $\mathcal{Behav}'_{TG} = \bigwedge_{1 \le i \le 6} TGi'$, and $\mathcal{Behav}'_{CB} = \bigwedge_{1 \le i \le 6} CBi'$, it must be shown that $\mathcal{RS}'$ *conforms*$_{rep}$ $\mathcal{RS}$.

rep (at DS.ip1.?)	=	at W.ip1.?
rep (after DS.ip1.?(p(x)))	=	after W.ip1.?(p(x))
rep (at DS.ip2.!(p(x))	=	at TG.ip2.!(p(x))
rep (after DS.ip2.!(p(x))	=	after TG.ip2.!(p(x))
rep (at DS.ip3.!(p(x))	=	at CB.ip3.!(p(x))
rep (after DS.ip3.!(p(x))	=	after CB.ip3.!(p(x))
rep ($\neg\varphi$)	=	$\neg$ rep (φ)
rep ($\varphi_1 \wedge \varphi_2$)	=	rep (φ_1) $\wedge$ rep (φ_2)
rep ($\forall x.\varphi$)	=	$\forall x.$ rep (φ)
rep ($\Box\ \varphi$)	=	$\Box$ rep (φ)
rep ([φ])	=	[rep (φ)]
rep (#[φ])	=	#[rep (φ)]
rep ($K_{DS}\varphi$)	=	$I_{\{W,TG,CB\}}$ rep(φ)
rep ($K'_{DS}\varphi$)	=	$I'_{\{W,TG,CB\}}$ rep(φ)
rep ($A_{DS}\varphi$)	=	$H_{\{W,TG,CB\}}$ rep(φ)

Table 7.12: The representation function rep

As explained in Chapter 3.3.9, conformance addresses both architectural and behavioural aspects. In particular, if $\mathcal{RS}'$ *conforms*$_{rep}$ $\mathcal{RS}$ is to be shown, then $\mathcal{Arch}'$ *refines* $\mathcal{Arch}$ (see Definition 2.3) must hold, which is the case for the refinement function ref: $AG \cup IP \rightarrow 2^{AG' \cup IP'}$ with ref(DS) = {W,TG,CB,ip4,ip5}, and ref(ip) = {ip} for ip ∈ {ip1,ip2,ip3}. To prove $\models_i \mathcal{Behav}' \supset rep(\mathcal{Behav})$, we define a representation function rep by mapping formulas of the more abstract description level to corresponding formulas of the lower level as shown in Table 7.12.

Note that apart from the atomic formulas and the additional building blocks, rep is identical to the representation function in Chapter 7.2.3. If we regard the proof obligations, it becomes clear why the properties W6c', W6d', TG4c', and CB4c' have been included in the refinement specification. They ensure that W, TG, and CB have combined knowledge of whether the number of request offers at ip4 and ip5 is greater or equal to the number of acceptances. It can then be shown that together with their individual knowledge, they always have combined knowledge of whether there are unsatisfied tea or coffee orders. With these preparations, conformance between $\mathcal{RS}'$ and $\mathcal{RS}$ is straightforward to prove.

7.2.7 Non-local epistemic properties

The specification of an agent is called "syntactically-local", if it refers to aspects which are local to this agent only; it is called "semantically-local" or "self-contained", if it can be implemented independently of its environment (see Chapter 3.3.8). Local aspects of an agent are the local state, local actions, and, in the epistemic framework, local knowledge. The previous specifications of drink server, waiter, tea girl, and coffee boy are syntactically-local. In particular, they describe for each agent what explicit knowledge it has about its local situation, and how to behave based on that knowledge. This is a necessary condition for semantical locality.

In general, specifications may contain non-local properties, i.e., properties referring to the state, the actions, or the knowledge of other agents. We can, for instance, specify that an agent acquires knowledge about remote situations. If φ states that all requests for tea have been satisfied by the tea girl, then $\Box (\varphi \supset \Diamond K_W \varphi)$ expresses that the waiter eventually attains knowledge of this fact. It is not revealed how the waiter acquires this knowledge, however, it can be concluded that some form of interaction between the waiter and the tea girl has to be introduced in order to implement this epistemic property.

Another kind of non-local epistemic properties refers to the knowledge of other agents. In the situation before, we can state that the tea girl acquires knowledge about the knowledge of the waiter. If φ is defined as in the last paragraph, then $\Box(\varphi \supset K_{TG}\Diamond K_W\varphi)$ expresses that the tea girl knows that the waiter will know φ, if φ is true. Since φ is a formula referring to local events of the tea girl, it can again be concluded that some interaction between the waiter and the tea girl has to be introduced in a later design stage.

A third kind of non-local epistemic properties expresses that remote events are triggered based on local information. If, for instance, φ states that the waiter has accepted orders for tea which it has not yet passed to the tea girl, and φ' states that the tea girl is ready to serve tea, then $\Box(K_W\varphi \supset \Diamond\varphi')$ is a property of this kind. To implement this property, suitable interaction has to be introduced.

If the specification of an agent contains non-local epistemic properties, the behaviour of that agent is in general not locally determined. To acquire knowledge about the local situation or the knowledge of other agents, or to trigger remote actions on the basis of local knowledge, suitable interaction between these agents has to be introduced. *It is only by means of interaction that agents can acquire knowledge about their environment, or that they can pass their knowledge to other agents.*

A specification containing non-local epistemic properties is in general more abstract in the sense that the behaviour of the agent is less determined. In particular, it is not specified what action has to be taken to acquire sufficient knowledge, or to trigger remote events. In an early design stage, this can be considered as irrelevant detail, but has to be added as the design evolves. Once the local behaviour of each agent is precisely defined, the non-local properties have to be proved from the joint behaviour of all agents.

We now reconsider the drink server example and add the requirement that if a drink is ordered, it has to be served before the next drink can be ordered. In other words, we require that the drink server works in rounds. The behaviour of the drink server can be captured by the specification in Table 7.8, where DS1' is replaced by DS1a' and DS1b' listed in Table 7.13.

DS1a' is a weaker requirement than DS1'. It states that DS must eventually be ready to take an order if it explicitly knows that all previous orders have been served. DS1b' expresses that in all other cases, DS must not be ready to take an order. DS1a' permits implementations that process each order before the next order is taken. DS1a' in conjunction with DS1b' enforces such implementations. Interestingly, DS1' can be proved from DS1a', DS1b', and the rest of the specification, if ip2 and ip3 always permit serving drinks, or if the environment of DS is ready to accept ordered drinks. Note that the specification of DS is syntactically-local.

$$\begin{aligned} &\text{DS1a'}.\ \Box\,(K'_{DS}\neg(\#[\text{after DS.ip1.?(order(tea))}] > \#[\text{after DS.ip2.!(serve(tea))}] \vee \\ &\qquad\qquad \#[\text{after DS.ip1.?(order(coffee))}] > \#[\text{after DS.ip3.!(serve(coffee))}]) \\ &\qquad \supset \Diamond\ \text{at DS.ip1.?}) \\ &\text{DS1b'}.\ \Box\,(\neg K'_{DS}\neg(\#[\text{after DS.ip1.?(order(tea))}] > \#[\text{after DS.ip2.!(serve(tea))}] \vee \\ &\qquad\qquad \#[\text{after DS.ip1.?(order(coffee))}] > \#[\text{after DS.ip3.!(serve(coffee))}]) \\ &\qquad \supset \neg\ \text{at DS.ip1.?}) \end{aligned}$$

Table 7.13: Modifications of the specification of DS

If DS1' is replaced by DS1a' and DS1b', the refinement of DS has to be modified, too. The behaviour of the waiter is now captured by the specification in Table 7.10, where W1', W7', and W8' are replaced by W1a', W1b', W7a', and W8a', respectively. The specifications of the tea girl and the coffee boy (see Chapter 7.2.5) remain unchanged.

$$\begin{aligned} &\text{W1a'}.\ \Box\,(K'_{W}\neg(\#[\text{after W.ip1.?(order(tea))}] > \#[\text{after TG.ip2.!(serve(tea))}] \vee \\ &\qquad\qquad \#[\text{after W.ip1.?(order(coffee))}] > \#[\text{after CB.ip3.!(serve(coffee))}]) \\ &\qquad \supset \Diamond\ \text{at W.ip1.?}) \\ &\text{W1b'}.\ \Box\,(\neg K'_{W}\neg(\#[\text{after W.ip1.?(order(tea))}] > \#[\text{after TG.ip2.!(serve(tea))}] \vee \\ &\qquad\qquad \#[\text{after W.ip1.?(order(coffee))}] > \#[\text{after CB.ip3.!(serve(coffee))}]) \\ &\qquad \supset \neg\ \text{at W.ip1.?}) \\ &\text{W7a'}.\ A_W q\ \text{ for all } q \in \{\ \text{at ag.ip.!(p(x)), after ag.ip.!(p(x)), at ag.ip.?,} \\ &\qquad\qquad \text{after ag.ip.?(p(x))}\ \},\ \text{where ag} = \text{W, ip} \in \mathit{Arch}'(\text{W}),\ \text{p} \in \text{P, and x} \in \text{X} \\ &\qquad\qquad \text{or ag} \in \{\text{TG,CB}\},\ \text{ip} \in \{\text{ip2,ip3}\},\ \text{p} \in \text{P, and x} \in \text{X} \\ &\text{W8a'}.\ \neg A_W q\ \text{ for all } q \in \{\ \text{at ag.ip.!(p(x)), after ag.ip.!(p(x)), at ag.ip.?, after} \\ &\qquad\qquad \text{ag.ip.?(p(x))}\ \},\ \text{where ag} \in \text{AG} \setminus \{\text{W}\},\ \text{ip} \in \{\text{ip4,ip5}\},\ \text{p} \in \text{P, and x} \in \text{X} \end{aligned}$$

Table 7.14: Modifications of the specification of W

W1a' and W1b' directly correspond to DS1a' and DS1b'. However, unlike DS1a' and DS1b', they are non-local properties, because both W1a' and W1b' refer to events occurring at ip2 and ip3. Certainly, W will not have implicit knowledge of the events occurring here, so under this specification, the waiter can be implemented such that W is never prepared to take orders. However, it turns out that this is not sufficient to prove that the refinement conforms to the drink server.

In order to show conformance, it has to be proved that $\models_i \mathcal{B}ehav' \supset rep(\mathcal{B}ehav)$, where $\mathcal{B}ehav'$ and $\mathcal{B}ehav$ are the behavioural specifications of the refinement and the drink server, respectively, and rep is the representation function from Table 7.12. Let $\varphi =_{Df} \neg$ (#[after W.ip1.?(order(tea))] > #[after TG.ip2.!(serve(tea))] $\vee$ #[after W.ip1.?(order(coffee))] > #[after CB.ip3.!(serve(coffee))]), and $G =_{Df}$ {W,TG,CB}. Conformance can be proved if the refinement satisfies the properties $\Box(\neg I'_G\varphi \supset \neg K'_W\varphi)$ and $\Box(I'_G\varphi \supset \Diamond K'_W\varphi)$. The first property is a valid formula and thus holds for any refinement. The second property cannot be proved from the refinement so far, therefore, we have to add it to the specification. In a later design stage, appropriate interaction between waiter, tea girl, and coffee boy can be added such that this property can be proved. We could, for instance, introduce an acknowledgement between the tea girl and the waiter after a tea has been served, and between the coffee boy and the waiter after a coffee has been served.

8 Conclusion

The design of open distributed systems has become central to computer science during the past 15 years. Broad international standardization activities in this area such as Open Systems Interconnection (OSI) and Open Distributed Processing (ODP), and a variety of related international conferences and journals indicate the great attention these systems are receiving from research and industry. Several design methodologies have been advocated, and a number of description techniques have been proposed for each design stage. Certainly, there will be no single answer to the question of how to design an open system well. However, there are a number of principles and basic concepts which can guide the design activity.

In this work, we have identified and investigated some principles and concepts of open distributed systems design which can be treated formally. We presented a framework in which architectural and behavioural aspects of open systems can be formally specified and verified. In particular, we have designed an appropriate temporal epistemic logic, and defined a notion of conformance taking behavioural and architectural aspects into account. We have used the temporal part of the logic to capture the semantics of the interaction point concept, and to specify and reason about communication services. We have used the epistemic part to illustrate the use of epistemic concepts in the design process.

In the context of open distributed systems, we believe it is essential both to model *and* to specify both behavioural *and* architectural requirements. The formalism presented in this work can express both aspects. We note that the formal description techniques currently used in the area of OSI cannot express system architecture. These techniques only permit structuring a specification in order to cope with problem complexity, but the structure imposes no architectural requirement.

We perceive system behaviour as being composed of events and interactions, and system architecture as consisting of agents and interaction points. These are general, *basic concepts* of open distributed systems which can be specialized and extended with respect to a given application area such as OSI and ODP. We have shown that none of these concepts can be omitted without leaving essential aspects of an open distributed system undefined.

Implicit and explicit formal description techniques have been proposed in the literature to specify requirements on system behaviour. Properties characterizing legal system behaviour can be expressed using implicit approaches, whereas explicit approaches allow the description of system behaviour in an operational manner. The temporal epistemic logic presented in this work belongs to the class of implicit techniques. We believe that implicit approaches are preferable during the early design stages, and in particular for formal reasoning and verification purposes. As the design evolves, they should be complemented by operational techniques.

To express *temporal properties* of system behaviour, various operators are incorporated into the logic to refer to past, present, and future. In particular, we introduce operators for event occurrence and for the construction of past time intervals. The future fragment of the logic is suited to specifying liveness properties of reliable and unreliable systems. We applied the temporal part of the logic to capture the semantics of interaction points, and to specify and reason about communication services. The logic is sufficiently expressive to avoid the use of history variables and state variables, leading to the specification of visible system behaviour on a high level of abstraction.

To express *epistemic properties* of system behaviour, the temporal part of the logic contains a number of operators referring to different kinds of knowledge. As knowledge can be ascribed to single agents as well as to sets of agents, we define operators to refer to individual knowledge and to group knowledge. Moreover, we distinguish between implicit and explicit knowledge. With implicit knowledge, agents are omniscient, i.e. they know all tautologies and all logical consequences of their knowledge. Explicit knowledge is more restrictive in the sense that an agent can only know facts it is aware of. We have shown how epistemic concepts can be used to improve the understandability and abstractness of the system design.

We have argued that the *interaction point* concept plays a fundamental role in the context of open distributed systems. When an open system is designed, the environment into which it will be embedded, or, in the context of OSI and ODP, the entities it will interoperate with, are in general not determined. Therefore, the open system has to be characterized by its ability to interact, which will result in actual behaviour only when it is placed into some environment. The interaction points of the open system conceptually model the locations where interaction can occur, thus establishing the boundary to as well as the link with the environment.

We have specified several generic properties of interaction points. To capture the semantics of the interaction point concept in a particular application area such as OSI, the properties can be selected and composed. We have also noted and proved several interdependencies between the listed properties. We have attempted to define the semantics of interaction point representations in formal description techniques for the area of OSI.

In hierarchical methods, a *notion of correctness* between levels of system specifications is required. We have defined correctness such that both behavioural *and* architectural aspects are taken into account. This reflects our point of view that the system architecture is an essential aspect of open distributed systems. Our notion of correctness is independent of the environment, which may in general lead to unexpected outcomes. To overcome this difficulty, we have identified a sufficient condition based on the semantics of interaction points, and shown that our notion of correctness satisfies this condition.

We have demonstrated in particular that the formalism of temporal logic can be successfully applied to specifying and reasoning about *communication services*. In the course of these studies, we have discovered that the service concept can be explained in terms of the interaction point concept. We have specified properties defining the service as perceived by the service users, and properties defining the service provider. We have then proved that if some restrictions on service users and interaction points are respected, the service provider is correct with respect to the service. We have shown how a distinction between successful and unsuccessful behaviour harmonizing with the notion of correctness can be made. Furthermore, we have drawn a clear distinction between the service and the service provider, which is not possible with operational description techniques.

The results of this work indicate that more research is needed in several directions. One interesting aspect is the formal treatment of dynamic system architectures. This is quite complex, since the notion of correctness will have to be extended to take dynamic aspects of the system architecture into account. Another important issue is the inclusion of further basic and derived architectural concepts. On the behavioural side, the temporal and epistemic operators we have used should be reconsidered after more experience with applications of practical importance. Tool support should be developed for the creation and maintenance of specifications as well as for formal reasoning.

References

[AlSc85] Alpern, B., Schneider, F. B.: Defining Liveness; Information Processing Letters 21, 1985, pp. 181-185

[Aum76] Aumann, R. J.: Agreeing to disagree, Annals of Statistics 4:6, 1976, pp. 1236-1239

[BaKuPn84] Barringer, H., Kuiper, R., Pnueli, A.: Now you may compose Temporal Logic Specifications, in: Proc. of the Sixteenth ACM Symposium on the Theory of Computing, 1984, pp. 51-63

[Bar88] Barwise, J.: Three Views of Common Knowledge, in: M. Y. Vardi (ed.), Proc. of the 2nd Conf. on Theoretical Aspects of Reasoning about Knowledge, Pacific Grove/USA, 1988, pp. 365-379

[Bau88] Baumgarten, B.: Structural Prerequisites for Unambigous Conformance Testing; Proc. of the 2nd Int. Symposium on Interoperable Information Systems, ISIIS'88

[BeBe79] Beeri, C., Bernstein, P. A.: Computational Problems Related to the Design of Normal Form Relational Schema, ACM Transactions on Database Systems, Vol. 4 (1979), No. 1, pp. 30-59

[BeHoTr88] Belina, F., Hogrefe, D., Trigila, S.: Modelling OSI in SDL, in: K. Turner (ed.), Formal Description Techniques, North-Holland, Amsterdam, 1988

[Boc78] Bochmann, G. v.: Finite State Description of Communication Protocols, Computer Networks 2, 4/5 (Oct. 78), pp. 361-372

[Boc80] Bochmann, G. v.: A General Transition Model for Protocols and Communication Services, IEEE Transactions on Communications, Vol. COM-28, No. 4, April 1980, pp. 643-650

[Boc82] Bochmann, G. v.: Hardware Specification with Temporal Logic: An Example, IEEE Transactions on Computers, Vol. C-31, No. 3, March 1982, pp. 223-231

[Boc83c] Bochmann, G. v.: Concepts for Distributed Systems Design, Springer-Verlag, Berlin 1983, 259p.

[BoGo86] Bochmann, G. v., Gotzhein, R.: Deriving Protocol Specifications from Service Specifications, in: Communications Architectures & Protocols, Proc. of the SIGCOMM'86 Symposium, August 5-7, 1986, Stowe, Vermont, USA, pp. 148-156

[BoBe89] Bochmann, G. v., Bellal, O. B.: Test Result Analysis in Respect to Formal Specifications, in: Proceedings of the 2nd International Workshop on Protocol Test Systems, Berlin (West), Germany, Obtober 3-6, 1989, pp. 272-294

[BrGoVo92] Bredereke, J., Gotzhein, R., Vogt, F. H.: Design of a Formal Estelle Semantics for Verification, Fifth International Conference on Formal Description Techniques (FORTE'92), Lannion, France, October 13-16, 1992, pp.161-176

[BrScSt86] Brinksma, E., Scollo, G., Steenbergen, C.: Process Specifications, their Implementations and their Tests, in: B. Sarikaya, G. v. Bochmann (eds.), Protocol Specification, Testing, and Verification VI, North-Holland, 1987, pp. 349-360

[Bri88a] Brinksma, E.: On the Design of Extended LOTOS - A Specification Language for Open Distributed Systems, Ph. D. thesis, University of Hengelo, Netherlands, 1988, 238p.

[BUL89] BULL S.A.: Estelle-to-C Compiler ec, User Reference Manual, BULL S. A., Direction Methodologie/MDL, 1989

[CCITT87] CCITT: Recommendation Z.100: Specification and Description Language SDL, CCITT SG X, Contribution Com X-R15-E, 1987

[ClMa81] Clark, H. H., Marshall, C. R.: Definite reference and mutual Knowledge, in: A. K. Joshi, B. L. Webber, J. A. Sag (eds.), Elements of Discourse Understanding, Cambridge University Press, 1981

[ClEmSi86] Clarke, E. M., Emerson, E. A., Sistla, A. P.: Automatic Verification of Finite-State Concurrent Systems using Temporal Logic Specifications, ACM TOPLAS Vol. 8, Nr. 2, April 1986, pp. 244-263

[COS87] COST 11-ter group on FDT/ABM: Architectural and Behavioural Modelling in Computer Communication, in: M. H. Barton, E. L. Dagless, G. L. Reijns (eds.), Distributed Processing, North-Holland, 1987, pp. 53-70

[Dat81] Date, C. J.: An Introduction to Database Systems, Third Edition, Addison-Wesley Publishing Company, 1981, 574p.

[Dav89] Davidson, J. C.: International Conformance Testing - Towards the Next Decade, in: J. de Meer, W. Effelsberg, L. Mackert (eds.), 2nd International Workshop on Protocol Test Systems, Addendum 1, Berlin (West), Germany, October 3-6, 1989, 13p.

[Dia89] Diaz, M., Ansart, J. P., Courtiat, J. P., Azema, P., Chari, V.: The Formal Description Technique Estelle, North-Holland, 1989

[Dij76] Dijkstra, E. W.: A Discipline of Programming, Englewood Cliffs, N. J., Prentice-Hall, 1976, 217p.

[DiSc90] Dijkstra, E. W., Scholten, C. S.: Predicate Calculus and Program Semantics, Springer, 1990

[EmHa85] Emerson, E. A., Halpern, J. Y.: Decision Procedures and Expressiveness in the Temporal Logic of Branching Time, Journal of Computer and System Sciences, Vol. 30, No. 1, 1985, pp. 1-24

[EmHa86] Emerson, E. A., Halpern, J. Y.: 'Sometimes' and 'not never' revisited: On branching time versus linear time, JACM 33, 1986, pp. 151-178

[FaHa85] Fagin, R., Halpern, J. Y.: Belief, Awareness, and Limited Reasoning, Proc. of the Ninth International Joint Conference on AI (IJCAI-85), 1985

[FaHa88] Fagin, R., Halpern, J. Y.: Belief, Awareness, and Limited Reasoning, Artificial Intelligence 34 (1988), pp. 39-76

[GlObTo83] Glubrecht, J. M., Oberschelp, A., Todt, G.: Klassenlogik, Bibliographisches Institut, Mannheim, 1983, 467p. (in german)

[Got88] Gotzhein, R.: Knowledge-oriented consideration of communication protocols, in: S. Aggarwal, K. Sabnani (eds.), Protocol Specification, Verification, and Testing VIII , North-Holland, 1988, pp. 295-306.

[Got89] Gotzhein, R.: On the Formal Definition and Representation of Architectural Concepts, Report Nr. FBI-HH-B-142/89, University of Hamburg, July 1989, 37p.

[Got90] Gotzhein, R.: The Formal Definition of the Architectural Concept 'Interaction Point', in: S. T. Vuong (ed.), Formal Description Techniques, II, North-Holland, 1990, pp. 67-81

[Got90a] Gotzhein, R.: Specifying Open Distributed Systems with Z, VDM'90 Symposium, April 17-21, 1990, Kiel/F.R.G., 16p.

[Got90b] Gotzhein, R.: Specifying Communication Services with Temporal Logic; in: L. Logrippo, R. L. Probert, H. Ural (eds.), Protocol Specification, Testing, and Verification X, Proceedings, North-Holland, 1990, pp. 295-309

[GoBo90] Gotzhein, R., Bochmann, G.v.: Deriving Protocol Specifications from Service Specifications Including Parameters, ACM Transactions on Computer Systems, Vol. 8, No. 4, 1990, pp. 255-283

[Got92a] Gotzhein, R.: On Conformance in the Context of Open Systems, 12th International Conference on Distributed Computing Systems, Yokohama, Japan, June 9-12, 1992, pp.236-243

[Got92b] Gotzhein, R.: Temporal Logic and Applications - A Tutorial, Computer Networks and ISDN Systems 24 (1992) 203-218

[Got92d] Gotzhein, R.: Formal Definition and Representation of Interaction Points, Computer Networks and ISDN Systems 25 (1992) 3-22

[GoVo92] Gotzhein, R., Vogt, F.H.: The Design of a Temporal Logic for Open Distributed Systems, in: J. de Meer, V. Heymer, R. Roth (eds.), Open Distributed Processing, North-Holland, 1992, pp.229-240

[GoYu84] Gouda, M. G., Yu, Y.: Synthesis of Communicating Finite-State Machines with Guaranteed Progress, IEEE Transactions on Communications, Vol. COM-32, No. 7, July 1984, pp. 779-788

[Gri89] van Griethuysen, J. J.: Open Distributed Processing, in: E. Brinksma, G. Scollo, C. Vissers (eds.), Protocol Specification, Testing, and Verification IX, Proceedings, June 6-9, 1989

[Hai82] Hailpern, B. T.: Verifying Concurrent Processes Using Temporal Logic, LNCS 129, Springer, 1982

[HaMo84] Halpern, J. Y., Moses, Y.: Knowledge and Common Knowledge in a Distributed Environment, IBM Research Report RJ 4421 (47909) 10/2/84, 28p.

[HaFa85] Halpern, J. Y., Fagin, R.: A Formal Model of Knowledge, Action and Communication in Distributed Systems: Preliminary Report, in: Proc. of the 4th Annual ACM Symposium on PoDC, Ontario, 1985, pp. 224-236

[HaMo85] Halpern, J. Y., Moses, Y.: A Guide to the Modal Logics of Knowledge and Belief: Preliminary Draft, IBM Research Report RJ 4753 (50521) 6/25/85, 11p.

[HaVa86] Halpern, J. Y., Vardi, M. Y.: The Complexity of Reasoning about Knowledge and Time, Proc. of the 18th Annual ACM Symposium on Theory of Computing, 1986, pp. 304-315

[Hal87] Halpern, J. Y.: Using Reasoning about Knowledge to Analyze Distributed Systems, Ann. Rev. Comput. Sci. 1987, No. 2, pp. 37-68

[HaMo87] Halpern, J. Y., Moses, Y.: Knowledge and Common Knowledge in a Distributed Environment, IBM Research Report RJ 4421 (47909), revised 18.8.87, 50p.

[HaVa87] Halpern, J. Y., Vardi, M. Y.: The Complexity of Reasoning about Knowledge and Time, I: Lower Bounds, IBM Research Report RJ 5764 (58103) 8/4/87, 44p.

[HaZu87] Halpern, J. Y., Zuck, L. D.: A Little Knowledge Goes a Long Way: Simple Knowledge-based Derivations and Correctness Proofs for a Family of Protocols, Proc. of the 6th Annual ACM Symposium on PoDC, 1987, pp. 269-280

[HaFa88] Halpern, J. Y., Fagin, R.: Modelling Knowledge and Action in Distributed Systems: Preliminary Report, in: F. Vogt (ed.), Concurrency 88, LNCS 335, Springer Verlag, pp. 18-32

[Hay87] Hayes, I.: Specification Case Studies, International Series in Computer Science, Prentice-Hall, 1987

[HeMi85] Hennessy, M., Milner, R.: Algebraic Laws for Nondeterminism and Concurrency, JACM 32, 1 (January 1985), pp. 137-161

[Her89] Herbert, A.: Distributed Systems and OSI, in: G. X. Ritter (ed.), Information Processing 89, North-Holland, 1989

[Hin62] Hintikka, J.: Knowledge and Belief, Cornell University Press, 1962

[Hin75] Hintikka, J.: Impossible Possible Worlds Vindicated, Journal of Philosophical Logic, Vol. 4, 1975, pp. 475-484

[Hoa69] Hoare, C. A. R.: An Axiomatic Basis for Computer Programming, Communications of the ACM, Vol. 12, 1969, pp. 576-583

[Hoa85] Hoare, C. A. R.: Communicating Sequential Processes, Englewood Cliffs, N. J., Prentice-Hall, 1985, 256p.

[Hog88] Hogrefe, D.: OSI Service Specification with CCITT-SDL, ACM Comp. Comm. Review, Vol. 18, Nos. 1 and 2, 1988, pp. 63-90

[Hog88a] Hogrefe, D.: Protocol and Service Specification with SDL: the X.25 case study, Report Nr. FBI-HH-B-134/88, University of Hamburg, 1988

[Hog89] Hogrefe, D.: SDL and OSI: On the use of CCITT-SDL in the context of OSI, Habilitationsschrift, Department of Computer Science, University of Hamburg, June 1989

[Hog89a] Hogrefe, D.: Estelle, LOTOS und SDL. Standard-Spezifikationssprachen für verteilte Systeme, Springer-Verlag, Berlin, 1989, 188p. (in german)

[Hog92] Hogrefe, D.: OSI Formal Specification Case Study: The InRes Protocol and Service, revised, Report No. IAM-91-012, Update May 1992, University of Bern, May 1992, 33p.

[HoRo89] Hooman, J. J. M., de Roever, W. P.: Design and Verification in Real-Time Distributed Computing: an Introduction to Compositional Methods, Protocol Specification, Testing, and Verification XI, June 6-9, 1989, Twente/Netherlands

[HuCr68] Hughes, G. E., Cresswell, M. J.: An Introduction to Modal Logic, Methuen and Co. Ltd., London, 1968, 388p.

[HuCr84] Hughes, G., Cresswell, M. J.: A Companion to Modal Logic; London, Methuen, 1984, 203p.

[ISO81] ISO/TC97/SC16: Data Processing - Open Systems Interconnection - Basic Reference Model, Computer Networks 5 (1981), pp. 81-118

[ISO86a] ISO/TC97/SC6: Formal Description of Transport Service in Estelle, ISO/TC97/SC6 N4393, 1986

[ISO86b] ISO/TC97/SC6: Formal Description of ISO 8073 (Transport Protocol) in Estelle, ISO/TC97/SC6 N4394, 1986

[ISO88] ISO/IEC JTC 1/SC21: Information Processing Systems - OSI - Service Definition for the Commitment, Concurrency and Recovery Service Element, ISO/IEC JTC 1/SC21, DIS 9804, 1988, 28p.

[ISO88b] ISO/IEC JTC1/SC21: Guidelines for the Application of Estelle, LOTOS, and SDL, ISO/IEC JTC1/SC21/WG1/N2549 rev., Dec. 1988, 344p.

[ISO88c] ISO/TC97/SC21: LOTOS - A Formal Description Technique Based on the Temporal Ordering of Observational Behaviour, ISO/TC97/SC21, IS 8807, 1988

[ISO88d] ISO/IEC JTC1/SC21: Architectural Semantics for FDTs (working draft); ISO/IEC JTC1/SC21 N3251, Dec. 1988

[ISO89] ISO/TC97/SC21: Estelle - A Formal Description Technique Based on an Extended State Transition Model, ISO/TC97/SC21, IS 9074, 1989, 179p.

[ISO90] ISO/IEC JCT1/SC21: OSI Conformance Testing Methodology and Framework, Part 3: The Tree and Tabular Combined Notation (TTCN); ISO/IEC JCT1/SC21, DIS 9646 Part 3

[ISO90a] ISO/IEC JTC1/SC6: Formal Description of ISO 8072 in LOTOS, ISO/IEC DTR 10023, ISO/IEC JTC1/SC6 Plenary, Sydney, Sept. 1990

[ISO90b] ISO/IEC JTC1/SC6: Formal Description of ISO 8073 in LOTOS, ISO/IEC DTR 10024, ISO/IEC JTC1/SC6 Plenary, Sydney, Sept. 1990

[JaJe89] Jard, C., Jezequel, J. M.: A Multi-Processor Estelle-to-C Compiler to Prototype Distributed Algorithms on Parallel Machines, in: G. Scollo, E. Brinksma, C. Vissers (eds.), Protocol Specification, Testing, and Verification, IX, North-Holland, 1988

[JaFo85] des Jardins, R., Foley, J. S.: Open Systems Interconnection: A Review and Status Report; Journal of Telecommunications Networks, 1985, pp. 194-209

[Koy87] Koymans, R.: Specifying Message Passing Systems Requires Extending Temporal Logic, Proc. of the Sixth Annual ACM Symposium on PoDC, 1987, pp. 191-204

[KrGo93] Kreuz, D., Gotzhein, R.: A Compiler for the Parallel Execution of Estelle Specifications, FOKUS-Band, Saur-Verlag, 1993

[Kri63] Kripke, S. A.: Semantical Analysis of Modal Logic I: Normal Modal Propositional Calculi, Zeitschrift für math. Logik und Grundlagen der Mathematik, Bd. 9, 1963, pp. 67-96

[Krö87] Kröger, F.: Temporal Logic of Programs, EATCS Monographs on Theoretical Computer Science, VIII, Springer, 1987, 148p.

[Lam77] Lamport, L.: Proving the Correctness of Multiprocess Programs; IEEE Trans. on Software Engineering SE-3, 2 (March 1977), pp. 125-143

[Lam80] Lamport, L.: "Sometime" is Sometimes "Not Never" - On the Temporal Logics of Programs, Proc. of the 7th Annual ACM Symposium on Principles of Programming Languages, Las Vegas/USA, 1980, pp. 174-185

[Lam83] Lamport, L.: What good is temporal logic?, in: R. E. A. Mason (ed.), Information processing 83, IFIP, North-Holland, 1983, pp. 657-668

[Lam83a] Lamport, L.: Specifying Concurrent Program Modules; TOPLAS 5,2 (1983), pp. 190-222

[Lam91] Lamport, L.: The Temporal Logic of Actions, DEC Research Report 79, Dec. 1991, 73p.

[Len78] Lenzen, W.: Recent Work in Epistemic Logic, Acta Philosophica Fennica 30, 1978, pp. 1-219

[LiPnZu85] Lichtenstein, O., Pnueli, A., Zuck, L.: The Glory of the Past, Workshop on Logics of Programs, Springer-Verlag, LNCS 193 (1985), pp. 196-218

[Lin88] Linn, R. J.: An Overview on Conformance Testing Methodology, in: S. Aggarwal, K. Sabnani (eds.), Eigth International Symposium on Protocol Specification, Testing and Verification, Tutorial Notes, Atlantic City/USA, June 7-10, 1988, 14p.

[MaNe87] Mackert, L. F., Neumeier-Mackert, I. B.: Communicating Rule Systems, Proc. of the IFIP TC6 Symposium on Protocol Specification, Testing and Verification VII, May 5-8, 1987

[Mel88] Melliar-Smith, P. M.: A Graphical Representation of Interval Logic; in: F. H. Vogt (ed.), Concurrency 88, LNCS 335, Springer, 1988, pp. 106-120

[Mil80] Milner, R.: A calculus of communicating systems, LNCS 92, 171p., Springer Verlag, 1980

[Mos86] Moszkowski, B. C. : Executing Temporal Logic Programs, Cambridge University Press, 1986

[NBS87] NBS (National Bureau of Standards): User Guide for the NBS Prototype Compiler for Estelle-Final Report, Report No. ICST/SNA-87/3, Oct. 1987, NBS, 73p.

[OwGr76] Owicki, S., Gries, D.: An Axiomatic Proof Technique for Parallel Programs; Acta Informatica 6 (1976), pp. 319-340

[Pnu77] Pnueli, A.: The Temporal Logic of Programs, 19th Annual Symposium on Foundations of Computer Science, Providence R. I., Nov. 1977

[Pnu79] Pnueli, A.: The Temporal Semantics of Concurrent Programs, Proc. Symp. on Semantics of Concurrent Computation, LNCS, Springer Verlag, 1979, pp. 1-20

[Pnu86] Pnueli, A.: Applications of Temporal Logic to the Specification and Verification of Reactive Systems: A Survey of Current Trends, in: Current Trends in Concurrency, LNCS 224, Springer Verlag, 1986, pp. 510-584

[Poi88] Poigné, A.: Partial Algebras, Subsorting and Dependent Types: Prerequisites of Error Handling in Algebraic Specification, in: D. Sannella, A. Tarlecki (eds.), Recent Trends in Data Type Specification, LNCS 332, Springer Verlag, 1988, pp. 208-234

[Pri57] Prior, A. N.: Time and Modality, Oxford University Press, 1957

[Pri67] Prior, A. N.: Past, Present, and Future; Oxford Press, 1967

[Rei86] Reisig, W.: Petri Nets in Software Engineering, in: W. Brauer, W. Reisig, G. Rozenberg (eds.), Petri Nets: Applications and Relationships to Other Models of Concurrency, Lecture Notes in Computer Science 255, 1986, pp.63-96

[ReUr71] Rescher, N., Urquhart, A.: Temporal Logic, Springer Verlag, 1971

[Ros85] Rosenschein, S. J.: Formal Theories of Knowledge in AI and Robotics, in: New Generation Computing, Vol. 3, No. 4, 1985, pp. 345-357

[Ros87] Rosenschein, S. J.: Formal Theories of Knowledge in AI and Robotics, in: New Generation Computing, Vol. 3, No. 4, Ohmsha Ltd., Tokyo, 1987

[RuWe82] Rubin, J., West, C.H.: An improved protocol validation technique, Computer Networks, 6 (1982), pp. 65-73

[Sch92] Schneider, J.: Protocol Engineering - A Rule-Based Approach, Advanced Studies in Computer Science, Vieweg (1992), 249p.

[ScMe82] Schwartz, R. L., Melliar-Smith, P. M.: From State Machines to Temporal Logic: Specification Methods for Protocol Standards, IEEE Transactions on Communications, No. 12, Dec. 1982, pp. 2486-2496

[ScMeVo83] Schwartz, R. L., Melliar-Smith, P. M., Vogt, F. H.: Interval Logic: A Higher-Level Temporal Logic for Protocol Specification, in: H. Rudin, C. H. West (eds.), Protocol Specification, Testing, and Verification III, North-Holland, 1983, pp. 3-18

[ScMeVo83a] Schwartz, R. L., Melliar-Smith, P. M., Vogt, F. H.: An Interval Logic for Higher-Level Temporal Reasoning, in: Proc. of the 2nd ACM Symposium on PoDC, Montréal/Canada, Aug. 17-19, 1983, pp. 173-186

[SiSt91] Sijelmassi, R., Strausser, B.: The Portable Estelle Translator: An Overview and User Guide, Technical Report NCSL/SNA-91/2, National Institute of Standards and Technology, 1991

[Spi89] Spivey, J. M.: The Z Notation - A Reference Manual, Prentice-Hall, 1989, 155p.

[Svo89] Svobodova, L.: Implementing OSI systems, IEEE Journal on Selected Areas in Communications, Vol. 7, No. 7, Sept. 1989, pp. 1115-1130

[Tur87] Turner, K.: An Architectural Semantics for LOTOS, in: H. Rudin, C. H. West (eds.), Protocol Specification, Testing, and Verification VII, Zurich, May 5-8, 1987

[Tur92] Turner, K. (ed.): Using Formal Description Techniques - An Introduction to Estelle, LOTOS and SDL, John Wiley & Sons, 1992

[ViLo85] Vissers, C. A., Logrippo, L.: The Importance of the Service Concept in the Design of Data Communications Protocols, in: M. Diaz (ed.), Protocol Specification, Testing, and Verification V, North-Holland, 1986, pp. 3-17

[Vog82] Vogt, F. H.: Event-Based Temporal Logic Specifications of Services and Protocols, in: C. Sunshine (ed.), Protocol Specification, Testing, and Verification II, 1982, North-Holland, pp. 63-73

[VuChCh88] Vuong, S. T., Chan, R. I., Chan, W. Y. L.: An Estelle-C Compiler for Automatic Protocol Implementation, in: S. Aggarwal, K. Sabnani (eds.), Protocol Specification, Testing, and Verification VIII, North-Holland, 1988, pp. 387-398

[Wer88] Werner, E.: Toward a Theory of Communication and Cooperation for Multiagent Planning, WISBER Report No. 22, University of Hamburg, Jan. 1988, 20p.

[WhRu10] Whitehead, A. N., Russell, B. A. W.: Principia Mathematica; Cambridge University Press, 3 Vols., First edition 1910-1913, Second edition 1923-1927

[Wol86] Wolper, P.: Expressing Interesting Properties of Programs in Propositional Temporal Logic (extended abstract), in: Proc. of the Thirteenth ACM Symposium on the Principles of Programming Languages, Florida/USA, Jan. 1986, pp. 184-193

[Zaf80] Zafiropulo, P., West, C. H., Rudin, H., Cowan, D. D., Brand, D.: Towards Analyzing and Synthesizing Protocols, IEEE Transactions on Communications, Vol. COM-28, No. 4, April 1980, pp. 651-661

[Zim80] Zimmermann, H.: OSI Reference Model - The ISO Model of Architecture for Open Systems Interconnection, IEEE Transactions on Communications, Vol. COM-28, No. 4, April 1980, pp. 425-432

Appendix

A.1 Theorems and valid formulas

<u>Theorems *Pr*</u>

Let $\varphi, \varphi_1, \varphi_2, \varphi_3, \varphi_4$ be formulas:

T1: $\vdash (\varphi_1 \supset \varphi_2) \equiv (\neg\varphi_2 \supset \neg\varphi_1)$ (law of transposition)

T2: $\vdash \varphi \equiv \neg\neg\varphi$ (law of double negation)

T3: $\vdash (\varphi_1 \supset \varphi_2) \wedge (\varphi_2 \supset \varphi_3) \supset (\varphi_1 \supset \varphi_3)$ (law of syllogism)

T4: $\vdash (\varphi_1 \wedge (\varphi_2 \vee \varphi_3) \equiv (\varphi_1 \wedge \varphi_2) \vee (\varphi_1 \wedge \varphi_3))$ (distributivity of conjunction)

T5: $\vdash (\varphi_1 \vee (\varphi_2 \wedge \varphi_3) \equiv (\varphi_1 \vee \varphi_2) \wedge (\varphi_1 \vee \varphi_3))$ (distributivity of disjunction)

T6: $\vdash (\varphi_1 \wedge \varphi_2) \supset \varphi_1$

T7: $\vdash (\varphi_1 \wedge \varphi_2) \supset \varphi_2$

T8: $\vdash (\varphi_1 \supset \varphi_2) \wedge (\varphi_1 \supset \neg\varphi_2) \equiv \neg\varphi_1$

T9: $\vdash (\varphi_1 \supset (\varphi_2 \supset \varphi_3)) \equiv (\varphi_1 \wedge \varphi_2 \supset \varphi_3)$

T10: $\vdash (\varphi_1 \vee \varphi_2) \equiv \neg(\neg\varphi_1 \wedge \neg\varphi_2)$

T11: $\vdash (\varphi_2 \supset \varphi_3) \supset ((\varphi_1 \supset \varphi_2) \supset (\varphi_1 \supset \varphi_3))$

T12: $\vdash (\varphi_1 \supset \varphi_3) \wedge (\varphi_2 \supset \varphi_4) \supset ((\varphi_1 \vee \varphi_2) \supset (\varphi_3 \vee \varphi_4))$

<u>Theorems *Q*</u>

Let φ_1, φ_2 be formulas where x is the only free variable:

T13: $\vdash \forall x. (\varphi_1 \supset \varphi_2) \supset (\forall x.\varphi_1 \supset \forall x.\varphi_2)$

T14: $\vdash \forall x. (\varphi_1 \wedge \varphi_2) \equiv \forall x.\varphi_1 \wedge \forall x.\varphi_2$

T15: $\vdash \forall x.\varphi_1 \vee \forall x.\varphi_2 \supset \forall x. (\varphi_1 \vee \varphi_2)$

T16: $\vdash \exists x. (\varphi_1 \wedge \varphi_2) \supset \exists x.\varphi_1 \wedge \exists x.\varphi_2$

T17: $\vdash \exists x. (\varphi_1 \vee \varphi_2) \equiv \exists x.\varphi_1 \vee \exists x.\varphi_2$

<u>Theorems F_L</u>

Let $\varphi, \varphi_1, \varphi_2$ be formulas:

T18: $\vdash \Box\varphi \equiv \Box\Box\varphi$

T19: $\vdash \Diamond\varphi \equiv \Diamond\Diamond\varphi$

T20: $\vdash \Diamond\Box\Diamond\varphi \equiv \Box\Diamond\varphi$

T21: $\vdash \Box \Diamond \Box \varphi \equiv \Diamond \Box \varphi$

T22: $\vdash \Box (\varphi_1 \wedge \varphi_2) \equiv \Box \varphi_1 \wedge \Box \varphi_2$

T23: $\vdash \Box \varphi_1 \vee \Box \varphi_2 \supset \Box (\varphi_1 \vee \varphi_2)$

T24: $\vdash \Diamond (\varphi_1 \wedge \varphi_2) \supset \Diamond \varphi_1 \wedge \Diamond \varphi_2$

T25: $\vdash \Diamond (\varphi_1 \vee \varphi_2) \equiv \Diamond \varphi_1 \vee \Diamond \varphi_2$

Theorems F_B

Let φ, φ_1, φ_2 be formulas:

T26: $\vdash$ AG $\varphi \supset$ AF φ

T27: $\vdash$ AF $\varphi \supset$ EF φ

T28: $\vdash$ AG $\varphi \equiv$ AG AG φ

T29: $\vdash$ EF $\varphi \equiv$ EF EF φ

T30: $\vdash$ AF $\varphi \equiv$ AF AF φ

T31: $\vdash$ AG $(\varphi_1 \wedge \varphi_2) \equiv$ AG $\varphi_1 \wedge$ AG φ_2

T32: $\vdash$ AG $\varphi_1 \vee$ AG $\varphi_2 \supset$ AG $(\varphi_1 \vee \varphi_2)$

T33: $\vdash$ AF $(\varphi_1 \wedge \varphi_2) \equiv$ AF $\varphi_1 \wedge$ AF φ_2

T34: $\vdash$ AF $\varphi_1 \vee$ AF $\varphi_2 \supset$ AF $(\varphi_1 \vee \varphi_2)$

T35: $\vdash$ EF $(\varphi_1 \wedge \varphi_2) \supset$ EF $\varphi_1 \wedge$ EF φ_2

T36: $\vdash$ EF $(\varphi_1 \vee \varphi_2) \equiv$ EF $\varphi_1 \vee$ EF φ_2

Theorems P

Let φ, φ_1, φ_2 be formulas:

T37: $\vdash \blacksquare \varphi \equiv \blacksquare \blacksquare \varphi$

T38: $\vdash \blacklozenge \varphi \equiv \blacklozenge \blacklozenge \varphi$

T39: $\vdash \blacksquare (\varphi_1 \wedge \varphi_2) \equiv \blacksquare \varphi_1 \wedge \blacksquare \varphi_2$

T40: $\vdash \blacksquare \varphi_1 \vee \blacksquare \varphi_2 \supset \blacksquare (\varphi_1 \vee \varphi_2)$

T41: $\vdash \blacklozenge (\varphi_1 \wedge \varphi_2) \supset \blacklozenge \varphi_1 \wedge \blacklozenge \varphi_2$

T42: $\vdash \blacklozenge (\varphi_1 \vee \varphi_2) \equiv \blacklozenge \varphi_1 \vee \blacklozenge \varphi_2$

Valid formulas E_P

Let φ, φ_1, φ_2 be formulas:

V1: $\models [\varphi] \supset \varphi$

V2: $\models [\varphi] \equiv [[\varphi]]$

V3: $\models [\varphi_1 \wedge \varphi_2] \equiv [\varphi_1] \wedge [\varphi_2]$

V4: $\models [\varphi_1 \vee \varphi_2] \supset [\varphi_1] \vee [\varphi_2]$

Valid formulas E_F

Let φ be a formula:

V5: $\models \exists n \in \mathbb{N}_0.\ \#[\varphi] = n$

V6: $\models \forall n_1, n_2 \in \mathbb{N}_0.\ (\#[\varphi] = n_1 \wedge \#[\varphi] = n_2 \supset n_1 = n_2)$

V5 and V6 express that the number of event occurrences is always well-defined, and that it is uniquely defined.

Valid formulas I

Let φ, φ_1, φ_2 be formulas, β be an interval term, δ, δ_1, δ_2, δ_3 be interval expressions:

V7: $\models \neg \langle \beta \rangle \varphi \supset \langle \beta \rangle \neg \varphi$

V8: $\models \langle \beta \rangle (\varphi_1 \wedge \varphi_2) \equiv \langle \beta \rangle \varphi_1 \wedge \langle \beta \rangle \varphi_2$

V9: $\models \langle \beta \rangle (\varphi_1 \vee \varphi_2) \equiv \langle \beta \rangle \varphi_1 \vee \langle \beta \rangle \varphi_2$

V10: $\models \langle \beta \rangle (\varphi_1 \supset \varphi_2) \equiv \langle \beta \rangle \varphi_1 \supset \langle \beta \rangle \varphi_2$

V11: $\models \langle \delta \Leftarrow \rangle \varphi \wedge \langle \Leftarrow \delta \rangle \varphi \supset \varphi$

V12: $\models \varphi \supset \langle \delta \Leftarrow \rangle \varphi \vee \langle \Leftarrow \delta \rangle \varphi$

V13: $\models \langle \delta_1 \Rightarrow \delta_2 \rangle \varphi \wedge \langle (\delta_1 \Rightarrow \delta_2) \Rightarrow \delta_3 \rangle \varphi \supset \langle \delta_1 \Rightarrow (\delta_2 \Rightarrow \delta_3) \rangle \varphi$

V14: $\models \langle \text{begin } [\varphi] \rangle \varphi$

V15: $\models \langle \text{end } [\varphi] \rangle \varphi$

V16: $\models \langle \text{begin } [\varphi_1] \rangle \varphi_2 \equiv \langle \text{end } [\varphi_1] \rangle \varphi_2$

V17: $\models \langle [\varphi_1] \Rightarrow [\varphi_1] \rangle \varphi_2 \equiv \langle \text{begin } [\varphi_1] \rangle \varphi_2$

V18: $\models \langle [\varphi_1] \Leftarrow [\varphi_1] \rangle \varphi_2 \equiv \langle \text{begin } [\varphi_1] \rangle \varphi_2$

V19: $\models \langle \delta \Rightarrow \rangle \varphi \equiv \langle \delta \Leftarrow \rangle \varphi$

V20: $\models \langle \Rightarrow \delta \rangle \varphi \equiv \langle \Leftarrow \delta \rangle \varphi$

V21: $\models \langle \Rightarrow ([\varphi_1] \Rightarrow \bullet[\varphi_1]) \rangle \varphi_2 \equiv \langle \Rightarrow \bullet[\varphi_1] \rangle \varphi_2$

V22: $\models \langle \Rightarrow (\bullet[\varphi_1] \Rightarrow \bullet[\varphi_1]) \rangle \varphi_2 \equiv \langle \Rightarrow \bullet\bullet[\varphi_1] \rangle \varphi_2$

V23: $\models \langle (\bullet[\varphi_1] \Leftarrow [\varphi_1]) \Leftarrow \rangle \varphi_2 \equiv \langle \bullet[\varphi_1] \Leftarrow \rangle \varphi_2$

V24: $\models \langle (\bullet[\varphi_1] \Leftarrow \bullet[\varphi_1]) \Leftarrow \rangle \varphi_2 \equiv \langle \bullet\bullet[\varphi_1] \Leftarrow \rangle \varphi_2$

<u>Theorems *K*</u>

Let φ, φ_1, φ_2 be formulas, ag, ag' $\in$ AG be agents:

T43: $\vdash K_{ag}\varphi \equiv K_{ag}K_{ag}\varphi$

T44: $\vdash K_{ag}(\varphi_1 \wedge \varphi_2) \equiv K_{ag}\varphi_1 \wedge K_{ag}\varphi_2$

T45: $\vdash K_{ag}\varphi_1 \vee K_{ag}\varphi_2 \supset K_{ag}(\varphi_1 \vee \varphi_2)$

T46: $\vdash K_{ag}K_{ag'}\varphi \supset K_{ag}\varphi$

<u>Theorems *K'*</u>

Let φ, φ_1, φ_2 be formulas, ag, ag' $\in$ AG be agents:

T47: $\vdash K'_{ag}\varphi \equiv K'_{ag}K'_{ag}\varphi$

T48: $\vdash K'_{ag}(\varphi_1 \wedge \varphi_2) \equiv K'_{ag}\varphi_1 \wedge K'_{ag}\varphi_2$

T49: $\vdash K'_{ag}K'_{ag}\varphi \supset K'_{ag}\varphi$

<u>Theorems *A*</u>

Let φ_1, φ_2 be formulas, ag $\in$ AG be an agent:

T50: $\vdash A_{ag}(\varphi_1 \vee \varphi_2) \equiv A_{ag}\varphi_1 \wedge A_{ag}\varphi_2$

T51: $\vdash A_{ag}(\varphi_1 \supset \varphi_2) \equiv A_{ag}\varphi_1 \wedge A_{ag}\varphi_2$

T52: $\vdash A_{ag}(\varphi_1 \equiv \varphi_2) \equiv A_{ag}\varphi_1 \wedge A_{ag}\varphi_2$

<u>Theorems *G*</u>

Let φ, φ_1, φ_2 be formulas, G, G' $\subseteq$ AG be groups of agents:

T53: $\vdash S_G\varphi \equiv S_GS_G\varphi$

T54: $\vdash S_G(\varphi_1 \wedge \varphi_2) \supset S_G\varphi_1 \wedge S_G\varphi_2$

T55: $\vdash S_G\varphi_1 \vee S_G\varphi_2 \supset S_G(\varphi_1 \vee \varphi_2)$

T56: $\vdash E_G(\varphi_1 \wedge \varphi_2) \equiv E_G\varphi_1 \wedge E_G\varphi_2$

T57: $\vdash E_G\varphi_1 \vee E_G\varphi_2 \supset E_G(\varphi_1 \vee \varphi_2)$

T58: $\vdash E_GE_{G'}\varphi \supset E_G\varphi$

T59: $\vdash I_G\varphi \equiv I_GI_G\varphi$

T60: $\vdash I_G(\varphi_1 \wedge \varphi_2) \equiv I_G\varphi_1 \wedge I_G\varphi_2$

T61: $\vdash I_G\varphi_1 \vee I_G\varphi_2 \supset I_G(\varphi_1 \vee \varphi_2)$

T62: $\vdash I_GI_{G'}\varphi \supset I_G\varphi$

T63: $\vdash C_G\varphi \equiv C_GC_G\varphi$

T64: $\vdash C_G(\varphi_1 \wedge \varphi_2) \equiv C_G\varphi_1 \wedge C_G\varphi_2$

T65: $\vdash C_G\varphi_1 \vee C_G\varphi_2 \supset C_G(\varphi_1 \vee \varphi_2)$

T66: $\vdash C_G C_{G'} \varphi \supset C_G\varphi$

Theorems A_G

Let φ_1, φ_2 be formulas, $G \subseteq AG$ be a group of agents:

T67: $\vdash R_G(\varphi_1 \vee \varphi_2) \supset R_G\varphi_1 \wedge R_G\varphi_2$

T68: $\vdash R_G(\varphi_1 \supset \varphi_2) \supset R_G\varphi_1 \wedge R_G\varphi_2$

T69: $\vdash R_G(\varphi_1 \equiv \varphi_2) \supset R_G\varphi_1 \wedge R_G\varphi_2$

T70: $\vdash D_G(\varphi_1 \vee \varphi_2) \equiv D_G\varphi_1 \wedge D_G\varphi_2$

T71: $\vdash D_G(\varphi_1 \supset \varphi_2) \equiv D_G\varphi_1 \wedge D_G\varphi_2$

T72: $\vdash D_G(\varphi_1 \equiv \varphi_2) \equiv D_G\varphi_1 \wedge D_G\varphi_2$

T73: $\vdash H_G(\varphi_1 \vee \varphi_2) \equiv H_G\varphi_1 \wedge H_G\varphi_2$

T74: $\vdash H_G(\varphi_1 \supset \varphi_2) \equiv H_G\varphi_1 \wedge H_G\varphi_2$

T75: $\vdash H_G(\varphi_1 \equiv \varphi_2) \equiv H_G\varphi_1 \wedge H_G\varphi_2$

Theorems G'

Let φ, φ_1, φ_2 be formulas, $G \subseteq AG$ be a group of agents:

T76: $\vdash S'_G\varphi \equiv S'_G S'_G\varphi$

T77: $\vdash S'_G(\varphi_1 \wedge \varphi_2) \supset S'_G\varphi_1 \wedge S'_G\varphi_2$

T78: $\vdash E'_G(\varphi_1 \wedge \varphi_2) \equiv E'_G\varphi_1 \wedge E'_G\varphi_2$

T79: $\vdash I'_G\varphi \equiv I'_G I'_G\varphi$

T80: $\vdash I'_G(\varphi_1 \wedge \varphi_2) \equiv I'_G\varphi_1 \wedge I'_G\varphi_2$

Valid formulas of mixed temporal logics

Let φ be a formula, β be an interval term, and φ' be a formula where x is the only free variable:

V25: $\models_L \Box \forall x.\ \varphi' \equiv \forall x.\ \Box \varphi'$ $\quad Q, F_L$

V26: $\models_L \exists x.\ \Box \varphi' \supset \Box \exists x.\ \varphi'$

V27: $\models_L \Diamond \forall x.\ \varphi' \supset \forall x.\ \Diamond \varphi'$

V28: $\models_L \exists x.\ \Diamond \varphi' \equiv \Diamond \exists x.\ \varphi'$

V29: $\models_B AG\ \forall x.\ \varphi' \equiv \forall x.\ AG\ \varphi'$ $\quad Q, F_B$

V30: $\models_B \exists x.\ AG\ \varphi' \supset AG\ \exists x.\ \varphi'$

V31: $\models_B AF\ \forall x.\ \varphi' \supset \forall x.\ AF\ \varphi'$

V32: $\models_B \exists x.\ AF\ \varphi' \supset AF\ \exists x.\ \varphi'$

V33: $\models_B EF\ \forall x.\ \varphi' \supset \forall x.\ EF\ \varphi'$

V34: $\models_B \exists x.\ EF\ \varphi' \equiv EF\ \exists x.\ \varphi'$

V35: $\models \blacksquare\ \forall x.\ \varphi' \equiv \forall x.\ \blacksquare\ \varphi'$ — *Q,P*

V36: $\models \exists x.\ \blacksquare\ \varphi' \supset \blacksquare\ \exists x.\ \varphi'$

V37: $\models \blacklozenge\ \forall x.\ \varphi' \supset \forall x.\ \blacklozenge\ \varphi'$

V38: $\models \exists x.\ \blacklozenge\ \varphi' \equiv \blacklozenge\ \exists x.\ \varphi'$

V39: $\models_L \Box \blacksquare \varphi \equiv \blacksquare \Box \varphi$ — P, F_L

V40: $\models_L \Box \blacksquare \varphi \supset \Box \varphi$

V41: $\models_L \Box \varphi \supset \Box \blacklozenge \varphi$

V42: $\models_L \blacksquare \Box \varphi \supset \blacksquare \varphi$

V43: $\models_L \blacksquare \varphi \supset \blacksquare \Diamond \varphi$

V44: $\models_{iL} \Box \varphi \supset \Box \blacksquare \varphi$

V45: $\models_B AG \blacksquare \varphi \equiv \blacksquare AG \varphi$ — P, F_B

V46: $\models_B AG \blacksquare \varphi \supset AG \varphi$

V47: $\models_B AG \varphi \supset AG \blacklozenge \varphi$

V48: $\models_B \blacksquare AG \varphi \supset \blacksquare \varphi$

V49: $\models_B \blacksquare \varphi \supset \blacksquare AF \varphi$

V50: $\models_{iB} AG \varphi \supset AG \blacksquare \varphi$

V51: $\models_L \forall n \in \mathbb{N}_0.\ (\Diamond \#[\varphi] = n \supset \#[\varphi] \leq n)$ — monotonicity of #[.]

V52: $\models_L \forall n \in \mathbb{N}_0.\ (\#[\varphi] = n \supset \Box \#[\varphi] \geq n)$ — monotonicity of #[.]

V53: $\models_B \forall n \in \mathbb{N}_0.\ (EF\ \#[\varphi] = n \supset \#[\varphi] \leq n)$ — monotonicity of #[.]

V54: $\models_B \forall n \in \mathbb{N}_0.\ (\#[\varphi] = n \supset AG\ \#[\varphi] \geq n)$ — monotonicity of #[.]

<u>Valid formulas of mixed epistemic logics</u>

Let φ be a formula, φ' be a formula where x is the only free variable, $G \subseteq AG$, $ag \in G$:

V55: $\models K_{ag}\varphi \supset S_G\varphi$ — K, K', A, G, G', A_G

V56: $\models A_{ag}\varphi \supset R_G\varphi$

V57: $\models K'_{ag}\varphi \equiv K_{ag}\varphi \wedge A_{ag}\varphi$

V58: $\models S'_G\varphi \supset S_G\varphi \land R_G\varphi$

V59: $\models E'_G\varphi \equiv E_G\varphi \land D_G\varphi$

V60: $\models I'_G\varphi \equiv I_G\varphi \land H_G\varphi$

V61: $\models K_{ag}\, \forall x.\, \varphi' \equiv \forall x.\, K_{ag}\varphi'$ — *Q,K,K',A*

V62: $\models \exists x.\, K_{ag}\varphi' \supset K_{ag}\, \exists x.\, \varphi'$

V63: $\models A_{ag}\, \forall x.\, \varphi' \equiv \forall x.\, A_{ag}\varphi'$

V64: $\models A_{ag}\, \exists x.\, \varphi' \equiv \forall x.\, A_{ag}\varphi'$

V65: $\models K'_{ag}\, \forall x.\, \varphi' \equiv \forall x.\, K'_{ag}\varphi'$

V66: $\models S_G\, \forall x.\, \varphi' \supset \forall x.\, S_G\varphi'$ — *Q,G,G',A_G*

V67: $\models \exists x.\, S_G\varphi' \supset S_G\, \exists x.\, \varphi'$

V68: $\models E_G\, \forall x.\, \varphi' \equiv \forall x.\, E_G\varphi'$

V69: $\models \exists x.\, E_G\varphi' \supset E_G\, \exists x.\, \varphi'$

V70: $\models I_G\, \forall x.\, \varphi' \equiv \forall x.\, I_G\varphi'$

V71: $\models \exists x.\, I_G\varphi' \supset I_G\, \exists x.\, \varphi'$

V72: $\models C_G\, \forall x.\, \varphi' \equiv \forall x.\, C_G\varphi'$

V73: $\models \exists x.\, C_G\varphi' \supset C_G\, \exists x.\, \varphi'$

V74: $\models R_G\, \forall x.\, \varphi' \supset \forall x.\, R_G\varphi'$

V75: $\models R_G\, \exists x.\, \varphi' \supset \forall x.\, R_G\varphi'$

V76: $\models D_G\, \forall x.\, \varphi' \equiv \forall x.\, D_G\varphi'$

V77: $\models D_G\, \exists x.\, \varphi' \equiv \forall x.\, D_G\varphi'$

V78: $\models H_G\, \forall x.\, \varphi' \equiv \forall x.\, H_G\varphi'$

V79: $\models H_G\, \exists x.\, \varphi' \equiv \forall x.\, H_G\varphi'$

V80: $\models E'_G\, \forall x.\, \varphi' \equiv \forall x.\, E'_G\varphi'$

V81: $\models I'_G\, \forall x.\, \varphi' \equiv \forall x.\, I'_G\varphi'$

<u>Valid formulas of mixed temporal epistemic logics</u>

Let φ be a formula, $G \subseteq AG$, $ag \in AG$:

V82: $\models_L A_{ag}\varphi \equiv \Box\, A_{ag}\varphi$ — *F_L,K,K',A,G,G',A_G*

V83: $\models_L R_G\varphi \equiv \Box\, R_G\varphi$

V84: $\models_L D_G\varphi \equiv \Box\, D_G\varphi$

V85: $\models_L H_G\varphi \equiv \Box\, H_G\varphi$

V86: $\models_B A_{ag}\varphi \equiv AG\, A_{ag}\varphi$ — *F_B,K,K',A,G,G',A_G*

V87: $\models_B R_G\varphi \equiv AG\ R_G\varphi$

V88: $\models_B D_G\varphi \equiv AG\ D_G\varphi$

V89: $\models_B H_G\varphi \equiv AG\ H_G\varphi$

V90: $\models A_{ag}\varphi \equiv \blacksquare\ A_{ag}\varphi$ *P,K,K',A,G,G',*A_G

V91: $\models R_G\varphi \equiv \blacksquare\ R_G\varphi$

V92: $\models D_G\varphi \equiv \blacksquare\ D_G\varphi$

V93: $\models H_G\varphi \equiv \blacksquare\ H_G\varphi$

V94: $\models \blacksquare\ K_{ag}\ \varphi \wedge \langle\ \beta\ \rangle\ \text{true} \supset \langle\ \beta\ \rangle\ \blacksquare\ K_{ag}\ \varphi$ *P,I,K*

A.2 Ordering properties for the service provider

C_M26. AG ∀n1,n2. ([after M.ip$_A$.!(RECconf(n1))] ∧ ◆ [after M.ip$_A$.!(RECconf(n2))]
⊃ ◆ ([after M.ip$_B$.?(RECresp(n1))] ∧ ◆ [after M.ip$_B$.?(RECresp(n2))]))

C_M27. AG ∀n. ([after M.ip$_A$.!(CONconf(n))] ∧ ◆ [after M.ip$_A$.!(DISind)]
⊃ ◆ ([after M.ip$_B$.?(CONresp(n))] ∧ ◆ [after M.ip$_B$.?(DISreq)]))

C_M28. AG ∀n. ([after M.ip$_A$.!(DISind)] ∧ ◆ [after M.ip$_A$.!(RECconf(n))]
⊃ ◆ ([after M.ip$_B$.?(DISreq)] ∧ ◆ [after M.ip$_B$.?(RECresp(n))]))

C_M29. AG ∀n. ([after M.ip$_A$.!(RECconf(n))] ∧ ◆ [after M.ip$_A$.!(DISind)]
⊃ ◆ ([after M.ip$_B$.?(RECresp(n))] ∧ ◆ [after M.ip$_B$.?(DISreq)]))

C_M30. AG ∀n1,n2.([after M.ip$_A$.!(CONconf(n1))] ∧ ◆ [after M.ip$_A$.!(RECconf(n2))]
⊃ ◆ ([after M.ip$_B$.?(CONresp(n1))] ∧ ◆ [after M.ip$_B$.?(RECresp(n2))]))

C_M31. AG ∀n1,n2. ([after M.ip$_A$.!(RECconf(n1))] ∧ ◆ [after M.ip$_A$.!(RECconf(n2))]
⊃ ◆ ([after M.ip$_B$.?(RECresp(n1))] ∧ ◆ [after M.ip$_B$.?(CONresp(n2))]))

C_M32. AG ∀n1,n2. ([after M.ip$_B$.!(CONind(n1))] ∧ ◆ [after M.ip$_B$.!(CONind(n2))]
⊃ ◆ ([after M.ip$_A$.?(CONreq(n1))] ∧ ◆ [after M.ip$_A$.?(CONreq(n2))]))

C_M33. AG ∀n1,n2. ([after M.ip$_B$.!(RECind(n1))] ∧ ◆ [after M.ip$_B$.!(RECind(n2))]
⊃ ◆ ([after M.ip$_A$.?(RECreq(n1))] ∧ ◆ [after M.ip$_A$.?(RECreq(n2))]))

C_M34. AG ∀n1,n2. ([after M.ip$_B$.!(CONind(n1))] ∧ ◆ [after M.ip$_B$.!(RECind(n2))]
⊃ ◆ ([after M.ip$_A$.?(CONreq(n1))] ∧ ◆ [after M.ip$_A$.?(RECreq(n2))]))

C_M35. AG ∀n1,n2. ([after M.ip$_B$.!(RECind(n1))] ∧ ◆ [after M.ip$_B$.!(CONind(n2))]
⊃ ◆ ([after M.ip$_A$.?(RECreq(n1))] ∧ ◆ [after M.ip$_A$.?(CONreq(n2))]))

C_M36. AG ∀n,x. ([after M.ip$_B$.!(CONind(n))] ∧ ◆ [after M.ip$_B$.!(DATind(x))]
⊃ ◆ ([after M.ip$_A$.?(CONreq(n))] ∧ ◆ [after M.ip$_A$.?(DATreq(x))]))

C_M37. AG ∀n,x. ([after M.ip$_B$.!(DATind(x))] ∧ ◆ [after M.ip$_B$.!(CONind(n))]
⊃ ◆ ([after M.ip$_A$.?(DATreq(x))] ∧ ◆ [after M.ip$_A$.?(CONreq(n))]))

C_M38. AG ∀n,x. ([after M.ip$_B$.!(RECind(n))] ∧ ◆ [after M.ip$_B$.!(DATind(x))]
⊃ ◆ ([after M.ip$_A$.?(RECreq(n))] ∧ ◆ [after M.ip$_A$.?(DATreq(x))]))

C_M39. AG ∀n,x. ([after M.ip$_B$.!(DATind(x))] ∧ ◆ [after M.ip$_B$.!(RECind(n))]
⊃ ◆ ([after M.ip$_A$.?(DATreq(x))] ∧ ◆ [after M.ip$_A$.?(RECreq(n))]))

Table A.1: Constraints for the service provider: ordering properties

A.3 Abbreviations

AI	Artificial Intelligence
BRM	Basic Reference Model
CCITT	The International Telegraph and Telephone Consultative Committee
CCS	Calculus of Communicationg Systems
CRS	Communicating Rule Systems
CSP	Communicating Sequential Processes
CTL	Computation Tree Logic
DAI	Distributed Artificial Intelligence
FDT	Formal Description Technique
FIFO	first-in-first-out
InRes	Initiator - Responder
ISO	International Standardization Organization
ISP	Internationally Standardized Profiles
ISS	interpreted symbolic structure
IUT	Implementation under Test
LOTOS	Language of Temporal Ordering Specification
ODP	Open Distributed Processing
OSI	Open Systems Interconnection
PCO	Point of Control and Observation
PICS	Protocol Implementation Conformance Statement
SAK	Situated-Automata Knowledge
SAP	Service Access Point
SDL	Systems Definition Language
TLA	Temporal Logic of Actions
TTCN	Tree and Tabular Combined Notation

A.4 Notation

abstracts	architectural abstraction relation
af	awareness function
ag, ag', ag_i	agents
AG, AG'	sets of agents
$\mathcal{Arch}$, $\mathcal{Arch}'$	system architectures
$\mathcal{Archf}$, $\mathcal{Archf}'$	architecture functions
B_i	awareness functions
$\mathcal{Behav}$, $\mathcal{Behav}'$	system behaviours
$\mathcal{Behav}_{ag}$	behaviour of agent ag
Cl	closure under formation rules
comp	interaction point compatibility relation
conf, *conf**	conformance relations
$conforms_{rep}$	conformance relation
D^s	set of objects
E	environment
f	function
$f_{s,s_1,...s_n}$	function symbol
$\mathcal{F}$	set of functions
G, G'	groups of agents
h	history function
i,j,k,l,m,n	variables ranging over $\mathbb{N}_0$
incomp	interaction point incompatibility relation
ip, ip', ip_i	interaction points
IP, IP'	sets of interaction points
lp	local proposition function
$\mathcal{M}$	Kripke structure
$\mathcal{M}_P$	model of propositional temporal logic
$\mathcal{M}_F$	model of many-sorted first-order temporal logic
$\mathcal{M}_L$	model of linear time temporal logic
$\mathcal{M}_B$	model of branching time temporal logic
$\mathcal{M}_{PL}$	model of propositional linear time temporal logic
$\mathcal{M}_{PB}$	model of propositional branching time temporal logic
$\mathcal{M}_{FL}$	model of many-sorted first-order linear time temporal logic
$\mathcal{M}_{FB}$	model of many-sorted first-order branching time temporal logic
$\mathcal{M}_{LE}$	model of linear time temporal epistemic logic
$\mathcal{M}_{BE}$	model of branching time temporal epistemic logic
$\mathcal{M}_{PLE}$	model of propositional linear time temporal epistemic logic

$\mathcal{M}_{PBE}$	model of propositional branching time temporal epistemic logic
$\mathcal{M}_{FLE}$	model of many-sorted first-order linear time temporal epistemic logic
$\mathcal{M}_{FBE}$	model of many-sorted first-order branching time temporal epistemic logic
$\mathbb{N}_0$	set of natural numbers
OP	set of abstract operations
p, q	propositional variables
p, p1, p2	variables ranging over interaction types
P	set of interaction types
$r(\pi)$	root of state tree π
ref	refinement function
refines	architectural refinement relation
rep	representation function
r	relation
$r_{s_1,...s_n}$	relation symbol
R, R_i	seeing-relations, epistemic accessibility relations
$\mathcal{R}$	set of relations
$\mathcal{RS}$, $\mathcal{RS}'$	requirement specifications
s, s_i	sorts
S	set of states
S_0	set of initial states
S^ω	set of infinite state sequences
S1, S2	specifications
$\mathcal{S}$	set of sorts
$\mathcal{S}eman_{ip}$	semantics of interaction point ip
t, t_i	terms
v	view function
V	value assignment
$\mathcal{V}$	set of individual variables
w, w'	worlds
W	set of worlds, states of affairs
x, x1, x2	variables ranging over parameter values
x^s	variable of sort s
X	set of parameter values
Φ	set of atomic propositions
φ, φ_1, φ_2	formulas
π, π'	state trees
Π	set of state trees

σ, σ'	state sequences
σ_n	(n+1)th element of state sequence σ
σ^{n-}	prefix of σ of length n+1
$\sigma^{i,j}$	subsequence of σ
Σ	set of state sequences
!, ?, §	abstract operations (offer, accept, inspect)

Index

Relative Complexities of First Order Calculi

by Elmar Eder

1992. vi, 173 pages (Artificial Intelligence, edited by Wolfgang Bibel and Walther von Hahn) Softcover
ISBN 3-528-05122-1

In this book various proof calculi of first order predicate logic are compared to each other with respect to their relative complexities in terms of length of shortest proofs. It is proved that resolution can simulate step by step one of the simpler versions of the connection method, but that, conversely, this connection calculus can not simulate resolution at polynomial cost. It is shown that the method of tableaux and the connection method are essentially equivalent.